Darwin's Universe

From Nothing,

By Nothing,

For Nothing

Survival for Nothing

Yan T Wee

All Scriptures are quoted from the Authorized King James Version

Shalom Baptist Church: shalom-baptist.org

ISBN: 978-981-18-2675-7

Dedication

To God who alone has made it possible to pen down
this book for His glory;

To the members of Shalom Baptist Church who have a big
part in my pastoral and writing ministry;

To my wonderful wife and four lovely children, whose love
and laughter, have made this earthly journey more
pleasurable;

And to those whose Christian faith have been devastated by
pseudo-science and vindicated by empirical science.

Preface

Most atheists do not give much thought as to where Darwinism is taking them. Like the pied piper of Hamelin who, as the legend says, led the town children away with his magical tune, and they were never to be seen again, Darwinism has a charming 'magical tune' that enchants millions of followers. But many are unaware of its true intent or the disastrous destination it is leading them.

Darwinists hope to kill God but, like conjoined twins, in killing God, they kill themselves. They end up being: *From Nothing, By Nothing, For Nothing.* Looking further ahead down the foggy road of Darwinism, it reveals a dark, gloomy and depressive landscape – life has no real meaning and survival has no ultimate purpose. Man is nothing more than a cosmic orphan, caged up in a dying universe, propagating his DNA, and waiting to return to stardust. Above all, most Darwinists are unaware that Darwin and Darwinism are *Killing them Softly*.

> "When Darwin deduced the theory of natural selection to explain the adaptations in which he had previously seen the handiwork of God, he knew that he was committing cultural murder. He understood immediately that if natural selection explained adaptations, and evolution by descent were true, then the argument from design was dead and all that went with it, namely the existence of a personal god, free will, life after death, immutable moral laws, and ultimate meaning in life." (William Provine)

Science encourages us to think critically and let us place Darwinism in the crosshairs and examine it in the light of empirical science – is it observable, falsifiable and repeatable? If not, it is not experimental science. And, as we shall see, Darwinism is an unobservable and unreproducible pseudo-science.

This book will walk us through cosmology, biology, philosophy and end with theology, the queen of the sciences. Empirical science buries Darwinism and resurrects Creationism. We are more than cosmic orphans lost in an accidental, uncaring and dying Universe; we are living souls, made in the image of God, and designed to have a wonderful relationship with an awesome Creator.

Contents

Chapter 1: From Nothing

Contents

CHAPTER 1

From Nothing

The First Dirt

A scientist approached God and said, "Listen, we've decided we no longer need you. Nowadays, we can clone people, transplant hearts, and do all kinds of things that were once considered miraculous."

God patiently heard him out, and then said, "All right. To see whether or not you still need me, why don't we have a man-making contest?"

"Okay, great!" the scientist said.

"Now, we're going to do this just like I did back in the old days with Adam," God said.

"That's fine," replied the scientist, and bent to scoop up a handful of dirt.

"Whoa!" God said, shaking his head in disapproval. "Not so fast, pal. You go get your own dirt!"[1]

'Get your own dirt' – that is basically the crux of the matter. Despite all the latest discoveries in every discipline of science, all the cosmologists, physicists and biologists will inevitably converge at the edge of a vast cosmic chasm they cannot cross – where did the 'first dirt' come from? And to go a step further, where did all the physical laws governing this material universe come from - from gravity to electromagnetism, the strong nuclear force, and the weak nuclear force? Who defines these and the many other laws of nature and calibrates them with such fine precision without which matter and life can never exist. Scientists today are both stunned and stumped by this exquisite fine-tuning of the universe and by what is now commonly known as the 'Anthropic Principle' – the universe appears to be patently contrived to permit intelligent life.

No matter how many theories of evolution we posit – from cosmic to biological, and no matter how far we kick the can down the road with regard to the beginning of the universe, we must end up in this curious cosmic cul-de-sac and stare in the face of this spooky conundrum: what was before all this came into being? It is like putting your hand outside the edge of the universe. This is where science ends – *ex nihilo nihil fit* (from nothing nothing comes) and the supernatural begins – "In the beginning God created the heaven and the earth."[2] (*Bible*)

The universe has a now scientifically proven, finite, one-time beginning in time past and the inexorable law of cause-and-effect must be called upon to explain its inception. The visible creation we see demands a necessary, causal Creator that transcends space, time, matter and energy. And, as this universe cannot bring itself into existence from no existence and by no existence, there must be an uncaused First Cause that brought into existence the 'first dirt' and set in motion everything we now see. Welcome to the world of God!

> "It isn't rational to argue that the world which is based
> on cause and effect is itself uncaused."[3]

References:

1.   Source Unknown

2.   *Bible*, Genesis 1:1

3.   Michael Green

Pseudo-Science is Religion

"Even if all the data point to an intelligent designer, such a hypothesis is excluded from science because it is not naturalistic."[1]

When Christians proclaim, "In the beginning there was nothing, and God created everything", the atheists would cringe in horror and label it as a fairy tale. But when secular cosmologists, with regard to the Big Bang theory, posit, "In the beginning there was nothing, and nothing created everything", they would unashamedly call it 'science'. Really, you got to be kidding? Nothing created everything? Doesn't it sound like another fairy tale?

Christians are stereotyped as 'religious' when they cannot answer the question: "If God created the universe, who created God?" But atheists are reckoned to be scientific even when they do not have the answer to: "If gravity created the universe, who created gravity?"

To have an inexplicable God that created this world is a lazy answer to the secular scientific community, but to have an inexplicable law of nature that birthed this universe seems justifiable by the same crowd. 'Shut up and calculate' is fine with the unexplained laws of nature but not with an unexplained God. This fundamentalist nature of pseudo-science is in plain sight.

Secular scientists are deemed to be very noble and honest when they admit that they do not know but are still figuring things out. But Christians are often condemned to be unscientific when they say, "We don't know and are still working on it."

According to the Darwinist, since there are so many religions and oftentimes they disagree with one another – therefore, none is true. In the same breath, they will tell us that there are many competing, scientific hypothesis - but, in this, we should celebrate! Okay, but why?

To believe that God created the world is a religious faith that is devoid of any evidence – we cannot see it happening – so say the Darwinist. But, to believe that nothing created the universe, or inorganic chemicals self-organized into the first living cell, or the first living critter blossomed into the Darwinian tree of life, is science – despite the fact that it has never been observed to have happened – no different from the belief in an unseen God or in Bertrand Russell's flying teapot orbiting the sun. This is the materialist's faith: "Even though we have never observed the mechanism of something from nothing, it must have happened!" Let us try this: "Even though we have not observed the mechanism of how God created the universe from nothing, it must have happened." What is the difference?

3

On the one hand, science boasts of being open-minded to all the possible explanations for the many mystifying and perplexing observations in the universe - no matter how counter-intuitive they may be – like the 'spooky action at a distance' in quantum mechanics. But strangely, on the other hand, secular scientists would slam the door shut on the supernatural – the only logical solution to this obvious conundrum – how did we get something from nothing apart from the uncaused First Cause, the Creator of this Universe? Occam's Razor would have shaved off all the other endless speculations on the origin of the universe and leave us with this most simple, elegant and logical uncaused First Cause that kick-started all the other secondary causes.

True science is not about the search for naturalistic truths, but all kinds of truth, and that includes the metaphysical and the supernatural. Objective science goes where the evidence leads – no matter how counter-intuitive it may be – even if it leads to a divine Designer that created the cosmos from nothing. Impartial science is bold as well as objective. It is not subjective or shackled by its own personal biasness. Let us see how skewed the mainstream, secular, scientific community is, and how pseudo-science (in contrast to objective science) today is the result of a faith-based, *a priori* bias towards only one set of conclusions in the search for truths – a materialistic explanation at the exclusion of all others, even if they make good, logical sense.

> "We take the side of science in spite of the patent absurdity of some of its constructs, in spite of its failure to fulfill many of its extravagant promises of health and life, in spite of the tolerance of the scientific community for unsubstantiated just-so stories, because we have a prior commitment, a commitment to materialism. It is not that the methods and institutions of science somehow compel us to accept a material explanation of the phenomenal world, but, on the contrary, that we are forced by our a priori adherence to material causes to create an apparatus of investigation and a set of concepts that produce material explanations, no matter how counter-intuitive, no matter how mystifying to the uninitiated. Moreover, that materialism is an absolute, for we cannot allow a Divine Foot in the door."[2] (R. Lewontin)

> "There is a kind of religion in sciences... every effect must have its cause; there is no First Cause... This religious faith of the scientist is violated by the discovery that the world had a beginning under conditions in which the known laws of physics are not valid, and as a product of forces or circumstances we cannot discover. When that happens, the scientist has lost control. If he really examined the

implications, he would be traumatized. As usual when faced with trauma, the mind reacts by ignoring the implications – in science this is known as 'refusing to speculate.'"[3] (Robert Jastrow)

Empirical science begins with the data and it gives the data a free hand to define the paradigm. Scientism commences with a yet-to-be-proven, materialistic paradigm that must be held on at all costs and rejects all others. Science is an objective discipline but Scientism is a religious faith that permits no other explanations. Science is a blessing but Scientism is a curse to science. Edward F. Blick lays it down squarely the protocol in objective science – it decides after it investigates, and not concludes before it exhausts its findings.

"To simply dismiss the concept of a Creator as being unscientific is to violate the very objectivity of science itself."[4]

In spite of all the charms about science – science is objective, science is self-correcting, and science goes where the evidence leads, there is a dark side to pseudo-science – it cannot tolerate a personal Causation to its existence because such a Creator will ruin the happiness of its ardent followers. They want Him out of their bedrooms, out of their sinful pleasures, and out of their cosmos. They do not want to be accountable to a God who someday will judge them for their sins. All non-personal causations to the existence of the universe are gladly welcome; any personal Causation will be thrown out of the window.

This is the religious nature of pseudo-science. It is, as Ben Stein puts it, the ABG hypothesis (Anything But God)[5]. It has scant little to do with evidence; it is more about a deep-seated prejudice – I don't want there to be a God. There is a world of difference between a statement made by a scientist and a scientific statement. At times, scientists do make incredibly baseless statement like: "Something can come from nothing."

My mind is made up. Don't confuse me with facts.

References:

1.   S. C. Todd, correspondence to *Nature* 410, 6752:423, 30 Sept 1999

2.   R. Lewontin, *Billions and Billions of Demons*, New York Review, 1997

3.   Robert Jastrow, *God and the Astronomers,* p. 113-114

4.   Dr. Edward F. Blick, *Special Creation vs. Evolution*, 1988, p. 29-31

5.   Ben Stein, *Expelled*

The Supernatural in the Natural

The Universe is objectively unnatural; it is astonishingly supernatural!

We have lived in this naturalistic world for so long that we forget that it is an unnatural world to begin with. It is unnatural to get something from nothing. It is unnatural to have a whole ocean of distinct, finely calibrated, subatomic particles materializing from nothing. It is unnatural to have random and unrelated physical laws governing the universe from nothing. It is even more intriguing for these laws of nature to be fine-tuned to sometimes one in a million million part to birth a life-permitting universe from nothing. And it is even more mind-boggling for these laws of nature to be exquisitely fine-tuned to each other to sustain this universe from nothing.

Gravity, electromagnetism, the strong nuclear force, and the weak nuclear force, and the whole plethora of subatomic particles are alien to the world of absolute nothing – the 'before' of the universe. We have lived so long with these matter and laws that we forget that they are exceedingly strange to a world of absolute nothing – for out of nothing, nothing comes. Objectively speaking, can nothing prefabricate these complex atomic structures from nothing, and then shackle them with even more complex laws of nature governed by even more complex mathematical equations to which they must subserviently obey? Is it not perfectly logical that the more improbable an event, the more it points to design and a designer?

If it is improbable to get an airplane or a car through chance or necessity, then it becomes a very scientific and logical proposition to attribute them to a designer. In this 'chance or design' explanation, the evidence to the contrary is the evidence – if chance cannot build a skyscraper or a space shuttle naturally, then design becomes the only alternative – there is no third option. Objective science knows when it runs out of options and turns to divine creation. Pseudo-science will carry on indefinitely believing in the impossible – even in the ridiculous notion of a naturalistic creation of something from nothing. The 'science of the gaps' argument has its limitations – scientism can never cause a wind mill, a car, a space shuttle, or an exquisitely, fine-tuned universe to appear naturally from nothing.

> "At what point is it fair to admit that science suggests that we cannot be the result of random forces... Doesn't assuming that an intelligence created these perfect conditions require far less faith than believing that a life-sustaining Earth just happened to beat the inconceivable odds to come into being?"[1]

And all this, according to the atheistic community, must be constructed from nothing and by nothing – a most ridiculous proposition by all accounts. And over time, we take it for granted that our milieu is 'natural' – it has always been like this. But for those observing from the outside or for the first time, it is unnatural or rather supernatural – how did we get all these complex atoms and the even more complex laws of nature from a simple Nothing without a brilliant Creator?

And to go a step further, because we are 'trapped' in this Cosmic Mall, the Universe, we can only look through the lens of natural science and interpret everything by its preset design often failing to realize its obvious implications and limitations. All that science is doing is discovering how this prefabricated Cosmic Mall works – $E=mc^2$, gravity attracts, light consists of photons, or the Higgs field gives mass to the particles. But the apparatus of science cannot extricate us from this Cosmic Mall and look at it objectively from without and answer the question: "Who created the Universe or why is there something rather than nothing?"

Max Planck, the father of quantum theory and Nobel Laureate for Physics, saw the obvious drawback of this restrictive science to explain how our universe came about in the first place. He writes:

> "Science cannot solve the ultimate mystery of nature. And that is because, in the last analysis, we ourselves are part of nature and therefore part of the mystery that we are trying to solve."[2]

It is akin to a bunch of natives who were locked in a shopping mall. Over time, they figured out how it worked – the lights, escalators and air conditioners. And imagine how foolish they would appear if they were to say that this is all to their whole existence? And they would further conclude that since we now understand how the mall works, there is therefore no need for the existence of the architect of the mall? We managed to squeeze out the 'architect of the gaps'. We don't need a designer to explain the mall. We now know how it works. Plain silly isn't it? Such thinking misses out the most obvious fact: who constructed the mall? It could not have materialized from nowhere. Someone has to build it and organize the whole running. The understanding of how a mall works does not do away with its builder. Instead, it helps us to appreciate his ingenuity even more. And the understanding of how the Universe works does not do away with its Maker, but rather, it reveals Him.

Science does not make God irrelevant, but instead, it is God that makes science possible. Without God, there is no science. Science is a slave, not the master. Science is the effect, not the cause. Science is the mechanism, not the Maker. That is the rightful place of science. But, secular scientists have grossly overexaggerated the importance of this humble slave called 'science', and elevated it to a pedestal it never meant to occupy.

Science may answer the question 'how', but it is not designed to answer the question 'why'. Science can tell us how gravity works, but it cannot tell us why there is gravity, and why it works the way it works. The 'how' questions belong to the world of a created science, but the 'why' questions are exclusive to the realm of a Mind, just as science may explain how a car works, but it cannot explain why there is a car in the first place. It takes a Mind to determine the 'what', 'why', and 'how' of everything in this universe – what is gravity, why gravity, how it came about to have a certain specific strength or constant, and to be fine-tuned to the rest of the other three fundamental forces to permit intelligent life to exist?

What is true of gravity is true of every other laws and matter in this universe – why space, why time, why matter, why energy, why gravity, why quantum mechanics, or why not nothing? Science is forever dumbfounded by the 'why' questions. It is 'over the head' for science because science is a humble creation of an awesome Creator. Erwin Schrödinger, the father of the quantum mechanics and Nobel Laureate for Physics, writes:

> "I am very astonished that the scientific picture of the real world around me is very deficient. It gives us a lot of factual information, puts all of our experience in a magnificently consistent order, but it is ghastly silent about all and sundry that is really near to our heart that really matters to us. It cannot tell us a word about red and blue, bitter and sweet, physical pain and physical delight; it knows nothing of beautiful and ugly, good or bad, God and eternity. Science sometimes pretends to answer questions in these domains but the answers are very often so silly that we are not inclined to take them seriously."[3]

And as for those secular scientists who are constantly ranting about the power of science to figure out everything in this Cosmic Mall, they forget that they are confined to a finite Universe with a one-time beginning and figuring out everything by its predetermined configurations. They are in a permanent cosmic lockdown. There are insuperable barriers and cosmic firewalls that natural science cannot cross. Scientism is forever incarcerated in this Cosmic Prison we call the Universe and spent its brief existence hopelessly banging its head incessantly and pitifully against the cold, impenetrable walls. We are like the frog that is consigned to a cosmic well, and we see our world with a tunnel vision – we feel convinced that science is the be-all and end-all. Or, as Arthur Schopenhauer puts it:

> "Everyone takes the limits of his own vision for the limits of the world."[4]

But science is the effect and not the cause of the universe. There was a time when there was no science. And there is a bigger world beyond our little cosmic well – the world of infinite power, infinite wisdom, and an awesome God! And all that fanciful science is doing is to take us for an endless tour in this exotic universe as more and more weird stuff are discovered. It is often a wearisome journey and we are unable to break free from its cosmic hold. And, as Steven Weinberg, Nobel Laureate in Physics, once commented:

> "The more the universe seems comprehensible, the more it seems pointless."[5]

The theists are not afraid of objective science as it leads them to the Creator and not away from Him. Science reveals God and buries atheism. Science says, "I rule supreme in the after of the creation event, but not in the 'before' – for I never did exist in the before." Empirical science points to its own demise in the white dot before the Big Bang, where all the laws of science break down, and where space, time, matter and energy, as we know it, do not exist. Scientism, naturalism and reductionism died before time began! Let us pause for a moment to read the obituary of a created science in the 'before' of the universe from the world-renowned theoretical physicist Stephen Hawking:

> "In real time, the universe has a beginning and an end at singularities that form a boundary to space-time and at which the laws of science breaks down."[6]

Science humbly bows before its Creator and reveals the ultimate Scientist that created this supernatural cosmos together with all its built-in science from nothing. Science points us to beyond a naturalistic science to the supernatural Science-Maker. From the Bible comes these revelations:

> "The heavens declare the glory of God; and the firmament sheweth (shows) his handywork."[7] (*Bible*)

> "All things were made by him; and without him was not any thing made that was made."[8] (*Bible*)

"For by him were all things created, that are in heaven, and that in earth, visible and invisible... And he is before all things, and by him all things consist."[9] (*Bible*)

"For the invisible things of him from the creation of the world are clearly seen, being understood by the things that are made, even his eternal power and Godhead; so that they are without excuse."[10] (*Bible*)

"People see God every day, they just don't recognize him."[11]

References:

1.   From the Documentary *Collision*, Christopher Hitchens vs Douglas Wilson, *italics mine*

2.   Max Planck, *Where is Science Going,* W. W. Norton & company, Inc, New York, p. 217, 1932

3.   Erwin Schrödinger, the founding father of the Quantum mechanics, Nobel Laureate for Physics in 1933, 'Nature and the Greeks' and 'Science and Humanism', Cambridge University Press, 1954, p. 95)

4.   Arthur Schopenhauer

5.   Steven Weinberg, *The First Three Minutes: A Modern View of the Origin of the Universe*, 1977, 1993, p. 154

6.   Stephen Hawking, *A Brief History of Time*, p. 139

7.   *Bible*, Psalms 19:1

8.   *Bible*, John 1:3

9.   *Bible*, Colossians 1:16-17

10.   *Bible*, Romans 1:20

11.   Pearl Bailey

Much Ado About Nothing

There was a time when things were simpler – nothing is nothing. And nothing can create nothing. And out of nothing comes nothing. If nothing can create something, then it cannot be nothing but something. And there was nothing too difficult to understand about nothing. And so says an old song: "Nothing comes from nothing, nothing ever could." In short, there is no 'free lunch'.

Today's definition of nothing is kind of convoluted – it is really not nothing, but something that is masqueraded as 'nothing' – that is, the quantum vacuum or empty space. Every three-dimension space in this finite universe – be it on this earth or in outer space – is not empty. It is a sea of subatomic energies – the world of quantum fluctuations where virtual particles appear and disappear in a brief moment, annihilating each other. In short, the empty space in this universe is not empty; it is literally a seething froth of quantum energies. And it is estimated that more than 95% of the mass-energy in the universe is in empty space – the so-called 'dark energy' and 'dark matter'.

In the Standard Big Bang model of the universe, theoretical physicists postulated that the universe brought itself into existence from no existence and by no existence some 13.8 billion years ago. Literally, nothing expanded through what is now called the Big Bang (nobody has a clue of what it is or how it works, but it is supposed to have happened), and the universe popped out from nowhere and became everything we now see – space-time and mass-energy suddenly appeared with all its accompanying laws of nature. Amazing! Although this sounds more like a fairy tale, yet it is accepted today as 'empirical science'.

"The Big Bang theory says nothing about what banged, why it banged, or what happened before it banged."[1] (Alan Guth)

The atheist's faith: "Once there was nothing, and nothing mysteriously exploded. And from it came a zoo of particles that magically turned into a zoo of living creatures. And it makes perfectly good sense! Hallelujah!"

In order to dodge the possibility of a Creator, secular theoretical physicists attempt to prove that something can come from nothing without a Designer through this Big Bang cosmology – the ultimate 'free lunch' of the universe. But their concept of 'nothing' is not nothing, but something – the quantum vacuum governed by the laws of nature, and popping with virtual particles. The problem is, before the Big Bang, there was literally nothing – no quantum vacuum, no quantum mechanics, and no anything. And nothingness cannot bring something into existence, much less, an inflating universe stuffed with billions of galaxies and myriads of stars, and a whole plethora of complex physical laws. We call this 'common sense', which is getting rarer and rarer by the day.

For others, they push the beginning of the universe further back into deep time through the Multiverse cosmology to some pre-existing primordial quantum vacuum, weak energy fields, or quantum froth. But the existence of this primordial quantum vacuum itself needs an explanation for its existence – it just cannot pop out of nowhere or the First Law of Conservation of energy will be violated (energy cannot be created or destroyed). There is no 'cheating' in this cosmic genesis.

A note from the Stanford Encyclopedia shows us this sleight of hand by secular cosmologists to replace an absolute nothing with a quantum something:

> "For one thing, how can empty space explode without there being matter or energy? Since space is a function of matter, if no matter existed, neither could space, let alone empty space, exist. Further, if the vacuum has energy, the question arises concerning the origin of the vacuum and its energy. In short, merely pushing the question of the beginning of the universe back to some primordial quantum vacuum does not escape the question of what brought this vacuum laden with energy into existence. A quantum vacuum is not nothing (as in Newtonian physics) but "a sea of continually forming and dissolving particles that borrow energy from the vacuum for their brief existence (Craig 1993, 143). Hence, he concludes, the appeal to a vacuum as the initial state is misleading. Defenders of the argument affirm that only a personal explanation can provide the sufficient reason for the existence of the universe.""[2]

Lawrence Krauss, in his book, *A Universe From Nothing: Why There is Something Rather than Nothing*, attempts to prove the universe can come from nothing without the hand of a Creator. But when he describes that 'nothing', it sounds a lot like something. Don't let him fool you with his 'nothing'. His 'nothing' is not nothing, but something – an already existing quantum vacuum or empty space peppered with the law of quantum mechanics and popping with virtual particles. He is no different from all the previous 'emperors with no clothes' in all of their cosmological parades seeking to fool the uninitiated into believing they were elegantly clothed in the latest, cutting-edge, scientific garb. All it takes is for the little boy in the street to honestly blurt out, "The emperor has no clothes", and soon the emperor will be sent scuttling red-faced to his palace.

Just look beyond all the wild cheering and silly praises by the journalistic crowds, and ask Krauss this simple question: "What is your definition of 'nothing'?" And soon you will see his gaudy underwear. His definition of nothing is: "Nothing is usually a boiling, bubbling brew of virtual particles popping in and out of existence..."[3] Incredible, his definition of 'nothing' is not nothing but a 'boiling, bubbling brew of virtual particles'. Any 5-year-old kid can see that it is not nothing, but something.

Krauss, like many of today's high-powered scientists, has to first redefine the long-established meaning of 'nothing' to mean the 'quantum vacuum laden with energy and governed by the laws of quantum mechanics' to prove that something can come from nothing without the hand of a Creator. In short, Krauss' 'nothing' is not nothing, but a something that consists minimally of space-time and the laws of quantum mechanics. His universe can never come from the conventional, ironclad definition of 'nothing' – no space-time, no mass-energy, no laws of physics, and no anything. His universe has to come from within an existing cosmos governed by the laws of nature, and not from the 'before' of the cosmos where there is absolutely nothing to begin with. Krauss may be a very educated and bright scientist, but he hasn't got a clue about 'nothing'. And it is no wonder his 'nothing', like him, is terribly unstable. Let us unravel his crafty shenanigan:

> "... 'something' and 'nothing' are physical concepts and therefore are properly the domain of science, not theology or philosophy."[4] (Lawrence Krauss)

> "But... surely 'nothing' is every bit as physical as 'something,' especially if it is to be defined as the 'absence of something.' It then behooves us to understand precisely the physical nature of both these quantities."[5] (Jerry Coyne)

First, science, not logic, calls the shots and does the defining of 'nothing'. Next, 'nothing' is now defined as something, not nothing – "nothing is every bit as physical as something". So Krauss' audacious claim of 'something from nothing' is no more than 'something from something' masquerading as 'something from nothing' – definitely donkey's definition and logic, and not empirical science. If you were to ask Krauss what did he eat for lunch, he might tell you that he ate 'nothing', and then followed by, "Boy, it was awesome and it sure tasted great." Or, if you were to asked him where did he go last summer, his answer might be 'nowhere', and then followed by, "But the scenery there was

13

breathtaking." You cannot help feeling exasperated when engaging Krauss on 'nothing' – there will never be any meeting of the minds with all these warped definitions of everyday terminologies.

Krauss' Tango:

Step 1:   First, redefine something as 'nothing'.
Step 2:   Next, show that that 'nothing' can produce something.
Step 3:   Voila! There you have it – something can come from 'nothing'.
Step 4:   And so, the universe came from 'nothing'. God is not necessary.

Even the *Skeptical Inquirer* magazine is skeptical about Lawrence Krauss' audacious claim of something coming from nothing:

> "In places throughout the book, and in a more sustained way in later chapters, Krauss returns to the question of whether the science that he has described shows that one can get Something from Nothing... If one uses a natural scientific definition of Nothing, namely the lowest-energy state of a system, then it is a simple consequence of Schrodinger's equation that this state will never evolve into any other state... So, as long as we are in the realm of conventional quantum mechanics, current science supports the theologians: Nothing will always lead to Nothing... At this point the science of Nothing is overwhelmed by so much ambiguity and speculation that I am not sure how much advantage it has over theology."[6]

David Albert, professor of philosophy at Columbia University and the author of *Quantum Mechanics and Experience*, brilliantly rips to shreds this deceptive proposition of *A Universe from Nothing* by Krauss. He writes:

> "Krauss seems to be thinking that these vacuum states amount to the relativistic-quantum-field-theoretical version of there not being any physical stuff at all... And that, in a nutshell, is the account he proposes of why there should be something rather than nothing.
>
> But that's just not right. Relativistic-quantum-field-theoretical vacuum states – no less than giraffes or refrigerators or solar systems – are particular arrangements of elementary physical stuff... The fact that some arrangements of fields happen to correspond to the existence of particles and some don't is not a whit more

mysterious than the fact that some of the possible arrangements of my fingers happen to correspond to the existence of a fist and some don't. And the fact that particles can pop in and out of existence, over time, as those fields rearrange themselves, is not a whit more mysterious than the fact that fists can pop in and out of existence, over time, as my fingers rearrange themselves. And none of these poppings – if you look at them aright – amount to anything even remotely in the neighborhood of a creation from nothing... Krauss is dead wrong and his religious and philosophical critics are absolutely right."[7]

Many thinking scientists do not buy Krauss' ridiculous notion of *A Universe from Nothing*. In his book, *Did Adam and Eve Have Navels?*, well-known humanist mathematician and science writer, Martin Gardner, writes:

"It is fashionable now to conjecture that the big bang was caused by a random quantum fluctuation in a vacuum devoid of space and time. But of course such a vacuum is a far cry from nothing."[8]

Let us hear what Alan Guth, professor of physics at M.I.T., has to say about the quantum vacuum or empty space:

"In this context, a proposal that the universe was created from empty space is no more fundamental than a proposal that the universe was spawned by a piece of rubber. It might be true, but one would still want to ask where the piece of rubber came from."[9]

Theoretical physicist Alexander Vilenkin, one of the founders of the *Borde-Guth-Vilenkin* theorem, debunks the idea that empty space is nothing. He concludes that the origin of the universe ultimately ends with this brick wall – the inexplicable laws of physics which, by his own admission, is not nothing.

"A quantum fluctuation of the vacuum assumes that there was a vacuum of some pre-existing space. And we now know that "vacuum" is very different from "nothing." Vacuum, or empty space, has energy and tension, it can bend and warp, so it is unquestionably something."[10]

"I say "nothing" in quotations because the nothing that we were referring to here is the absence of matter, space and time. That is as close to nothing as you can get, but what is still required here is the laws of physics. So the laws of physics should still be there, and they are definitely not nothing."[11]

To sum it up, there is an 'absolute nothing' before the Big Bang, with no laws of nature, no space-time, no mass-energy, no anything, and can create nothing. And there is a 'false nothing' (false vacuum), the quantum vacuum, the empty space, that is everywhere in this created universe and bubbling with all kinds of virtual particles. And secular theoretical physicists attempt to replace an 'absolute nothing' with a 'false nothing' – the empty space bloated with space-time, mass-energy, and the inexplicable laws of nature – with this sleight of hand to prove that whole universes can be conjured up from nothingness.

It is truly an amazing cosmic performance designed to enthrall the simplistic populace. They saw what they always wanted to see – a world without God, without accountability, and, in the long run, without purpose. And a universe appearing from nothing fits perfectly. But the only problem is that that 'nothing' is not nothing but a pre-existing and created something.

A more accurate tittle for Lawrence Krauss' book, *A Universe from Nothing: Why there is Something rather than Nothing,* would be: *A Universe from Something masquerading as Nothing: Why there are Some Donkeys rather than No Donkeys*. In trying to propagate his 'something from nothing', Krauss inevitably ends up to be more of a comical 'nothing from something'.

"Do advances in modern physics and cosmology help us address these underlying questions, of why there is something called the universe at all, and why there are things called "the laws of physics," and why those laws seem to take the form of quantum mechanics, and why some particular wave function and Hamiltonian? In a word: no. I don't see how they could. Sometimes physicists pretend that they are addressing these questions, which is too bad, because they are just being lazy and not thinking carefully about the problem."[12]
(Sean Carroll)

"Scientists tell us the universe is made up of electrons, protons and neutrons.
They forgot to mention morons."[13]

16

References:

1. Neil, Swidey, *Alan Guth, What made the Big Bang,* The Boston Globe, May 2014

2. *Stanford Encyclopaedia of Philosophy*, first published Jul 13, 2004; substantive revision, Oct 26, 2012

3. Transcript for Lawrence Krauss & Marcelo Gleiser on *Something from Nothing.* Lawrence Krauss, *A Universe From Nothing,* YouTube

4. Krauss, in Harris, *'Everything and Nothing: An Interview with Lawrence M. Krauss'*

5. Jerry Coyne, *'David Alberts pans Lawrence Krauss' New Book'*, p. 8-9

6. Review of *"A universe from nothing"*, Lawrence Krauss, Published in Skeptical Inquirer, Nov/Dec 2012, by Mark Alford

7. David Albert, *On the Origin of the Universe*, The New York Times, March 23, 2012

8. Martin Gardner, 2000, *Did Adam and Eve Have Navels?* New York: W.W. Norton, p. 303

9. Alan Guth, *The Inflationary Universe*, New York: Perseus Books, 1997, p. 273

10. Vilenkin, Alex, *Many Worlds in One: The Search for Other Universes*, New York: Hill and Wang, 2006, p. 185

11. Jacqueline Mitchell, *In the Beginning Was the Beginning*, Tufts Now, May 29, 2012

12. Carroll, Sean, *A Universe from Nothing?* Cosmic Variance Blog, April 28, 2012

13. Avinash Wandre

Something from Nothing = God

"Astronomers now find they have painted themselves into a corner because they have proven, by their own methods, that the world began abruptly in an act of creation to which you can trace the seeds of every star, every planet, every living thing in this cosmos and on the earth. And they have found that all this happened as a product of forces they cannot hope to discover... That there are what I or anyone would call supernatural forces at work is now, I think, a scientifically proven fact."[1] (Robert Jastrow)

"This is an exceedingly strange development, unexpected by all but the theologians. They have always accepted the word of the Bible: In the beginning God created the heaven and the earth... It is unexpected because science has had such extraordinary success in tracing the chain of cause and effect backward in time. For the scientist who has lived by his faith in the power of reason, the story ends like a bad dream. He has scaled the mountains of ignorance; he is about to conquer the highest peak; as he pulls himself over the final rock, he is greeted by a band of theologians who have been sitting there for centuries."[2] (Robert Jastrow)

Science takes pride in projecting itself as an empirical discipline. It makes careful deductions of the events it observes and then subjects them to rigorous scrutiny – are they testable, falsifiable and repeatable, and do the observations tally with the predictions? Secular scientists are usually very scientific in the 'after' of the Big Bang but not in the 'before'. As they approach the 'before' of the Big Bang where all the laws of nature break down, they literally commit academic suicide en masse – they just jump off the cosmic cliff. They suddenly become very unashamedly unscientific. Are you ready for this? They consider this to be the most cutting-edge discovery of all time: "YES, SOMETHING CAN COME FROM NOTHING!" In a quantum second, the jealously-guarded and time-proven, cause-and-effect explanation for all physical phenomena is unapologetically thrown out of the window and murdered in cold blood.

Everything physical we see demands a logical causation, and science has meticulously provided those explanations. But when it comes to the birth of this finite universe, these cosmologists just went insane – they irrationally held on to a causeless Big Bang – it just banged, and not only banged, it is capable of orchestrating its own banging, fine-tuned to 1 part in 10^{123} in the first instant, to spit out the billions of bizarre, spiral galaxies and the myriads of orbiting planets. What? You have got to be kidding – nothingness, with no laws of nature and no anything, can bang into existence 'something' with all the accompanying ironclad, complex, varied, limited, fine-tuned laws governing the even weirder, fine-tuned subatomic particles? And this complex universe can pop out of nothingness?

Even a high school kid with two grains of common sense between the ears would find this laughable. Is it possible for rocks and pebbles to appear from the empty space in the classroom? These kids would be scorned by these giants of science for even suggesting such a possibility. Yet, the same secular cosmological think-tank will tell you with a straight face that this vast, dazzling universe with its predictable general theory of relativity and its bizarre quantum mechanics can materialize from nothing without the hand of a Creator. We suppose pseudo-science today has reached its zenith in this hilarious cosmic play entitled: *A Big Bang without a Starter Gun*. It probably outsells *Chitty Chitty Bang Bang*.

It is just unbelievable what these cutting-edge 'nothing theorists' have to say about a causeless universe appearing from nothing:

> "Our universe is simply one of those things which happen from time to time."[3] (Edward P. Tryon)

> "... the universe is probably the result of a random quantum fluctuation in a spaceless, timeless void... So what had to happen to start the universe was the formation of an empty bubble of highly curved space-time. How did this bubble form? What caused it? Not everything requires a cause. It could have just happened spontaneously as one of the many linear combinations of universes that has the quantum numbers of the void... Much is still in the speculative stage, and I must admit that there are yet no empirical or observational tests that can be used to test the idea of an accidental origin."[4] (Stenger, Victor J.)

> "What produced the energy before inflation? This is perhaps the ultimate question. As crazy as it might seem, the energy may have come out of nothing! The meaning of "nothing" is somewhat ambiguous here. It might be the vacuum in some pre-existing space and time, or it could be nothing at all – that is, all concepts of space and time were created with the universe itself."[5] (Alexei V. Filippenko and Jay M. Pasachoff)

"There's no such thing as a free lunch, or so the saying goes, but that may not be true on the grandest, cosmic scale. Many physicists now believe that the universe arose out of nothingness during the Big Bang which means that nothing must have somehow turned into something. How could that be possible?"[6] (Amanda Gefter)

Ralph Estling articulated in the *Skeptical Inquirer* a stinging rebuke of the idea that the cosmos can create itself out of nothing. In his article, curiously titled, *"The Scalp-Tinglin', Mind-Blowin', Eye-Poppin', Heart-Wrenchin', Stomach-Churnin', Foot-Stumpin', Great Big Doodley Science Show!!!"*, he wrote:

"The problem emerges in science when scientists leave the realm of science and enter that of philosophy and metaphysics, too often grandiose names for mere personal opinion, untrammeled by empirical evidence or logical analysis, and wearing the mask of deep wisdom.

And so they conjure us an entire Cosmos, or myriads of cosmoses, suddenly, inexplicably, causelessly leaping into being out of – out of Nothing Whatsoever, for no reason at all, and thereafter expanding faster than light into more Nothing Whatsoever. And so cosmologists have given us Creation ex nihilo... And at the instant of this Creation, they inform us, almost parenthetically, the universe possessed the interesting attributes of Infinite Temperature, Infinite Density, and Infinitesimal Volume, a rather gripping state of affairs, as well as something of a sudden and dramatic change from Nothing Whatsoever. They then intone equations and other ritual mathematical formulae and look upon it and pronounce it good.

I do not think that what these cosmologists, these quantum theorists, these universe-makers, are doing is science. I can't help feeling that universes are notoriously disinclined to spring into being, ready-made, out of nothing. Even if Edward Tryon (ah, a name at last!) has written that "our universe is simply one of those things which happen from time to time..." Perhaps, although we have the word of many famous scientists for it, our universe is not simply one of those things that happen from time to time."[7]

20

To get something from nothing looks more like a cosmic magic show for children than serious science. It is like the conjuring of a rabbit from an empty magician's hat. David Darling was brutally frank when he penned down this sarcastic note:

> "What is the big deal – the biggest deal of all – is how you get something out of nothing... Don't let the cosmologists try to kid you on this one. They have not got a clue either – despite the fact that they are doing a pretty good job of convincing themselves and others that this is really not a problem. 'In the beginning,' they will say, 'there was nothing – no time, space, matter or energy. Then there was a quantum fluctuation from which...' Whoa! Stop right there. You see what I mean? First there is nothing, then there is something. And the cosmologists try to bridge the two with a quantum flutter, a tremor of uncertainty that sparks it all off. Then they are away and before you know it, they have pulled a hundred billion galaxies out of their quantum hats..."[8]

Renowned British astronomer Sir Fred Hoyle viewed with much dissatisfaction the notion of a universe expanding from nothing. He writes:

> "This most peculiar situation is taken by many astronomers to represent the origin of the universe. The universe is supposed to have begun at this particular time. From where? The usual answer, surely an unsatisfactory one, is: from nothing!"[9]

Let us hear what renowned philosopher David Hume has to say regarding a known effect without a cause:

> "I have never asserted so absurd a proposition as that anything might arise without cause."[10]

In their irrational attempts to get rid of God, secular scientists have neither qualm nor shame about throwing rationality out of the window. They can't see the cosmic madman in their cosmic mirror. George Orwell's well-worded insult has found a permanent home in the world of these absurd, ridiculous, unscientific cosmologists:

> "One has to belong to the intelligentsia to believe things like that: no ordinary man could be such a fool."[11]

21

A statement made by a scientist is not the same as a scientific statement. At times, it is just an unsubstantiated, stupid statement. Just pose this simple question to these 'nothing theorists': Have you observed, tested, and repeated this prediction of 'something materializing from nothing'? If not, or if it can't be done, then where did you get the mandate to pronounce this naturalistic 'something out of nothing' as a scientific theory and circulate it around in the many science journals and TV programs until it morphs into an almost foregone conclusion and beyond dispute? The poor public swallows it hook, line and sinker – an untested hypothesis that is peddled as an established scientific theory. Just listen to all the talk shows on the Big Bang or the Multiverse. It sounds like it is a proven fact that something can indeed materialize from nothing.

Richard Lieu of the Department of Physics, University of Alabama, highlights the ridiculous latitude these absurd cosmologists would accord themselves in inventing unknowns to explain the unknown:

> "Cosmology is not even astrophysics: all the principal assumptions in this field are unverified (or unverifiable) in the laboratory, and researchers are quite comfortable with inventing unknowns to explain the unknown."[12]

In contrast, many down-to-earth, candid scientists are fully aware of this impossible, cosmic chasm that cannot be crossed – the realm where all the laws of science break down – the 'before' of the Big Bang. From Albert Einstein to Stephen Hawking, they find themselves entering into the domain where one can only speculate but not calculate. There are no laws of science to work with in that absolute nothingness – the 'before' of the inflation of the universe. To Einstein, it is the frustrating "curtain that cannot be lifted"[13]; to Hawking, in his frank moment, it is the place where "one would have to appeal to religion and the hand of God"[14]; to Andre Linde, "this problem lies somewhere at the boundary between physics and metaphysics"[15]; and to Barry Parker, "a creation of some sort is forced upon us."[16]

As atheistic as some of these scientists may be, they do not spit out the usual, scathing rhetoric by many of the superficial cosmologists against the theists in their claim of God creating the cosmos – the accusation of resorting to the 'God of the gaps' (whatever we cannot understand, we attribute to God), the argument from incredulity (if things are just too complex to have happened, they must have been created by God), or just being plain lazy (when science cannot explain the unexplainable, God must be the One who did it). These renowned men of science saw the depth of the problem and humbly recognized that scientism is not omnipotent but has its physical limitations. And they saw where all the evidence were gravitating to – from the material reality to an immaterial causation.

There is a cosmic chasm that science just simply cannot cross. It is void of the physical laws that science finds solace in. Science can only come to the edge of this vast cosmic chasm and meekly acknowledge that beyond the wide horizon, the Supernatural must provide the bridge to bring one across. The laws of nature cannot provide for that bridge between nothing and something because there are no laws of nature in nothingness to construct it. This physically-impossible bridge can only be fabricated with the materials that transcend space, time, matter and energy, and that inevitably points to the Great Architect of the Universe who is spaceless, timeless and immaterial.

Renowned agnostic astronomer Robert Jastrow had pondered long and hard over this impenetrable cosmic barrier. He saw no hope for any naturalistic explanation for the inexplicable commencement of the universe. Instead, he saw the end of science in this cosmic beginning.

> "But the latest astronomical results indicate that at some point in the past the chain of cause and effect terminated abruptly. An important event occurred – the origin of the world – for which there is no known cause or explanation within the realm of science. The Universe flashed into being, and we cannot find out what caused that to happen.
>
> This is a distressing result for scientists because, in the scientist's view, given enough time and money, he must be able to find an explanation for the beginning of the Universe on his own terms – an explanation that fits into the framework of natural rather than supernatural forces.
>
> So, the scientist asks himself, what cause led to the effect we call the Universe? And he proceeds to examine the conditions under which the world began. But then he sees that he is deprived – today, tomorrow, and very likely forever – of finding out the answer to this critical question...
>
> This is a very surprising conclusion. Nothing in the history of science leads us to believe there should be a fundamental limit to the results of scientific inquiry. Science has had extraordinary success in piecing together the elements of a story of cosmic evolution that adds many details to the first pages of Genesis. The scientist has traced the history of the Universe back in time from the appearance of man to the lower animals, then across the threshold of life to a time when the earth did not exist,

and then back farther still to a time when stars and galaxies had not yet formed and the heavens were dark. Now he goes farther back still, feeling he is close to success – the answer to the ultimate question of beginning – when suddenly the chain of cause and effect snaps. The birth of the Universe is an effect for which he cannot find the cause."[17]

In another book, *Until the Sun Dies*, Jastrow laments:

"This great saga of cosmic evolution, to whose truth the majority of scientists subscribe, is the product of an act of creation that took place twenty billion years ago [by evolutionary estimates – BT]. Science, unlike the Bible, has no explanation for the occurrence of that extraordinary event. The Universe, and everything that has happened in it since the beginning of time, are a grand effect without a known cause. An effect without a cause? That is not the world of science; it is world of witchcraft, of wild events and the whims of demons, a medieval world that science has tried to banish. As scientists, what are we to make of this picture? I do not know."[18]

Albert Einstein, despite his brilliance, saw the same depressing picture of the hopelessness of any possible naturalistic explanation for the unnatural commencement of the universe. He writes:

"Scientists live by their faith in causation, and the chain of cause and effect. Every effect has a cause that can be discovered by rational arguments. And this has been a very successful program, if you will, for unraveling the history of the universe. But it just fails at the beginning... So time, really, going backward, comes to a halt at that point. Beyond that, that curtain can never be lifted... And that is really a blow at the very fundamental premise that motivates all scientists."[19]

Renowned astrophysicist Stephen Hawking too, acknowledges this inescapable cosmic cemetery where the laws of science were buried in the white dot before the Big Bang. In *A Brief History of Time,* he wrote the obituary for scientism:

"In real time, the universe has a beginning and an end at singularities that form a boundary to space-time and at which the laws of science breaks down."[20]

Over and over again, all the brightest minds could do was to throw up their hands on this unnatural cosmic genesis. Russian cosmologist, A. D. Linde, pens down this pensive thought:

> "The most difficult aspect of this problem is not the existence of the singularity itself, but the question of what was before the singularity... This problem lies somewhere at the boundary between physics and metaphysics."[21]

World-renowned British astrophysicist, Sir Arthur Eddington, freely admits:

> "The beginning seems to present insuperable difficulties unless we agree to look on it as frankly supernatural."[22]

Let us hear from Max Planck, a legend in the world of quantum physics:

> "As a man who has devoted his whole life to the most clear headed science, to the study of matter, I can tell you as a result of my research about atoms this much: There is no matter as such. All matter originates and exists only by virtue of a force which brings the particle of an atom to vibration and holds this most minute solar system of the atom together. We must assume behind this force the existence of a conscious and intelligent mind. This mind is the matrix of all matter."[23]

Nobel Laureate in Physics and a UC Berkeley professor Charles Townes sums it up neatly:

> "In my view the question of origin seems always left unanswered if we explore from a scientific point of view alone. Thus, I believe there is a need for some religious or metaphysical explanation. I believe in the concept of God and in His existence."[24]

When the atheist runs from a supernatural Creator, he must run into an insuperable conundrum – how do we get something from nothing? He merely sidesteps the supernatural and bumps into the metaphysical – the very thing that he is desperately trying to avoid. Cosmological tooth fairies must be invoked time and again by secular cosmologists to prove that something can come from nothing without the hand of the Divine. And his most comical tooth fairy is: "Give me the first miracle (the Big Bang) and we will explain the rest." But that is a blatant, cosmic cheating condemned in the field of empirical science.

Nothing cannot birth something because Nothing is no existence, no laws, and no anything. It is 'what rocks dream about'. If something did appear from nothing, then, there has to be a preexistent, uncaused First Cause to birth it. The Universe cannot 'bootstrap' itself from nothing! Keith Ward, in his book *God, Chance and Necessity,* writes:

> "Between the hypothesis of God and the hypothesis of a cosmic bootstrap, there is no competition. We were always right to think that persons, or universes, who seek to pull themselves up by their own bootstraps are forever doomed to failure."[25]

If something is highly improbable, it needs a miracle; if it is totally impossible, it needs a Creator. Something from Nothing = God.

"No material thing can create itself."[26]

References:

1.   *A Scientist Caught Between Two Faiths: Interview with Robert Jastrow,* Christianity Today, August 6, 1982, p. 15, 18

2.   Robert Jastrow, *God and the Astronomers,* 1978, p. 116

3.   Edward P. Tryon, professor of physics, Hunter College, Manhattan, as quoted in Trefil, 1984, 92[6]:100

4.   Stenger, Victor J., particle physicist, *Was the Universe Created?* Free Inquiry, 7[3]:26-30, Summer, 1987

5.   Alexei V. Filippenko and Jay M. Pasachoff in an article, *'A Universe from Nothing'*

6.   Amanda Gefter, *Existence: Why is there a universe?* New Scientist, 26 July 2011

7.   Estling, Ralph, *Letter to the Editor, Skeptical Inquirer,* 19[1]:69-70, January/February, 1994, 18[4]:430, emph. Added

8.   David Darling, *On creating something from nothing,* New Scientist, 151 (2047), 1996, p. 49

9.   Sir Fred Hoyle, *Astronomy Today,* London: Heinemann, 1975, p. 165

10.   J. Y. T. Greid, ed., *The Letters of David Hume,* Oxford: Clarendon Press, 1932, p. 187

11. George Orwell, *Notes on Nationalism*, p. 45

12. Lieu, R., *LCDM cosmology: how much suppression of credible evidence, and does the model really lead its competitors, using all evidence?* 17 May 2007, arXiv:0705.2462

13. As quoted in *Heeren*, 1995, p. 303

14. Lisa Grossman, *Why Physicists can't avoid a Creation Event*, New Scientist, 11 January 2012

15. A. D. Linde, *Inflationary Universe*, p. 976

16. Barry Parker, *Creation - the Story of the Origin and Evolution of the Universe*, New York & London: Plenum Press, 1988, p. 202

17. Robert Jastrow, *Message from Professor Robert Jastrow*

18. Robert Jastrow, *Until the Sun Dies*, 1977, p. 21

19. As quoted in *Heeren*, 1995, p. 303

20. Stephen Hawking, *A Brief History of Time*, p. 139

21. A. D. Linde, *Inflationary Universe*, p. 976

22. Arthur Eddington, *The Expanding Universe*, New York: Macmillan, 1933, p. 178

23. Max Planck, physicists, founder of the quantum theory, Das Wesen der Materie [*The Nature of Matter*], speech at Florence, Italy, 1944, from Archiv zur Geschichte der Max-Planck-Gesellwft, Abt. Va, Rep. 11 Planck, Nr. 1797

24. Charles Townes, Nobel laureate, quoted by Henry F. Schaeffer III in *Stephen Hawking, the Big Bang, and God*, 1994

25. Keith Ward, *God, Chance and Necessity,* Oxford: One World Publications, 1996, p. 49

26. George Davis, Physicist

The Cosmic Genesis

"All the evidence we have says that the universe had a beginning."[1] (A. Vilenkin)

"Almost everyone now believes that the universe, and time itself, had a beginning at the big bang."[2] (Stephen Hawking)

"About thirty years ago science solved the mystery of the birth and death of stars, and acquired new evidence that the Universe had a beginning... Now both theory and observation pointed to an expanding Universe and a beginning in time."[3] (Robert Jastrow)

The secular, scientific community loathes the idea that the universe had a beginning. If the universe had a beginning, then one is forced to confront the possibility of a supernatural cause – God – because something cannot come from nothing apart from a supernatural Creator that transcends space and time. For years, they labored long and hard to seek out a naturalistic explanation for the existence of this finite universe. 'We cannot allow a Divine Foot in the door' is their battle cry as they look for just-so stories to explain why there is something rather than nothing and yet, without a beginning or a supernatural Causation. They keep kicking the can further down the road – postulating one model of the universe after another – from the Steady State to the Big Bang, and onto the Multiverse – to avoid the much dreaded 'beginning'.

Even the renowned astrophysicist Stephen Hawking recognized this self-evident truth that if the universe has a beginning then the hand of God has to come into play:

> "So long as the universe had a beginning, we could suppose it had a creator (the cosmological argument). But if the universe is really completely self-contained, having no boundary or edge, it would have neither beginning nor end: it would simply be. What place, then, for a creator?"[4]

Stephen Hawking labored for years to get rid of this troubling 'beginning' of the universe but the Borde-Guth-Vilenkin Theorem shows that there is no way to dodge this inescapable cosmic genesis.

The Eternal Universe

First on the scene is the Eternal Universe that postulates a cosmos without a beginning. As Carl Sagan put it, "The Cosmos is all that is, or ever was, or ever will be."[5] This is commonly believed to avoid the troubling 'beginning' of the universe that points directly to a supernatural Creator. However, if the universe has eternally been like this, then it poses the following problems:

First, it is hard to conceive something like the finite universe to be eternal. How did something come from nothing, absolute nothing? Who introduced the original energy into this finite universe? How did space, time, matter and energy appear from nowhere and become the 'eternal universe'? It violates the First Law of Thermodynamics – energy cannot be created or destroyed. So the obvious question is: where did the initial energy in the universe come from? It cannot materialize from thin air.

Secondly, if the universe has been around for a long eternal past – trillions and trillions of years – the sun and all the stars in the night sky would have long burnt out and we would be in a Big Freeze or a Heat Death. The Second Law of Thermodynamics tells us that the usable energy in an isolated system will always decrease, and the process is irreversible. The usable energy from the sun will be converted into light and heat, and they cannot be reconverted back to become the sun again. Someday, the universe will be nothing more than a cold, dark, lifeless, expanding cosmos. In short, who wound up this cosmic clock that is running down in what is known as entropy? The universe is getting darker and colder by the minute.

Thirdly, it is observed that all the galaxies are moving away from each other at great speed. This suggests that the universe had a beginning somewhere in time past when they were closer together. If the universe has been around for a long eternal past, all the galaxies would have moved to realms beyond our visual horizon, and the only galaxy we will know of today is our Milky Way. And yet, we are able to observe the billions of galaxies around us. This shows that this is a relatively young universe. The Eternal Universe was blown apart by the Big Bang with a finite beginning.

In *God and the Astronomers*, Robert Jastrow explains why all attempts to prove an eternal universe have failed miserably. He writes:

> "Now three lines of evidence – the motions of the galaxies, the laws of thermodynamics, and the life story of the stars – pointed to one conclusion; all indicated that the Universe had a beginning."[6]

Barry Parker put paid to the Eternal Universe:

> "We do, of course, have an alternative. We could say that there was no creation, and that the universe has always been here. But this is even more difficult to accept than creation."[7]

The Big Bang

Next in line is the Big Bang model of the universe, a term coined by the Steady State proponent, Sir Fred Hoyle, who used it in a derogatory manner against the Big Bang theorists in 1950 during a BBC radio broadcast. The Standard Big Bang theory tells of a beginning where all the mass-energy and space-time in the universe were once compressed into an infinitesimal small area, smaller than an atom. And then, for some unknown reason, it exploded or, more accurately, it expanded. And through the process of time, it organized itself into what we see today – the billions of exotic galaxies that litter the cosmic landscape.

The discovery by Edwin Hubble in 1929 of the redshift of the light from distant galaxies supposedly points to an expanding universe. In 1964, Arno Penzias and Robert Wilson chanced upon the cosmic microwave background (CMB) radiation which many believed is the echo or the after-glow of the Big Bang. These, together with Albert Einstein's General Theory of Relativity (without the fudge factor), seem to confirm the Big Bang theory.

However, instead of pointing us away from the need for a Creator, it actually forces upon us the possibility of His existence. Since there is an unavoidable beginning of the universe, there must be a cosmic 'Starter Gun' that sets off the 'Big Bang'. Our human rationality and common sense would oblige us to conclude that there must be an intelligent and powerful Someone that is able to 'bang' something out of nothing. Let us hear what some candid physicists and cosmologists have to say about the Big Bang theory:

> "The big bang theory requires a recent origin of the Universe that openly invites the concept of creation."[8]
> (Sir Fred Hoyle)

> "If we accept the big bang theory, and most cosmologists now do, then a 'creation' of some sort is forced upon us."[9]
> (Barry Parker)

"Even for a die-hard naturalist, naturalism ends prior to 10^{-43} s after this creation event. There is a singularity, where the laws of the universe break down (can no longer be applied). The "Big Bang" is a theory of creation! It is not a naturalistic theory of origins! Philosophically, the notion of a beginning of the present order of Nature is repugnant to me... I should like to find a genuine loophole."[10] (Sir Arthur S. Eddington)

"The seed of everything that has happened in the Universe was planted in that first instant; every star, every planet and every living creature in the Universe came into being as a result of events that were set in motion in the moment of the cosmic explosion... It was literally the moment of Creation. The Universe flashed into being, and we cannot find out what caused that to happen."[11] (Robert Jastrow)

"We have this very solid conclusion that the universe had an origin, the Big Bang. Fifteen billion years ago, the universe began with an unimaginably bright flash of energy from an infinitesimally small point. That implies that before that, there was nothing. I can't imagine how nature, in this case the universe, could have created itself. And the very fact that the universe had a beginning implies that someone was able to begin it. And it seems to me that had to be outside of nature."[12] (Robert Jastrow)

"At this singularity, space and time came into existence; literally nothing existed before the singularity, so, if the Universe originated at such a singularity, we would truly have a creation *ex nihilo*."[13] (John Barrow and Frank Tipler)

"The big bang cries out for a divine explanation and it forces us to a conclusion that nature had a definite beginning. I cannot see how nature could have created itself; only a supernatural force that is outside of space and time could have done that."[14] (Francis Collins)

The Oscillating Universe

The Oscillating Universe was introduced in an attempt to achieve what the Big Bang and the Eternal Universe models could not do – that is, to get rid of the 'beginning' of the universe. John Gribbin writes:

> "The biggest problem with the Big Bang theory of the origin of the universe is philosophical – perhaps even theological – what was there before the bang? This problem alone was sufficient to give a great initial impetus to the Steady State theory; but with that theory now sadly in conflict with the observations, the best way round this initial difficulty is provided by a model in which the universe expands from a singularity, collapses back again, and repeats the cycle indefinitely."[15]

In the Oscillating model of the universe, it is opined that the universe first expands due to inflation, then contracts due to the gravitational pull of the entire universe, and then expands again, and contracts again – the 'Big Bang' contracts into the 'Big Crunch' and expanded back into the 'Big Bang' again ad infinitum. However, all the evidence today points to a universe that is never going to contract. Instead, it is accelerating faster and faster in what many cosmologists now believe will lead to a 'Big Rip' where the universe will literally tear itself apart in the far distant future.

This ghost of the 'beginning' of the universe just won't go away even with the Oscillating Universe. In *Fabric of the Cosmos*, physicist Brian Greene explains:

> "The cyclic model has its own share of shortcomings... consideration of entropy buildup (and also of quantum mechanics) ensures that the cyclic model's cycles could not have gone on forever. Instead, the cycles began at some definite time in the past, and so, as with inflation, we need an explanation of how the first cycle got started."[16]

And from a page from renown Christian apologist William Lane Craig's writing:

> "The prospects of the Oscillating Model were severely dimmed in 1970, however, by Penrose and Hawking's formulation of the Singularity Theorems which bear their names. The theorems disclosed that under very generalized conditions an initial cosmological singularity is inevitable, even for inhomogeneous and non-isotropic universes. Reflecting on the impact of this discovery,

Hawking notes that the Hawking-Penrose Singularity Theorems 'led to the abandonment of attempts (mainly by the Russians) to argue that there was a previous contracting phase and a non-singular bounce into expansion'. Instead almost everyone now believes that the universe, and time itself, had a beginning at the big bang."[17]

The Multiverse

The Eternal Universe model did bring about some temporary relief to secular cosmologists as it seemed to do away with the need for a beginning and a supernatural Creator – the universe has been eternally like this. But it contradicts all the other observations and is now dead. The Big Bang theory unsettles many because of its metaphysical implication – there is a beginning to the universe at the singularity and science can't explain why the universe exist other than a creation of some sort. Many cosmologists initially shy away from the Big Bang, but with the introduction of the 'Multi-Universes' or Multiverse model, the same crowd is now back in business with the hope that there is finally a naturalistic explanation for the inception of this fine-tuned universe without any supernatural causality. They posit that our universe is just one of the many universes that spawned from some kind of primordial quantum vacuum and that it happened to have the right combination of the physical laws to produce matter and life. Other universes were not so fortunate to have struck this 'cosmic lottery' and they ended up sterile and lifeless.

The steady state, inflating or cyclic model all try to outdo the other to get rid of the ghostly 'beginning' of the universe that has been haunting the theoretical physicists for years. But try as they would, they just could not do away with the 'time before time' conundrum – what was 'before', what caused the universe to begin, and why is there something rather than nothing?

In reality, all that is taking place in the world of these 'nothing theorists' is that they are just kicking the can further down the road – to push the 'before' of the universe, the 'why there is something rather than nothing', further back into deep time in their search for the mythical 'beginningless' and causeless universe. And it is not just the problem of when time begins but why nothing can kick-start the universe with all its exquisitely defined, carefully calibrated and fine-tuned physical laws from nothing? Candidness would have propelled us into the realm of the metaphysical and the supernatural – there has to be a Mind behind the laws and matter to churn out the universe or universes, if there is such a thing as the multiverse. And a 'universe-generating factory' would still need a transcendent Agency to build it; it cannot assemble itself from nothing.

In an article *Why Physicists Can't Avoid a Creation Event,* Lisa Grossman shows that, after all these years and after the whole plethora of multiverse models posited, physicists still are unable to get rid of this pesky genesis of the universe. The following is quite revealing:

> "The big bang may not have been the beginning of everything – but new calculations suggest we still need a cosmic starter gun. You could call them the worst birthday presents ever. At the meeting of minds convened last week to honour Stephen Hawking's 70th birthday – loftily titled "State of the Universe" – two bold proposals posed serious threats to our existing understanding of the cosmos.
>
> One shows that a problematic object called a naked singularity is a lot more likely to exist than previously assumed (see "Naked black-hole hearts live in the fifth dimension") The other suggests that the universe is not eternal, resurrecting the thorny question of how to kick-start the cosmos without the hand of a supernatural creator.
>
> While many of us may be OK with the idea of the big bang simply starting everything, physicists, including Hawking, tend to shy away from cosmic genesis. "A point of creation would be a place where science broke down. One would have to appeal to religion and the hand of God," Hawking told the meeting, at the University of Cambridge, in a pre-recorded speech.
>
> For a while it looked like it might be possible to dodge this problem, by relying on models such as an eternally inflating or cyclic universe, both of which seemed to continue infinitely in the past as well as the future. Perhaps surprisingly, these were also both compatible with the big bang, the idea that the universe most likely burst forth from an extremely dense, hot state about 13.7 billion years ago.
>
> However, as cosmologist Alexander Vilenkin of Tufts University in Boston explained last week, that hope has been gradually fading and may now be dead. He showed that all these theories still demand a beginning. His first target was eternal inflation..."[18]

An article from *Astrophysics and Space Science* shows that there has to be a cosmic beginning despite all the proposed models of the universe to avoid it:

> "The absolute origin of the universe, of all matter and energy, even of physical space and time themselves, in the Big Bang singularity contradicts the perennial naturalistic assumption that the universe has always existed. One after another, models designed to avert the initial cosmological singularity – the Steady State model, the Oscillating model, Vacuum Fluctuation models – have come and gone. Current quantum gravity models, such as the Hartle-Hawking model and the Vilenkin model, must appeal to the physically unintelligible and metaphysically dubious device of "imaginary time" to avoid the universe's beginning. The contingency implied by an absolute beginning *ex nihilo* points to a transcendent cause of the universe beyond space and time. Philosophical objections to a cause of the universe fail to carry conviction."[19]

Here is a piece of wisdom from Sir Fred Hoyle and professor Chandra Wickramasinghe, in their book *Evolution from Space*:

> "Be suspicious of a theory if more and more hypotheses are needed to support it as new facts become available, or as new considerations are brought to bear."[20]

From Creation Wiki comes this article on the inescapable cosmic genesis:

> "The BGV theorem though holds independently of any physical description of the very early universe before Planck time. In fact it can support a wide variety of inflationary cosmological models, or completely different physics of a universe within a multiverse. So that even if our universe is just one part of a much grander set of universes called the multiverse, the multiverse itself then would require a beginning, or what has been called by some as a 'beginning of beginnings'. It maintains sweeping generality making very few assumptions, not even assuming the material content of the universe or that Albert Einstein's general relativity equations actually work. If tweaking needs to be done to Einstein's theory of gravity for the quantum level interactions of particles during the very early universe then so be it.

The BGV theorem even remains consistent with "higher dimensional cosmologies based on string theory." (Question 74: *CERN Probes Big Bang* By William Lane Craig) This is because "brane worlds" which are posited by string theory create "collisions of bubbles nucleating in an inflating higher-dimensional bulk spacetime." The "higher-dimensional bulk spacetime" cannot be "past-complete" or in other words, they cannot be past eternal. (Borde, A. Guth and A. Vilenkin, *Inflationary, space-times are not past-complete*, Phys. Rev. Lett. 90 151301, 2003, p. 4) The primary assumption made by Borde, Guth and Vilenkin however is that the cosmic expansion rate will never get to a nonzero value. There cannot be past-eternal inflation, there must be a beginning or singularity. (Alex Vilenkin, *Many Worlds In One: The Search for Other Universes*, Hill and Wang 2006, pg. 175)

The result is that the BGV theorem covers a wide range of cosmogonies (theories on the origin of the universe) because there need only be on average an expansion rate along the geodesic of more than zero for there to be a space-time boundary and therefore cosmic beginning."[21]

Hence Alexander Vilenkin concludes his painstaking research with this insightful statement:

"It is said that an argument is what convinces reasonable men and a proof is what it takes to convince even an unreasonable man. With the proof now in place, cosmologists can no longer hide behind the possibility of a past-eternal universe. There is no escape: they have to face the problem of a cosmic beginning."[22]

However, most secular scientists do not respond too well to a universe with a cosmic genesis. Robert Jastrow writes:

"Theologians generally are delighted with the proof that the universe had a beginning, but astronomers are curiously upset. It turns out that the scientist behaves the way the rest of us do when our beliefs are in conflict with the evidence. We become irritated, we pretend the conflict does not exist, or we paper it over with meaningless phrases..."[23]

Today's biased science is akin to the world of witchcraft in which one cosmic incantation is pronounced after another in the hope that some naturalistic spirit will materialize to exorcise the secular cosmologist from the ghostly 'beginning' of the universe. But try as they might, secular cosmologists could not do away with it. Ironically, it is objective science and not religion that keeps resurrecting this ghost of the beginning of the universe. Let us hear from agnostic physicist, cosmologist and astrobiologist Paul Davies:

> "There are many physical processes occurring in the universe that proceed at a finite rate, and are irreversible. For example, the formation and death of stars, and the emission of starlight into space. You can't run these processes backwards. But if the universe is infinitely old, then these irreversible processes would have all run their course by now, and the entire universe would have reached its final state. But that hasn't happened yet, so the universe can't have existed for ever. We know there must have been an absolute beginning a finite time ago."[24]

And if the universe has a one-time beginning, then the God hypothesis becomes a very scientific inference to the best explanation – for it takes an external Agency outside space-time to create space-time. "In the beginning God created the heaven and the earth" makes perfect sense as time itself has a beginning, and a Beginner is needed to begin it. And that sounds the death knell for materialism, naturalism, reductionism, and eventually, evolutionism. The universe was never past infinite. Materialism died and Creationism is resurrected. Science points us beyond the material beginning to an immaterial Causation.

'So long as the universe had a beginning, we could suppose it had a creator.'[25]
(Stephen Hawking)

References:

1. A. Vilenkin, cited in *"Why physicists can't avoid a creation event"*, New Scientist, 11 January, 2012

2. Stephen Hawking, *The Nature of Space and Time*, Princeton, N. J., Princeton University Press, 1996, p. 20

3. Robert Jastrow, *God and the Astronomers*, 1978, p. 105

4. S. Hawking, *A Brief History of Time*, pp. 140-141

5. Carl Sagan, in *Cosmos,* 1980, p. 4

6. Robert Jastrow, *God and the Astronomers*, p. 113-114

7. Barry Parker, *Creation—the Story of the Origin and Evolution of the Universe,* New York & London: Plenum Press, 1988, p. 202

8. Fred Hoyle, *The Intelligent Universe,* New York: Holt, Rinehard, and Winston, 1983, p. 13

9. Barry Parker, *Creation – the Story of the Origin and Evolution of the Universe*, New York & London: Plenum Press, 1988, p. 201-202

10. Sir Arthur S. Eddington, *Nature* 127, 1931, 450

11. Robert Jastrow, *God and the Astronomers*, W. W. Norton, p. 106

12. Robert Jastrow, *God and the Astronomers*, 1978, p. 111

13. John Barrow and Frank Tipler, *The Anthropic Cosmological Principle*, Oxford: Clarendon Press, 1986, p. 442

14. Francis Collins, *The Language of God*, Simon & Shuster, Inc., 2006, p. 67

15. John Gribbin, *Oscillating Universe Bounces Back*, Nature, 259 [1976]: 15

16. Brian Greene, *The Fabric of the Cosmos: Space, Time, and the Texture of Reality*, p. 410

17. William Lane Craig, *The Ultimate Question of Origins: God and the Beginning of the Universe*

18. Lisa Grossman, *Why physicists can't avoid a creation event,* New Scientist Magazine, issue 2847, 11 January 2012

19. *Astrophysics and Space Science*, 269-270 (1999): 723-740

20. Fred Hoyle & Chandra Wickramasinghe, *Evolution from Space*, 1981, p. 135

21. William Lane Craig and J. P. Moreland, *The Blackwell Companion to Natural Theology,* Blackwell Publishing 2009, p. 142

22. Alex Vilenkin, *Many Worlds In One: The Search for Other Universes*, Hill and Wang, 2006, pg. 176

23. Robert Jastrow, *God and the Astronomers*, 1978, p. 16

24. Paul Davies, *The Big Questions: In the Beginning*, ABC Science Online, interview with Phillip Adams, http://www.abc.net.au/science/bigquestions/s460625.htm, accessed February 23, 2014

25. Stephen Hawking, *A Brief History of Time*

Additional Resources:

1. *Borde-Guth-Vilenkin Theorm – Scientific Evidence for the Beginning of the Universe. And How Atheists Take Alexander Vilenkin (& the BVG Theorem) Out Of Context – William Lane Craig* (YouTube)

2. *Lawrence Krauss Deliberately Lies About Science (Atheists and the Borde Guth Vilenkin Theorem)* [YouTube]

The Elephant in the Room

> If we were to leave a few marbles on the table, they will remain where they are. But to have those marbles circling around a marble in the middle of the table requires some invisible law to make them do so. This is a crude description of the laws of nature. The physical laws are not only differentiated from the objects they control but they are also endowed with certain, specific constants. The operation of the laws can be observed in the electrons spinning around the neutrons and protons in the nucleus of the atom, and in the planets orbiting around the sun in our solar system. The laws of nature is the 'unseen and unexplained hand' that moves objects and compel matters to behave the way they behave. And that unseen hand inevitably points to an unseen Mind.

Sometimes, even the best minds refuse to acknowledge the elephant in the room – the physical laws behind the physical universe. Why are there laws of nature governing the behaviors and properties of every atom and particle in this universe? Where did they come from? Who defined them? Who calibrated them? Who fine-tuned them? Why are there those exact and necessary laws in the universe? Why are there not some 'missing laws' – like gravity or electromagnetism - which will render our present universe impossible, or additional laws that could have destroyed it?

The 'first dirt' is not as crucial as the 'first law' that governs it. The law is the real elephant in the room. Where did it come from? Without it, the universe would be a non-entity. No space can be inflated; no time can commence; no matter can emerge; and no energy can be unleashed. There will be nothing to bang the Big Bang! Instead of the 'Big Bang', it will be the 'Big Dud' – a true 'nothing comes from nothing, nothing ever could'. Or, as Linde puts it, "If there was no law, how did the Universe appear?"[1]

The real epicenter of the clashes of the Titans down the centuries between biblical Christianity and pseudo-science lies here – where did the laws of nature governing everything physical come from? Darwinian evolution cannot account for it. There is no cosmic natural selection and no stellar mutation to spawn the cosmos. The laws and their preset physical constants are mysteriously 'just there' and 'just right', period, and balanced on a razor edge. All the other discussion and debates from cosmic to organic evolution are mere sideshows compared to this crucial reality – where did the physical laws emanate from and who defined them? This is the ultimate 'Proof of God' inference – it takes a Mind to prefabricate, define, calibrate and harmonize all the known laws of nature to permit intelligent life.

A mindless, immaterial 'Absolute Nothing' is incapable of defining, generating and fine-tuning these essential laws of physics and breathe life into this universe. And science cannot answer this fundamental question: How did these laws emerge from absolute nothingness? Statistical and physical improbability put paid to the possibility that physical laws can spontaneously arise from nothing as nothingness does not know how many laws of nature are needed, what physical constants to give to each one of them, what their unique roles are, how to fine-tune them (in many cases they are fine-tuned to 1 in a million million parts) to generate the 'star dust' for life to exist, when to turn on the elusive Higgs field, how much of the speculative 'dark matter' and 'dark energy' is needed to hold the galaxies together and to expand the universe, and a host of mind-boggling demands for this universe to come into being and be sustained. This is the smoking gun that leads us to the ultimate, intelligent Lawgiver who alone can manufacture all these physical laws, enforce them, and breathe life into this finite universe.

> "Our concept of time begins with the creation of the universe. Therefore if the laws of nature created the universe, these laws must have existed prior to time; that is the laws of nature would be outside of time. What we have then is totally non-physical laws, outside of time, creating a universe. Now that description might sound somewhat familiar. Very much like the biblical concept of God: not physical, outside of time, able to create a universe."[2] (Gerald Schroeder)

Many physicists and cosmologists are beginning to see the 'second tier' of this cosmic conundrum — first, where did matter come from, and secondly, even more intriguing, where did the physical laws governing it originate from? Let us probe into their candid struggles and empathize with their hopeless endeavors.

In the round table discussion on Discovery Channel, Paul Davies commented:

> "You need to know where those laws come from. That's where the mystery lies — the laws... [they] are simply, for most scientists, unexplained. So, either you have an unexplained God or you have unexplained laws."[3]

In his book, *Did Adam and Eve Have Navels*, Martin Gardner writes:

> "Imagine that physicists finally discover all the basic waves and their particles, and all the basic laws, and unite everything in one equation. We can then ask, "Why that equation?" It is fashionable now to conjecture that the big

bang was caused by a random quantum fluctuation in a vacuum devoid of space and time. But of course such a vacuum is a far cry from nothing. There had to be quantum laws to fluctuate. And why are there quantum laws... There is no escape from the super ultimate questions: Why is there something rather than nothing, and why is the something structured the way it is?"[4]

Russian theoretical physicist A. D. Linde laments this chicken-and-egg enigma on the inception of the universe:

"The first, and main, problem is the very existence of the big bang. One may wonder, what came before? If space-time did not exist then, how could everything appear from nothing? What arose first: the universe or the laws governing it? Explaining this initial singularity – where and when it all began – still remains the most intractable problem of modern cosmology."[5]

British cosmologist John Barrow saw the light of this conundrum on the origin of the laws of nature when he penned down these words:

"At first, the absence of a beginning appears to be an advantage to the scientific approach. There are no awkward starting conditions to deduce or explain. But this is an illusion. We still have to explain why the Universe took on particular properties – its rate expansion, density, and so forth – at an infinite time in the past."[6]

Nobel Laureate Steven Weinberg recognized this irreducible mystery of the physical laws when he wrote:

"I have to admit that, even when physicists will have gone as far as they can go, when we have a final theory, we will not have a completely satisfying picture of the world, because we will still be left with the question 'why?' Why this theory, rather than some other theory? For example, why is the world described by quantum mechanics? Quantum mechanics is the one part of our present physics that is likely to survive intact in any future theory, but there is nothing logically inevitable about quantum mechanics; I can imagine a universe governed by Newtonian mechanics instead. So there seems to be an irreducible mystery that science will not eliminate."[7]

Bernard Haisch, in his book, *The God Theory,* states:

> "First of all, quantum fluctuations are a key ingredient of inflation theories that attempt to address how our universe, and myriad others, came into being. The problem is that quantum fluctuations presuppose the existence of quantum laws. If there truly were no quantum laws or any other laws whatsoever, nothing could happen. No laws, no action. The origin of universes as a result of quantum laws, inflation fields, or other arcane properties of string theory depends upon the pre-existence of those laws or fields. And so even the skeptical scientist cannot avoid taking that on faith."[8]

Professor Alexander Vilenkin of Tufts University concludes that the laws of physics precedes the existence of the universe. Like all others, he has no inklings as to the origin of the laws of nature.

> "What I am starting with are the laws of physics... and these laws are assumed to exist... why these laws, who gives these laws, it is a deep mystery... I don't have much to say about that."[9]

> "This seems to suggest the laws were there before the universe. The laws are more fundamental than the universe and have some plutonic existence."[10]

Albert Einstein too, recognized that the laws of nature are never the products of some haphazard, cosmic recipe, but stem from an unseen, superb intelligence:

> "The scientist is possessed by the sense of universal causation... His religious feeling takes the form of a rapturous amazement at the harmony of natural law, which reveals an intelligence of such superiority that, compared with it, all the systematic thinking and acting of human beings is an utterly insignificant reflection."[11]

One of the greatest scientists of the space age, Dr. Werner von Braun, who is credited with the invention of the Saturn V rocket that sent the Apollo team to the moon stated:

> "One cannot be exposed to the law and order of the universe without concluding that there must be design and purpose behind it all... The better we understand the

intricacies of the universe and all it harbors, the more reason we have found to marvel at the inherent design upon which it is based... To be forced to believe only one conclusion – that everything in the universe happened by chance – would violate the very objectivity of science itself..."[12]

Agnostic theoretical physicist Paul Davies acknowledges that there will always be the element of faith in the uncanny appearance of the laws of nature. 'Shut up and calculate', as adopted by most secular physicists, is never a statement of science, but an expression of a religious faith. And even if there is such a thing as the multiverse, there will still be the unexplained meta-physical laws governing such universes.

"Over the years I have often asked my physicist colleagues why the laws of physics are what they are. The answers vary from "that's not a scientific question" to "nobody knows." The favorite reply is, "There is no reason they are what they are – they just are"... But until science comes up with a testable theory of the laws of the universe, its claim to be free of faith is manifestly bogus...

The multiverse theory is increasingly popular, but it doesn't so much explain the laws of physics as dodge the whole issue. There has to be a physical mechanism to make all those universes and bestow by-laws on them. This process will require its own laws, or meta-laws. Where do they come from? The problem has simply been shifted up a level from the laws of the universe to the meta-laws of the multiverse.

Clearly, then, both religion and science are founded on faith – namely, on belief in the existence of something outside the universe, like an unexplained God or an unexplained set of physical laws, maybe even a huge ensemble of unseen universes, too..."[13]

Secular cosmologists will have to travel the same path as the old-time theologians – an inescapable conclusion in an unseen Something or Someone to manufacture those varied, unrelated, necessary, fine-tuned, exquisite laws. But if there is nothing in the beginning, and nothing can only create nothing, then there is only one option left – a logical, unseen Someone with intelligence, wisdom and power to create those exquisitely fine-tuned laws from nothing.

And, as Nobel Laureate Dr. Charles Townes put it:

> "Somehow intelligence must have been involved in the laws of the universe."[14]

The claims of materialism will end at this cosmic brick wall – the laws of nature cannot explain how the laws of nature come about. They can only describe how they govern the objects in the universe. And there was a time where there were no laws of nature. The Theory of Everything (TOE) will have to end with the God of Design (GOD). Without GOD, there will be no TOE!

> "The great delusion of modernity, is that the laws of nature explain the universe for us. The laws of nature describe the universe, they describe the regularities. But they explain nothing."[15] (Ludwig Wittgenstein)

The understanding of the laws of nature may explain away the 'God of the gaps' – of how things work; but they cannot explain away the 'God of the laws' – the One who makes things work. And the laws of nature will ultimately point us to the inescapable Lawgiver and Law Enforcer.

> "For by him were all things created, that are in heaven, and that in earth, visible and invisible... And he is before all things, and by him all things consist."[16] (*Bible*)

> "For the invisible things of him from the creation of the world are clearly seen, being understood by the things that are made, even his eternal power and Godhead; so that they are without excuse."[17] (*Bible*)

> "Who created these laws? There is no question but that a God will always be needed."[18]

References:

1. A. D. Linde, as quoted in Overbye, 2001

2. Gerald Schroeder, *The Big Bang Creation: God or the Laws of Nature*

3. Discovery Channel, *'Curiosity', The Creation Question: A Curiosity Conversation*

4. Martin Gardner, *Did Adam and Eve Have Navels?: Discourses on Reflexology, Numerology, Urine Therapy, and Other Dubious Subjects*, 2000, p. 303

5. A. D. Linde, *Scientific American*, 1994, 271[5]:48

6. Barrow, John D, *The Book of Nothing: Vacuums, Voids, and the Latest Ideas about the Origins of the Universe*, New York: Pantheon, 2000, p. 296

7. Steven Weinberg, Professor of Physics, University of Texas at Austin, Winner of the 1979 Nobel Prize in Physics, *A Designer Universe?*

8. Bernard Haisch, *The God Theory, Universes, Zero-Point Fields, and What's Behind It All*, 2009 Red Wheel/Weiser, LLC

9. Alexander Vilenkin, *Why is There 'Something' Rather Than 'Nothing'?* Closer to Truth, YouTube

10. Alexander Vilenkin, *A Universe From Nothing, The Search for the Theory of Everything*, YouTube

11. *The Quotable Einstein*, Princeton University Press

12. Dennis R. Petersen, *Unlocking the Mysteries of Creation*, Vol. 1, El Cajon: Master Books, 1988, p. 63, as quoted from the Bible Science Newsletter, May 1974, p. 8

13. Paul Davies, *Taking Science on Faith*, Nov. 24, 2007

14. *Science Finds God*, Newsweek, 7/20/98, p. 48

15. Ludwig Wittgenstein

16. *Bible*, Colossians 1:16-17

17. *Bible*, Romans 1:20

18. Heeren, F., *Show Me God*. Wheeling, IL, Searchlight Publications, 1995, p. 223

The Emperor's New Wheelchair

"Because there is a law such as gravity, the universe can and will create itself from nothing. Spontaneous creation is the reason there is something rather than nothing, why the universe exists, why we exist... it is not necessary to invoke God to light the blue touch paper and set the universe going."[1] (Stephen Hawking)

The late Stephen Hawking, in his book *The Grand Design,* made an audacious claim that there is no need for God to create the universe. Instead, gravity alone could do the job. He said, "Because there is a law such as gravity, the universe can and will create itself from nothing." He set out to make gravity the negative energy to balance matter, the positive energy, so that, at the end of the day, there is no net gain of the energy in the universe (zero-energy universe), and the law of conservation of energy is not violated. In short, because gravity exists, its counterpart, matter, will exist. Subsequently, through the process of cosmic evolution, this universe as we know it somehow came into being – case closed, the mystery solved, end of story.

Hawking's bold assertion does not make any philosophical, scientific or even common sense. Why? Because gravity is not nothing! From a physicist's viewpoint, it is undeniably a something – it describes, enforces and has a fine-tuned, physical constant. Hawking's declaration tantamounts to: "Because there is something (gravity), the universe can and will create itself from nothing." And if there is something (gravity) already existing prior to the universe, then the universe cannot be created from nothing! We are back to square one – the universe was created by something (gravity), not nothing! As it is wont to say, "Physicists often make bad philosophers."

Who prefabricated gravity, calibrated its exact specific constant, defined its role, and then intelligently fine-tuned it to harmonize with the other three fundamental forces – electromagnetism, strong and weak nuclear force, so as to permit the atoms to coalesce and life to exist? Hawking quietly bypassed this fundamental question: how did gravity come into the picture? After which, he conveniently moved on to make it the 'creator' of all things.

But Hawking did not explain how gravity came about in the first place. What he had done is liken to the promoting of a robotic factory that churned out cars as the 'creator' of cars, and then quietly bypassing the question of how a complex, robotic factory came into being in the first place. It could not have just existed eternally. Someone had to build that factory first before cars could be produced. And Someone had to create gravity first before it could create all the matter in the universe. A mindless gravity cannot create itself from nothing, and then define its role, and finally, be able to spit out matter into the universe. It takes an intelligent Creator to create gravity and then differentiate it from matter. Hawking dodged the super ultimate question: where did the law of gravity come from? And if you were to ask Hawking what created gravity, the answer would probably be 'turtle all the way down' – something (we haven't figured out yet) created that something (we haven't figured out yet) that created gravity ad infinitum – no difference from the infinite regress of 'who created God'? His TOE will need a prior TOE ad infinitum for its existence.

C. S. Lewis, an intellectual giant of his day, proved conclusively that the existence of the laws of nature could not give rise to the existence of matter. The laws of nature merely define how matter should behave but they cannot create anything. It takes a separate creative event to do that.

> "The law of nature produce no event, they state the pattern to which every event have only and can be induced to happen must conform. Just as the rules of Arithmetic state the pattern to which all transactions with money must conform, if only if you can get hold of any money. Thus in one sense the laws of nature covers the whole field of space and time. In another what they leave out is precisely the whole real universe. The incessant torrent of actual events, which makes up true history, that must come from somewhere else; to think the laws can produce it is like thinking you can create real money by doing sums. For every law says in the last resort: "If you have A, then you will get B". But first catch your A."[4]

Simply put, just try mentally adding $1,000 to $1,000 without money, and then produce $2,000 of real money. The law of Arithmetic alone cannot give you real money until you first have the money to begin with. The laws of the universe cannot produce the universe; it requires a separate creative event to produce all those atoms and particles to construct the universe. The laws can only describe how they will function. As professor John Lennox succinctly puts it, "Laws are descriptive and predictive, but not creative."

Furthermore, why is there a need to choose between gravity and God in the creation of the cosmos? Hawking's mind seemed terribly muddled up in his attempt to put into the same basket a physical law called 'gravity', which needed a Creator, and the Creator Himself who birthed gravity. It is a confusion of category. They both complement each other and are needed in the creation of the universe. They do not compete with each other. God is the Agent and gravity is the mechanism He uses to run the universe. Professor John Lennox from the university of Oxford sums it up elegantly:

> "What Hawking appears to have done is to confuse law with agency. His call on us to choose between God and physics is a bit like someone demanding that we choose between aeronautical engineer Sir Frank Whittle and the laws of physics to explain the jet engine. That is a confusion of category. The laws of physics can explain how the jet engine works, but someone had to build the thing, put in the fuel and start it up. The jet could not have been created without the laws of physics on their own – but the task of development and creation needed the genius of Whittle as its agent... Similarly, the laws of physics could never have actually built the universe. Some agency must have been involved."[5]

To put it in another way – why should our knowledge of how a car works do away with the maker of the car, or our understanding of how the plane flies do away with the designer of the plane, or our acquaintance of how the universe works do away with the Creator of the universe? There is a world of difference between the 'God of the gaps' and the 'God of the universe'! Without the God of the whole show, there will not be the God of the gaps – the present unknowns in our understanding of how the universe works.

Emeritus Rouse Ball Professor of Mathematics at Oxford Sir Roger Penrose, who formulated the *Penrose–Hawking Singularity Theorems* with Stephen Hawking, debunks Hawking's 'M-theory' in *The Grand Design* as an untestable and unobservable hypothesis. He writes:

> "What is referred to as M-theory isn't even a theory. It's a collection of ideas, hopes, (*and*) aspirations. It's not even a theory and I think the book is a bit misleading in that respect. It gives you the impression that here is this new theory, which is going to explain everything. It is nothing of the sort. It is not even a theory and certainly has no observational (*evidence*)... I think the book [*The Grand Design*] suffers rather more strongly than many (*others*). It's not an uncommon thing in popular descriptions of science to latch onto some idea, particularly things to do with string theory, which have absolutely no support from observations... They are very far from any kind of observational (*testability*). Yes, they are hardly science."[6]

> "Gravity explains the motions of the planets, but it cannot explain who sets the planets in motion."[7]

References:

1. Stephen Hawking, *The Grand Design*

2. Gerald Schroeder, *The Big Bang Creation: God or the Laws of Nature*

3. Stephen Hawking, *The Theory of Everything*, New Millennium, 2002C.

4. C. S. Lewis, *Miracles*, 1974, p. 93-94

5. Professor John Lennox, *As a scientist I'm certain Stephen Hawking is wrong. You can't explain the universe without God*, Mail Online, 3 September 2010

6. Sir Roger Penrose, former close colleague of Stephen Hawking, *Roger Penrose Debunks Stephen Hawking New Book The Grand Design,* (YouTube)

7. Sir Isaac Newton, *Principia Mathematica*

Fingerprints of the Fine-Tuner

"Yet, the discoveries of modern physics and cosmology in the last 50 years have shown that the structure of the universe is set in an extraordinarily precise way for the existence of life; if its structure were slightly different, even by an extraordinarily small degree, life would not be possible. In many people's minds, the most straightforward explanation of this remarkable fine-tuning is some sort of divine purpose behind our universe. This fine-tuning falls into three categories: the fine-tuning of the laws of nature, the fine-tuning of the constants of physics, and the fine-tuning of the initial conditions of the universe."[1] (Robin Collins)

"The really amazing thing is not that life on Earth is balanced on a knife-edge, but that the entire universe is balanced on a knife-edge and would be total chaos if any of the natural 'constants' were off even slightly. You see, even if you dismiss man as a chance happening, the fact remains that the universe seems unreasonably suited to the existence of life – almost contrived – you might say a 'put-up job.'"[2] (Paul Davis)

"There are some atheists who deny the fine-tuning, but these atheists are in firm opposition to the progress of science. The more science has progressed, the more constants, ratios and quantities we have discovered that need to be fine-tuned. Science is going in a theistic direction."[3] (Dr. Walter L. Bradley)

When man first peered into the night sky, the universe seemed mundane and simple – there were just the 'twinkle, twinkle little stars' that punctuated the cosmos above. But with great advances made in astronomy, astrophysics and cosmology, suddenly, the whole universe literally bursts open before us in astonishing ways – it is no longer as simple as it first appeared. In fact, it has become fascinating and troubling – fascinating, because there seems to be a deliberate, intricate order behind our universe that provides for intelligent life and troubling (to the atheists), because it seems to point to a Mind that is able to fine-tune with incredible precision every physical constant to birth and sustain this remarkable universe. Secular scientists today are stumped by this mind-boggling 'conspiracy' or what is now commonly known as the 'Anthropic Principle' or the 'Goldilocks Enigma' – the universe appears to be designed with an extremely narrow margin of error for the existence of intelligent life.

When we go behind the curtains of this physical universe, an intriguing hidden world opens up to our astonishment – a world of exceptionally finely-tuned laws and sub-atomic particles that defies any natural explanation as to its precise orders. And this fine-tuning is not only restricted to the microscopic world, but extended also to the macroscopic universe too – from a stable, right mass, 'right age' sun – to the existence of a large moon that stabilizes the earth's inclined rotation – and on to our safe, galactic location between the spiral arms of the millions of burning stars in the Milky Way.

The existence of the physical laws and matter from nothing are already troubling enough to the naturalists, but their extreme fine-tuning goes right through the roof of their 'lucky chance'. It is like the winning of the lottery a thousand times in a row. To date, there are more than 200 parameters that have to be fine-tuned for life to be possible on this privileged pale blue dot we called 'Earth'. And many more are being discovered to reveal the Fine-Tuner behind this amazing, contrived universe. Below is just a sample of the many estimated, fine-tuned constants:

Initial Entropy:	$1:10^{123}$
Gravitation Constant:	$1:10^{60}$
Cosmological Constant:	$1:10^{120}$
Mass Density of Universe:	$1:10^{59}$
Ratio of Electron to Proton:	$1:10^{37}$
Expansion Rate of the Universe:	$1:10^{55}$
Ratio of Electromagnetic Force to Gravity:	$1:10^{40}$

It is estimated that there are about 10^{80} atoms and 10^{22} stars in the observable universe. In the study of probability, anything beyond 1 chance in 10^{50} is an improbability – in short, it is almost impossible for it to have happened accidentally. The fine-tuned constants point more to design than brute force. In *God the Evidence*, Patrick Glynn provides more evidence of these fine-tuned constants:

> "Gravity is roughly 10^{39} times weaker than electromagnetism. If gravity had been 10^{33} times weaker than electromagnetism, 'stars would be a billion times less massive and would burn a million times faster.'"

> The nuclear weak force is 10^{28} times the strength of gravity. Had the weak force been slightly weaker, all the hydrogen in the universe would have been turned to helium (making water impossible, for example).

A stronger nuclear strong force (by as little as 2 percent) would have prevented the formation of protons – yielding a universe without atoms. Decreasing it by 5 percent would have given us a universe without stars.

If the difference in mass between a proton and a neutron were not exactly as it is – roughly twice the mass of an electron – then all neutrons would have become protons or vice versa. Say good-bye to chemistry as we know it – and to life.

The very nature of water – so vital to life – is something of a mystery (a point noticed by one of the forerunners of anthropic reasoning in the nineteenth century, Harvard biologist Lawrence Henderson). Unique amongst the molecules, water is lighter in its solid than liquid form: Ice floats. If it did not, the oceans would freeze from the bottom up and earth would now be covered with solid ice. This property in turn is traceable to the unique properties of the hydrogen atom.

The synthesis of carbon – the vital core of all organic molecules – on a significant scale involves what scientists view as an astonishing coincidence in the ratio of the strong force to electromagnetism. This ratio makes it possible for carbon-12 to reach an excited state of exactly 7.65 MeV at the temperature typical of the centre of stars, which creates a resonance involving helium-4, beryllium-8, and carbon-12 - allowing the necessary binding to take place during a tiny window of opportunity 10^{-17} seconds long."[4]

From *The Craig-Pigliucci Debate: Does God Exist:*

"The complex order in the universe. During the last 30 years, scientists have discovered that the existence of intelligent life depends upon a complex and delicate balance of initial conditions given in the Big Bang itself. We now know that life-prohibiting universes are vastly more probable than any life-permitting universe like ours. How much more probable?

The answer is that the chances that the universe should be life-permitting are so infinitesimal as to be incomprehensible and incalculable. For example, Stephen

Hawking has estimated that if the rate of the universe's expansion one second after the Big Bang had been smaller by even one part in a hundred thousand million million, the universe would have re-collapsed into a hot fireball. (Stephen W. Hawking, *A Brief History of Time,* New York: Bantam Books, 1988, p. 123)

Paul C. W. Davies has calculated that the odds against the initial conditions being suitable for later star formation (without which planets could not exist) is one followed by a thousand billion billion zeros, at least." (P. C. W. Davies, *Other Worlds*, London: Dent, 1980, pp. 160-161, 168-169)

John Barrow and Frank Tipler estimate that a change in the strength of gravity or of the weak force by only one part in 10^{100} would have prevented a life-permitting universe." (John Barrow and Frank Tipler, *The Anthropic Cosmological Principle,* Oxford: Clarendon Press, 1986)

There are around 50 such quantities and constants present in the Big Bang which must be fine-tuned in this way if the universe is to permit life. And it's not just each quantity which must be exquisitely fine-tuned; their ratios to one another must be also finely-tuned. So improbability is multiplied by improbability by improbability until our minds are reeling in incomprehensible numbers."[5]

Francis Collins, American physician-geneticist, director of National Human Genome Research Institute, has this to say:

"When you look from the perspective of a scientist at the universe, it looks as if it knew we were coming. There are 15 constants – the gravitational constant, various constants about the strong and weak nuclear force, etc. – that have precise values. If any one of those constants was off by even one part in a million, or in some cases, by one part in a million million, the universe could not have actually come to the point where we see it. Matter would not have been able to coalesce; there would have been no galaxy, stars, planets or people. That's a phenomenally surprising observation. It seems almost impossible that we're here. And that does make you wonder – gosh, who was setting those constants anyway? Scientists have not been able to figure that out."[6]

Paul Davies, British-born theoretical physicist, cosmologist, astrobiologist and noted author, echoed the same amazement on this fine-tuning phenomenon:

> "I belong to a group of scientists who do not subscribe to a conventional religion but nevertheless deny that the universe is a purposeless accident. Through my scientific work I have come to believe more and more strongly that the physical universe is put together with an ingenuity so astonishing that I cannot accept it merely as a brute fact. There must, it seems to me, be a deeper level of explanation. Whether one wishes to call that deeper level 'God' is a matter of taste and definition. Furthermore, I have come to the point of view that mind – i.e., conscious awareness of the world – is not a meaningless and incidental quirk of nature, but an absolutely fundamental facet of reality."[7]

> "I hope the foregoing discussion will have convinced the reader that the natural world is not just any old concoction of entities and forces, but a marvelously ingenious and unified mathematical scheme... these rules look as if they are the product of intelligent design. I do not see how that can be denied."[8]

Eminent astrophysicist Arno Penzias, who was co-awarded the Nobel Prize in Physics for the discovery of the cosmic microwave background radiation writes:

> "Astronomy leads us to a unique event, a universe which was created out of nothing, one with the very delicate balance needed to provide exactly the conditions required to permit life, and one which has an underlying (one might say 'supernatural') plan."[9]

World-renowned physicist Stephen Hawking acknowledges:

> "If the rate of expansion one second after the big bang had been smaller by even one part in a hundred thousand million million, the universe would have recollapsed before it ever reached its present size."[10]

> "The universe and the laws of physics seem to have been specifically designed for us. If any one of about 40 physical qualities had more than slightly different values, life as we

know it could not exist: Either atoms would not be stable, or they wouldn't combine into molecules, or the stars wouldn't form the heavier elements, or the universe would collapse before life could develop, and so on...”[11]

Astrophysicist George Ellis, who co-authored the book *The Large Scale Structure of Space-Time* with Stephen Hawking, reaffirms this uncanny fine-tuning of the universe:

“Amazing fine tuning occurs in the laws that make this [complexity] possible. Realization of the complexity of what is accomplished makes it very difficult not to use the word ‘miraculous’ without taking a stand as to the ontological status of the word.”[12]

American Astronomer George Greenstein states:

“As we survey all the evidence, the thought insistently arises that some supernatural agency – or, rather, Agency – must be involved. Is it possible that suddenly, without intending to, we have stumbled upon scientific proof of the existence of a Supreme Being? Was it God who stepped in and so providentially crafted the cosmos for our benefit?”[13]

With regard to the near-impossible window of opportunity for the formation of carbon atoms in the furnace of the stars, British astronomer Sir Fred Hoyle states:

“A common sense interpretation of the facts suggests that a super intellect has monkeyed with physics, as well as chemistry and biology, and that there are no blind forces worth speaking about in nature. The numbers one calculates from the facts seem to me so overwhelming as to put this conclusion almost beyond question.”[14]

World-renowned astronomist and winner of the Crawford prize in astronomy Alan Sandage concludes:

“I find it quite improbable that such order came out of chaos. There has to be some organizing principle. God to me is a mystery but is the explanation for the miracle of existence, why there is something instead of nothing.”[15]

Physicist Tony Rothman, who was the scientific editor of Andrei Sakharov's Memoirs and had contributed to numerous magazines, including *Scientific American, Discover, The New Republic* and *History Today,* writes:

> "When confronted with the order and beauty of the universe and the strange coincidences of nature, it's very tempting to take the leap of faith from science into religion. I am sure many physicists want to. I only wish they would admit it."[16]

Martin Ree, British cosmologist, astrophysicist, Astronomer Royal since 1995, and President of the Royal Society between 2005 and 2010, states:

> "These six numbers constitute a 'recipe' for a universe. Moreover, the outcome is sensitive to their values: if any one of them were to be 'untuned', there would be no stars and no life. Is this tuning just a brute fact, a coincidence? Or is it the providence of a benign Creator?"[17]

John Lennox, Professor of Mathematics and Philosophy of Science at Green Templeton College, Oxford, packs it together neatly:

> "We should note that the preceding arguments are not 'God of the gaps' arguments; it is advance in science, not ignorance of science, that has revealed this fine-tuning to us. In that sense there is no 'gap' in the science, The question is rather: how should we interpret the science? In what direction is it pointing?"[18]

Many of these leading secular scientists, when confronted with the exquisite fine-tuning of the universe, do not resort to the excuse of the 'God of the gaps' argument – since we don't know, we attribute it to God, but they saw where all the evidence were leading them to – beyond the natural to the supernatural. How did the universe appear from nothing? How did nothing selectively create the required number of the essential physical laws and then fine-tune them to a 'million million parts' in some cases?

These scientists were not lazy, on the contrary, they worked harder, thought deeper, researched painstakingly more than many of the superficial New Atheists – the 'four fuzzy, horsy men' – Richard Dawkins, Christopher Hitchens, Sam Harris and Daniel Bennett. And many of these giants of science are atheists or agnostics themselves, and have little to do with Christianity. These brilliant astrophysicists, cosmologists and physicists, after gleaning through their findings, reluctantly, but honestly, acknowledge that it inexorably gravitates towards a causal Agency that transcends space, time, matter and energy.

"All the seemingly random and unrelated constants in physics have one strange thing in common – these are precisely the values you need if you want to have a universe capable of producing life... Today the concrete data point strongly in the direction of the God hypothesis. It is the simplest and most obvious solution to the anthropic puzzle."[19] (Patrick Glynn)

"When I began my career as a cosmologist some twenty years ago, I was a convinced atheist. I never in my wildest dreams imagined that one day I would be writing a book purporting to show that the central claims of Judeo-Christian theology are in fact true, that these claims are straightforward deductions of the laws of physics as we now understand them. I have been forced into these conclusions by the inexorable logic of my own special branch of physics."[20] (Frank Tipler)

"If nature is so 'clever' as to exploit mechanisms that amaze us with their ingenuity, is that not persuasive evidence for the existence of intelligent design behind the universe? If the world's finest minds can unravel only with difficulty the deeper workings of nature, how could it be supposed that those workings are merely a mindless accident, a product of blind chance?"[21] (Paul Davies)

"Today there are more than 200 known parameters necessary for a planet to support life - every single one of which must be perfectly met, or the whole thing falls apart... The odds against life in the universe are simply astonishing."[22] (Eric Mataxas)

"At what point is it fair to admit that science suggests that we cannot be the result of random forces... Doesn't assuming that an intelligence created these perfect conditions require far less faith than believing that a life-sustaining Earth just happened to beat the inconceivable odds to come into being?"[23]

Science ultimately leads us to the intelligent Grand Designer who is able to create this material universe from nothing, define its laws, and exquisitely fine-tune their physical constants, for intelligent life to exist. Science does not lead a thinking person away from God but instead, as agnostic Paul Davies observes, it offers a surer path to God than religion:

"It may seem bizarre, but in my opinion science offers a surer path to God than religion... science has actually advanced to the point where what were formerly religious questions can be seriously tackled."[24]

The 'Atheist of the gaps' is getting smaller and smaller by the day even for the most infinitesimal demands of life.

"The physicists are getting things down to the nitty-gritty, they've really just about pared things down to the ultimate details and the last thing they ever expected to happen is happening. God is showing through... They hate it, but they can't do anything about it. Facts are facts... God, the Creator, Maker of Heaven and Earth... He made it, we can now see, in that first instant with such incredible precision that a Swiss watch is just a bunch of little rocks by comparison."[25] (John Updike)

"If anyone claims not to be surprised by the special features that the universe has, he is hiding his head in the sand. These special features are surprising and unlikely."[26] (Dr. David D. Deutsch)

"The exquisite order displayed by our scientific understanding of the physical world calls for the divine."[27] (Dr. Vera Kistiakowski)

"Nothing has shaken my atheism as much as this discovery (*the fine*-tuning)."[28]

References:

1. Robin Collins, *Why a Fine-Tuned Universe?*, Science + Religion Today

2. Paul Davies, BBC science documentary, *The Anthropic Principle, 1987*

3. Dr. Walter L. Bradley, *The Formation of the Elements required for Complex Embodied Life is Fine-tuned*

4. Patrick Glynn, *God: The Evidence: The Reconciliation of Faith and Reason in a Postsecular World,* Prima Publishing, 1997

5. William Lane Criag, *The Craig-Pigliucci Debate: Does God Exist?*

6. Francis Collins, *The Believer*, an interview with Steve Paulson, Aug 7, 2006

7. Paul Davies, *The Mind of God: The Scientific Basis for a Rational World*, 1992

8. Paul Davies, *The Cosmic Blueprint*, Templeton Foundation, 1988

9. Arno Penzias, *Cosmos, Bios, and Theos*, Margenau, H and R. A. Varghese, ed., La Salle, Illinois: Open Court Publishing, 1992, p. 83

10. Stephen Hawking, *A Brief History Of Time*, Bantam Press, London: 1988, p. 121-125

11. Stephen Hawking, *Austin American Statesman*, October 19, 1997

12. George Ellis, *The Anthropic Principle: Laws and Environments*, F. Bertola and U. Curi, ed., New York, New York: Cambridge University Press, 1993, p. 30

13. George Greenstein, *The Symbiotic, Universe: Life and Mind in the Cosmos*, New York: William Morrow, 1988, pp. 26-27

14. Fred Hoyle, *The Intelligent Universe: A New View of Creation and Evolution*, London: Michael Joseph Limited 1983

15. Alan Sandage, J. N. Willford, *Sizing up the Cosmos: An Astronomers Quest*, New York Times, March 12, 1991, p. B9

16. Casti, J. L., *Paradigms Lost*, New York, Avon Books, 1989, p. 482-483

17. Martin J. Rees, Astronomer Royal, *Just Six Numbers – The Deep Forces that Shape the Universe*

18. Lennox, John, *God's Undertaker. Has Science Buried God?* 2007, Lion Hudson

19. Patrick Glynn, *The Making and Unmaking of an Atheist, in: God: The Evidence*, Rocklin, Calif.: Forum, 1997, p. 53

20. Frank Tipler, F. J., *The Physics Of Immortality*, New York, Doubleday, Preface, 1994

21. Paul Davies, *Superforce*, p. 235-36

22. Eric Mataxas, *Science Increasingly Makes the Case for God*, Wall Street Journal, December 25, 2014

23. From the Documentary *Collision*, Christopher Hitchens vs Douglas Wilson, *italics mine*

24. Paul Davies, *God and the New Physics*, Penguin, 1983, p. 9

25. John Updike, *Roger's Version*, New York: Fawcett Crest, p. 9-10, 1986

26. Dr. David D. Deutsch, *The Guardian*, 8th January 2009

27. Dr. Vera Kistiakowski, professor of physics emeritus, MIT

28. Professor Sir Fred Hoyle, cited by David Wilkinson, *God, The Big Bang & Stephen Hawking,* Monarch, 1993, p. 108

Missing the Obvious

The Lone Ranger and Tonto are camping in the desert, set up their tent, and are asleep. Some hours later, The Lone Ranger wakes his faithful friend. "Tonto, look up and tell me what you see."

Tonto replies, "Me see millions of stars."

"What does that tell you?" asks The Lone Ranger.

Tonto ponders for a minute. "Astronomically speaking, it tells me that there are millions of galaxies and potentially billions of planets. Astrologically, it tells me that Saturn is in Leo. Time wise, it appears to be approximately a quarter past three. Theologically, it's evident the Lord is all powerful and we are small and insignificant. Meteorologically, it seems we will have a beautiful day tomorrow." "What it tells you, Kemo Sabi?"

The Lone Ranger is silent for a moment, then speaks, "Tonto, you Dumb Hoss, someone has stolen our tent." (Source Unknown)

While Tonto may have missed seeing the obviously stolen tent, many of today's high-powered, secular scientists choose to reject the obvious implication that the fine-tuning of the universe points to a logical Fine-Tuner.

<u>The first objection to the fine-tuning of the universe pointing to a divine Fine-Tuner: The Multiverse.</u>

The first objection to the fine-tuning of the universe leading to an intelligent and necessary First Cause is the Multiverse hypothesis, which postulates that our universe is just one of an infinite number of universes in the cosmos – like the bubbles in a glass of champagne. Our universe happens to have the right conditions to permit intelligent life. Other universes were not so fortunate and they remained in a state of cosmic comatose or lifelessness.

Simply put, if there were an infinite number of universes in the cosmos, then intuitively, there might be the possibility that some of these universes will have the right physical laws and physical constants for a life-permitting universe. But one of the obvious problems is that infinity is only an abstract idea, a mathematical construct, that does not exists in physical reality. There is no such thing as an infinite number of events or universes!

First, for the sake of argument, even if there were an infinite number of universes, there is no guarantee that we will get such a complex universe as ours with its razor-sharp, fine-tuned, physical composition, laws and constants. A case in point is that there can be an infinite number of hurricanes on planet earth, but they can never produce a highly complex space shuttle or build the Empire State Building. The materials are there but all these natural catastrophes can never organize them into these man-made structures and engineering marvels. If the thousands of observable hurricanes produce only destruction, what makes one thinks that more of it will produce things with specified complexity like the space-shuttle or the Empire State Building? It takes a lot of blind faith to believe that it can. An infinite number of events is no silver bullet to creating everything, especially, complex structures like our universe.

Secondly, at best, the Multiverse hypothesis seeks only to explain or explain away the fine-tuning of the universe. It still leaves unanswered the enigmatic question of where those matter and laws come from? Simply put, you cannot get something from nothing without a supernatural Creator. Let us hear what the world's most notorious atheist-turned-deist, Anthony Flew, has to say about the multiverse:

> "So multiverse or not, we still have to come to terms with the origin of the laws of nature. And the only viable explanation here is the divine mind".[1]

Thirdly, the Multiverse, together with all of its cosmic stepchildren, is just an untested hypothesis; they do not qualify as a scientific theory. They are not observable, falsifiable or repeatable. Here is an excerpt from an article in *Discover Magazine* (which is hostile to theism and Christianity):

> "Short of invoking a benevolent creator, many physicists see only one possible explanation: Our universe may be but one of perhaps infinitely many universes in an inconceivably vast multiverse. Most of those universes are barren, but some, like ours, have conditions suitable for life.
>
> The idea is controversial. Critics say it doesn't even qualify as a scientific theory because the existence of other universes cannot be proved or disproved. Advocates argue that, like it or not, the multiverse may well be the only viable non-religious explanation for what is often called the "fine-tuning problem" – the baffling observation that the laws of the universe seem custom-tailored to favor the emergence of life."[2]

In his NY Times article, *A Brief History of the Multiverse*, Paul Davies, offers a variety of arguments that Multiverse theories are blatantly non-scientific:

> "For a start, how is the existence of the other universes to be tested? To be sure, all cosmologists accept that there are some regions of the universe that lie beyond the reach of our telescopes, but somewhere on the slippery slope between that and the idea that there are an infinite number of universes, credibility reaches a limit. As one slips down that slope, more and more must be accepted on faith, and less and less is open to scientific verification. Extreme multiverse explanations are therefore reminiscent of theological discussions. Indeed, invoking an infinity of unseen universes to explain the unusual features of the one we do see is just as ad hoc as invoking an unseen Creator. The multiverse theory may be dressed up in scientific language, but in essence it requires the same leap of faith."[3]

Here is another damaging article from *Scientific American* on the Multiverse theory – it is more science fiction than a scientific theory:

> "These multiverse theories all share the same fundamental defect: They can be neither confirmed nor falsified. Hence, they don't deserve to be called scientific, according to the well-known criterion proposed by the philosopher Karl Popper... Multiverse theories aren't theories – they're science fictions, theologies, works of the imagination unconstrained by evidence."[4]

In his desperate attempt to hang on to the unobservable Multiverse theory to explain away the fine-tuning evidence of a Designer, Richard Dawkins suddenly seems unashamedly oblivious to his own definition of faith, which is 'believing without evidence'. From an article by David Couchman:

> "The biggest single objection to the idea of multiple universes is that there is (at least, so far) no evidence for it. Richard Dawkins says that, 'Scientific belief is based on publicly checkable evidence.' (*Daily Telegraph Science Extra*, Sept 11th 1989) But he also advances multiple universes as an explanation for cosmic fine tuning, without any supporting evidence. This is self-contradictory.

As Rodney Holder says: 'Curiously enough someone like Richard Dawkins says 'no, I believe in a multiverse. That will explain [*the fine-tuning*].' On the other hand, Richard Dawkins tells you that you should only believe things on the basis of evidence. Well, there's a massive contradiction there within the thought of Richard Dawkins.'

(Of course, in Dawkins' own mind, there may not be a contradiction: given that cosmic fine-tuning is a reality, given that there are only two possible explanations, and given that he rules out the 'God' explanation in principle, a multiverse is the only option that is left. However, this does seem to put the cart before the horse.)"[5]

Even Lawrence Krauss, a good friend of Richard Dawkins, and no friend to the creationists, refutes the idea that string theory, which gives rise to the Multiverse hypothesis, is even worthy to be called a scientific theory:

"I wrote a piece where I argued that is a disservice to evolutionary theory to call string theory a theory, for example. Because it's clearly not a theory in the same sense that evolutionary theory is, or that quantum electrodynamics is, because those are robust theories that make rigorous predictions that can be falsified. And string theory is just a formalism now that one day might be a theory. And when I'm lecturing, talking about science, people say to me, evolution is just a theory, I say, in science theory means a different thing, and they say, what do you mean? Look at string theory, how can you falsify that? It's no worse than intelligent design."[6]

Peter Woit articulates his deep concerns on how the Multiverse has morphed uncritically from a speculative hypothesis into a scientific theory in the many current text books today:

"My own moral concerns about the multiverse have more to do with worry that pseudo-science is being heavily promoted to the public, leading to the danger that it will ultimately take over from science, first in the field of fundamental physics, then perhaps spreading to others... One of the lessons of superstring theory unification is that if a wrong idea is promoted for enough years, it gets into the textbooks and becomes part of the conventional wisdom about how the world works. This process is now well underway with multiverse pseudo-science, as some theorists who should know better choose to heavily promote it, and others abdicate their responsibility to fight pseudo-science as it gains traction in their field."[7]

The secular cosmological community often accuses the theologians of wild superstition, but today the gun is turned on them. Faye Flam writes:

"Cosmologist Michael Turner of the University of Chicago recently coined the rule that, in a cosmological theory, you can't invoke the tooth fairy twice. His tooth fairy is not a mystical being replaces lost teeth with quarters, but any wild, whimsical assumption dreamed up to answer some problem. In a field like cosmology, where the questions are vast and data scarce, you would expect to have to summon a tooth fairy from time to time. But today, to hear many cosmologists talk, the population of tooth fairies is exploding. 'In some of the newer theories, we are inventing a new physical principle for every new observational fact,' complains astronomer Marc Davis of the University of California, Berkley... The field of cosmic structure is opening up to creative speculation."[8]

Bernard Carr, writing in *Discoverer Magazine,* states:

"If there is only one universe, you might have to have a fine-tuner. If you don't want God, you'd better have a multiverse."[9]

In conclusion, on one level, the scientific community would often demand the evidence for a Creator God from the theists, and yet, on another level, they would openly and unashamedly promote the Multiverse as a scientific theory without any shred of evidence. The creationists too, have the rights to counter demand from these unethical cosmologists: "Just the evidence, ma'am; just the evidence." The Multiverse hypothesis is not testable, falsifiable and reproducible, period. It is not even a scientific theory by all accounts. Yet, it is unscrupulously promoted as such. No wonder, many conclude that the Multiverse hypothesis is really the 'last resort for the desperate atheist' (Neil Manson). To use what you cannot observe (the multiverse) to explain away what you can observe (the fine-tuning) is both unscientific and anti-science.

<u>The second objection to the fine-tuning of the universe pointing to a divine Fine-Tuner: The universe is 'dying'.</u>

Another common objection to the fine-tuning of the universe pointing to a Creator is that the universe will eventually die the 'Heat Death', where all the stars will burn out, leaving behind a cold, lifeless, ever-expanding darkness with no traces of life. If our universe is fine-tuned by God, why then is it running down into disorder and death?

If we were to find Paley's watch on the beach, we can correctly assume that there was a designer for that intricate watch. But, would it not be foolish and illogical to conclude that since it was found to be rusting and breaking down, it proves it was never designed? On the contrary, we should seek to know the reason why it broke down. In this case, it is traced to entropy – where everything in an isolated system will eventually turn into disorder – every house will collapse and every car will rust, if nothing is done to preserve them. It does not prove the lack of design or a designer.

In the case of this universe we are living in, we have not arrived yet. This temporal world is a broken down world, with its sins and rebellion. Man knows its effect but does not know of its cause – only the Bible, the Word of God, can reveal its true history – the history of a once beautiful, perfect and pristine Garden of Eden; of Man's failure to obey God; of his sin, judgment and misery; and of a promised return back to Paradise someday if he submits to God's plan of redemption through his faith in the Lord Jesus Christ, the Son of God.

This imperfect, temporal world is God's testing ground to prove man's heart. The atheist is entitled to his rights and story; the Christian too, is entitled to his belief in a Divine Book that delineates his history. The unspoken atheistic story is quite depressing: we are *From Nothing, by Nothing, and for Nothing,* a curious accident in the backwater of the universe heading into oblivion. The Christians, at the other end, have a more vibrant outlook in life – we are *From Someone, by Someone, and for Someone*, having the assurance of a wonderful relationship with God both here and thereafter.

This world in which we are right now is not home yet. Someday, we will be in our eternal home, where all the tears, sorrows and imperfections will be a thing of the past. But while we are here, we have ample evidence of God's existence and His creative power in this visible universe. His fingerprints are plastered all over the cosmos, and one of the many proofs of God along a long trail of evidence He left us is this exquisite, mystifying, mind-boggling, cosmic fine-tuning of the Universe. The Bible has much to say of the transient nature of this world. One of which is this:

"But the day of the Lord will come as a thief in the night; in the which the heavens shall pass away with a great noise, and the elements shall melt with fervent heat, the earth also and the works that are therein shall be burned up... Nevertheless we, according to his promise, look for new heavens and a new earth, wherein dwelleth righteousness"[10] (*Bible*). Incidentally, this is the Bible's Big Bang.

The third objection to the fine-tuning of the universe pointing to a divine Fine-Tuner: The vast expanse of the universe is uninhabitable.

Here, the objection to a Designer for this fine-tuned universe is the extravagance of a wasteful universe to produce just one habitable planet called 'earth'. In short, if there is a purposeful Creator, why this cosmic wastage with possibly billions of planets that are inhospitable to life?

But that argument can be turned around. Today's astrophysicists and cosmologists acknowledge that every star and every planet in the universe is needed to birth and sustain this earth teeming with life. The mass density of the universe is fine-tuned to $1:10^{59}$ (Dr. Edward Wright, Ph.D., Professor of Astronomy at UCLA) to keep this earth going! Any infinitesimal addition or subtraction to the mass-energy of the universe will see it either expanding too fast for stars to coalesce or imploding on itself. God not only feeds the sparrows on this earth, but He hangs the very last star in the night sky to keep us going. And, as English cosmologist and theoretical physicist John Barrow puts it:

"Many philosophers, from Bertrand Russell backwards, have argued that the enormous size and emptiness of the universe is a signature that it is neither sympathetic nor terribly conducive to the development of life within it. Now modern astronomy changes this whole perception of the universe completely... If the universe was significantly smaller, say just the size of our Milky Way galaxy, it would be little more than a month old, it could barely pay off your credit card bill let alone produce complexity in life. The universe would have to be just as large as it is to support even one lonely outpost of life."[11]

What an awe-inspiring and caring God! Above all, God, being God, is entitled to use the whole of the universe to create this one precious speck of dirt in space we called 'earth' - a holding place for fallen mankind. He can well afford to be extravagant for the people whom He loves and is preparing for eternity. Besides, the universe is made of 'cheap stuff' – the ubiquitous and varied arrangements of atoms governed by His amazing, carefully-crafted laws.

68

In the final analysis, the argument for God or Nothing creating the cosmos is a probabilistic argument – which is more probable – an intelligent God creating this amazingly fine-tuned universe or a dumb, immaterial Nothing devoid of matter and laws? The evidence to the contrary is the evidence – if Nothing did not and could not do it, then an intelligent and infinitely powerful Creator will be its only default candidate! There are only two possibilities to the creation of a car or a building – either by chance or by design. If you rule out one, the other will be the likely candidate. Take your pick! This is a free world.

The late Christopher Hitchens, like many other atheists, in his candor, realized that the fine-tuning of the physical constants of the laws of nature is probably the most powerful and compelling argument for the existence of God – it points to the ultimate Fine-Tuner. Let us hear his candid admission:

> "At some point, certainly, we are all asked, "Which is the best argument you come up against from the other side [*the creationists*]." I think everyone of us picks the 'fine-tuning' as one of the most intriguing. The fine-tuning that... one hair difference [*will turn the universe into*] nothing... that even though it doesn't prove a design, doesn't prove a designer, could of all happened... you have to spend time thinking about it, working on it. It is not trivial, we all say that."[12] [*italics mine*]

No, Hitchens, you don't have to spend a lot of time thinking about this cosmic fine-tuning. It is God's unmistakable signature on His cosmos in plain sight.

> "For the invisible things of him from the creation of the world are clearly seen, being understood by the things that are made, even his eternal power and Godhead; so that they are without excuse."[13] (*Bible*)

It is what you want to do about it – humbly believe it or irrationally reject it. Sadly, you have thrown away your only hope to a meaningful and wonderful life beyond the grave.

> "Because that, when they knew God, they glorified him not as God, neither were thankful; but became vain in their imaginations, and their foolish heart was darkened. Professing themselves to be wise, they became fools..."[14] (*Bible*) / "The fool hath said in his heart, There is no God."[15] (*Bible*)

> It isn't that the atheists can't see the solution;
> it is that they can't see the problem.

69

References:

1. Anthony Flew, *There is a God: How the World's Most Notorious Atheist Changed His Mind*, p. 37

2. Tim Folger, *Science's Alternative to an Intelligent Creator: the Multiverse Theory,* Discover Magazine, December 2008

3. Davies, Paul, *A Brief History of the Multiverse*, New York Times,12 April 2003

4. John Horgan, *Is speculation in multiverses as immoral as speculation in subprime mortgages?,* Scientific American, January 28, 2011)

5. David Couchman, *Which is the better explanation of cosmic fine-tuning? A multiverse or a creator God?* March 2010

6. *The Energy of Empty Space that isn't Zero, A Talk With Lawrence M. Krauss,* Edge [7.5.06]

7. Peter Woit, *Is the Multiverse Immoral? Not Even Wrong,* January 29, 2011

8. Faye Flam, *In Search of a New Cosmic Blueprint,* Science, 254, 22 Nov. 1991: 1106

9. Bernard Carr, *Discoverer Magazine,* November 26, 2008

10. *Bible,* 2 Peter 3:10-13

11. John Barrow, *The Anthropic Principle,* The Science Show, 27 January 2007

12. From the Documentary *Collision,* Christopher Hitchens vs Douglas Wilson, italics mine

13. *Bible,* Romans 1:20

14. *Bible,* Romans 1:21-22

15. *Bible,* Psalms 14:1

Whodunit?

> "It is absurd for the Evolutionist to complain that it is unthinkable for an admittedly unthinkable God to make everything out of nothing, and then pretend that it is more thinkable that nothing should turn itself into everything."[1] (G. K. Chesterton)

In the final analysis, there are only three possible options for the existence of this universe.

1) The Universe is Eternal
2) The Universe created Itself
3) The Universe was created by a personal Agency

With regard to the first, that theory is long dead as we have seen in the previous studies. If the universe had been around for trillions and trillions of years, all the stars would have long burnt out and the galaxies would have drifted beyond our visual horizon. The Second Law of Thermodynamics, the birth and death of the stars, and the expanding universe, all point to a beginning to the Universe. It has never existed eternally and it is 'dying' every moment in the inevitable entropy. And if it is 'dying', then, there must have been a beginning to the universe for it to begin the process of decay.

The only other two possible candidates left for the existence of this universe are an impersonal 'Dumb Nothing' and a personal 'Creator of Everything'. There is nothing in-between. And all parties agree that there are no scientific proofs for one or the other – both are hypotheses or working models at best. You cannot put Nothing or God into some laboratory to test, observe and collaborate results from it, or to go back in time to see which of these two candidates did the job. Science cannot prove or disprove Nothing or God creating the universe from nothing. We can only deduce from the inference to the best explanation – which of the two candidates is a more logical and rational explanation? Both Creationism and Evolutionism are unrepeatable and unobservable past events, and both are accepted based on faith and not on testable and repeatable science. And the ultimate question is: which faith fits the facts?

The First Candidate: Nothing

For the sake of discussion, 'Nothing' is powerful enough to ignite the Big Bang from nothing. 'Nothing' can miraculously bring forth a whole ocean of distinct, subatomic particles from nothing. 'Nothing' is so musically talented as to cause different 'strings' in the cosmos to vibrate with different harmonics to produce the different subatomic particles from nothing (String Theory).

'Nothing' is so intelligent as to define the laws of nature to govern these particles, and again, from nothing. 'Nothing', with nothing in its head, is really smart to be able to decide what physical constant to assign to each physical law for a life-permitting universe. 'Nothing', hats off to it, is clever enough to fine-tune the laws of nature to, in some cases, one part in a million million.

'Nothing', and this really takes my breath away, is able to do complex mathematics to formulate all the laws of nature and to fine-tune their relationships to each other for life to exist. And above all, a 'Dumb Nothing', beyond man's wildest imagination, is able to bring a 'Smart Something' into existence without any help from Richard Dawkins or Stephen Hawking. Today's cosmological 'Nothing' is truly awesome! It is all-powerful and all-knowing - and it sounds a lot like Someone we are familiar with - God.

Some would point to the possibility of chance in the creation of the universe, like the winning of a lottery in a million to one chance. But that argument is patently flawed as in the case of a lottery with a fixed number of tickets, there will be a winning ticket. For the cosmos, there can be no 'winning ticket' - nothing leading to nothing! In reality, Nothing and her twin sister, Chance, are hopeless in the creation of the cosmos.

> "The fact is, however, we have a no-chance chance creation... What are the real chances of a universe created by chance? Not a chance. Chance is incapable of creating a single molecule, let alone an entire universe. Why not? Chance is no thing. It is not an entity. It has no being, no power, no force. It can effect nothing for it has no causal power within it, it has no 'itness' to be within. Chance... is a word which describes mathematical possibilities which, by a curious slip of the fallacy of ambiguity, slips into discussion as if it were a real entity with real power, indeed, supreme power, the power of creativity."[2] (Robert Charles Sproul, John Henry Gerstner, Arthur Lindsley)

'Nothing' cannot create this amazing Universe with its exquisite, fine-tuned laws from nothing. 'Nothing' can only create nothing. And 'Nothing' will always remain as nothing. 'Nothing' is no thing, no something and, in essence, no existence, period. When will the 'nothing theorists' get it? If 'Nothing' can create this universe from nothing, prove it – subject it to testing, falsification, and repetition? If not, it is nothing more than a religious faith called 'Evolutionism'.

Question:	Why is there something instead of nothing?
Atheist:	There just is, it just happened to have happened. Time did it, chance did it, matter did it, evolution did it. It is an accidental coincidence.
Question:	Why did the universe come into existence?
Atheist:	There just is, it just happened to have happened. Time did it, chance did it, matter did it, evolution did it. It is an accidental coincidence.
Question:	Why did the laws of the universe come to be established?
Atheist:	There just is, it just happened to have happened. Time did it, chance did it, matter did it, evolution did it. It is an accidental coincidence.
Question:	Why did the universe come to be fine-tuned?
Atheist:	There just is, it just happened to have happened. Time did it, chance did it, matter did it, evolution did it. It is an accidental coincidence.
Question:	What is the absolute, ultimate, objective meaning of life?
Atheist:	There is none. Just make something up and remember to be nice for some reason or other. Of course, this is not an absolute. (Source Unknown)

Today's 'Science of Nothing' is akin to the world of medieval witchcraft, and the 'nothing theorists', the semi-naked witch doctors, in ecstatic trances, pounding their chests and chanting endlessly strange and incoherent cosmic incantations: "Something from nothing, something from nothing; but how, how, how? We don't know how, but never mind how, just keep chanting something from nothing, something from nothing, and soon those idiots out there will believe it. And so, something from nothing, something from nothing, blah, blah, blah." When will all this mumbo jumbo, voodoo science end?

The idea that the universe created itself from nothing and by nothing is absurd, both philosophically and scientifically. It is not right; it is not 'even wrong'. And it is worse than an oxymoron! If this cosmic genesis came from the Bible instead of Massachusetts Institute of Technology (MIT), it would have been long laughed out of town and frowned upon as a preposterous myth concocted by some ignorant, Stone Age theologians. And yet today, it is pontificated as 'brilliant science'. And if 'Nothing' can create this universe out of nothing, it will be a piece of cake for God to create the cosmos out of nothing!

The Second Candidate: A Creator God

The First Law of Thermodynamics points to a Creator God

When we are lost, we look for signposts to direct us to our destination. Few people realize with the discovery of the First Law of Thermodynamics, man has unintentionally stumbled upon the unmistakable cosmic signpost that points to a Creator God.

The First Law of Thermodynamics states that matter cannot be created or destroyed in our finite cosmos. The implication is that the existing matter was in some finite past 'introduced' to create the universe. After which, the First Law is unbreachable. Mark Eastman and Chuck Missler show us why it inevitably leads us to a necessary First Cause:

> "In effect, the First Law states that you and I can neither create nor destroy matter. Therefore, it follows that if something which exists (you and I) cannot create matter, then something which doesn't exist cannot create it either!"[3]

In short, nothing creates nothing. Next, they logically conclude:

> "Matter cannot create itself and, in the real world, cannot arise from nothing. Within the bounds of natural law all effects must have a cause. Because of this fact, the spontaneous appearance of hydrogen atoms out of nothing (ex nihilo creation) is a definite breach of the First Law of Thermodynamics which asserts that matter, under natural circumstances, can neither be created nor destroyed. Therefore, since it is not a natural event, it is by definition a supernatural event – a miracle!"[4]

Or, in the words of agnostic physicist and astrobiologist, Paul Davies:

> "[The big bang] represents the instantaneous suspension of physical laws, the sudden abrupt flash of lawlessness that allowed something to come out of nothing. It represents a true miracle – transcending physical principles."[5]

A layman's interpretation: "Since nothing cannot create anything, and if something did appear from nothing, then a miracle has taken place."

From Nothing = The Big Bang = Something = A Miracle

Isn't it ironical? The same atheistic crowd that scorns the miracle of the origin of the universe by a Creator must now embrace another unintended and even more impressive and absurd miracle that our universe was supernaturally brought into existence from no existence and by no existence. So, miracles are possible after all! Isn't that great? And no matter how far back in time secular cosmologists would want to extrapolate, this miracle of the beginning is inescapable.

The atheist, like the theist, must now accept by faith the miracle that something can come from nothing. For the Christian, that miracle is God; for the atheist, that miracle is: 'we are still working on it'; 'we refuse to speculate'; or 'science will figure it out some day'. In short, it is a cop-out – an obvious supernatural event without a supernatural cause. Without exception, no physical existence always leads to no physical reality. The immutable First Law of Thermodynamics seals its fate forever. If something did come from nothing, then it becomes a permanent, cosmic signpost that points us to a supernatural event – a miracle – and ultimately to a Creator.

The Second Law of Thermodynamics points to a Creator God

The next sign post is the Second Law of Thermodynamics which states that the usable energy in the universe is decreasing in entropy and that process is irreversible. In short, the universe is getting more and more disorderly – the sun and the stars are burning out and that process is irreversible. It is like a wound-up clock that is running down every moment and that cannot wind it up again. And that begs the question: Who wound it up in the finite past? The Second Law of Thermodynamics is an inviolable law.

> "The law that entropy always increases (the Second Law of Thermodynamics) holds, I think, the supreme position among the laws of nature. If someone points out to you that your pet theory of the universe is in disagreement with Maxwell's equations [on electricity], then so much the worse for Maxwell's equations... But if your theory is found to be against the Second Law of Thermodynamics, I can give you no hope; there is nothing for it but to collapse in deepest humiliation."[6] (Sir Arthur Eddington)

The first hint of God creating the cosmos is found in the First Law of Thermodynamics where the present energy in the universe was intentionally introduced into this universe. The second hint is that the initial usable energy in our universe was raised to such a 'maximum level' to permit for life to exist. Without the sun, life would have been impossible. If this universe had originally existed in darkness (maximum entropy) without suns or stars, life as we know it would be impossible.

> "The time asymmetry of the universe is expressed by the Second Law of Thermodynamics, that entropy (randomness) increases with time as order is transformed into disorder. The mystery is not that an ordered state should become disordered but that the early universe was in a highly ordered state..."[7] (Don Page)

First, why is the initial usable energy at such low entropy? Could it be the work of an intelligent First Cause who intends to birth and sustain life in this universe? It sure looks like it. Innate energy cannot 'wind up' itself – the Second Law works against it – an external Source is needed to wind it up. Or, to put it in another way, what is winding down must have been once wound up. And the million dollar question is: "By who?" It cannot be 'by what', for 'what' (the physical realm) can only wind down and not up as according to the Second Law. A 'Divine Hand' is needed to wind it up.

Secondly, when we extrapolate the Second Law of Thermodynamics back into time past, it will wind its way to a 'creation event', the lowest entropy possible. In his book, *The Mysterious Universe*, Cambridge University astronomer, Sir James Jeans, declares that the orderly state of the universe requires a 'creation' event at a finite time in the past.

> "A scientific study of the universe has suggested a conclusion that may be summed up... in the statement that the universe appears to have been designed by a pure mathematician... The more orthodox scientific view is that the entropy (randomness or disorder) of the universe must forever increase to its final value. It has not yet reached this: we should not be thinking about if it had. It [entropy or randomness] is still increasing rapidly... there must have been what we may describe as 'creation' at a time not infinitely remote."[8]

Isaac Asimov was unsettled by the puzzling low entropy in the commencement of the universe. How did nature manage to wind up the universe?

> "As far as we know, all changes are in the direction of increasing entropy, of increasing disorder, of increasing randomness, of running down. Yet the universe was once in a position from which it could run down for trillions of years. How did it get into that position?"[9]

Actually, it is quite simple Isaac - "In the beginning, God created the heaven and the earth"[10] (*Bible*). Nature can only wind down the universe; only God can wind it up.

The Law of Cause-and-Effect points to a Creator God

All physical effects must have their antecedent physical causes. And the chain of cause-and-effect events must regress to the point of the beginning – the first link. The cause-and-effect mechanism cannot regress indefinitely (a physical impossibility); it must logically and necessarily terminate at a 'first link'. And when the physical causes culminate in this 'first link', there will be no more physical causes to speak of. Beyond that, there is literally nothing – no quantum vacuum, no quantum mechanics, no anything – just nothing. Science runs out of naturalistic causation and explanation – only the metaphysical and supernatural can adequately explain how this naturalistic 'first link' appears from 'no link'.

One can keep pushing the 'beginning' of the universe further back into deep time – from the universe coming from some primordial quantum vacuum, and the primordial vacuum coming from a previous 'weak energy field', and the weak energy field coming from an earlier quantum foam, et al. But, sooner or later, it will run out of natural causes to trigger the Big Bang. It must necessarily terminate at nothing. Someone that transcends space-time and mass-energy must now come into play. And the only logical explanation of getting the 'first link' from 'no link' is in the Divine.

The now famous Kalam Cosmological Argument made popular by William Lane Craig states:

> Whatever begins to exist has a cause;
> The universe began to exist;
> Therefore, the universe has a cause.[11]

Let us hear from Oxford philosopher Richard Swinburne on his observation of the two possible explanations for the origin of the universe:

> "... scientific explanations in terms of laws and initial conditions and personal explanations in terms of agents and their volitions. A first state of the universe cannot have a scientific explanation, since there is nothing before it, and therefore it can be accounted for only in terms of a personal explanation."[12]

A sharper perspective comes from a page of the Stanford Encyclopedia of Philosophy:

> "We have seen that one cannot provide a natural causal explanation for the initial event, for there are no precedent events or natural existents to which the laws of physics apply. The line of scientific explanation runs out at the initial singularity, and perhaps even before we arrive at the singularity (at 10^{-35} seconds). If no scientific explanation (in terms of physical laws) can provide a causal account of the origin of the universe, the explanation must be personal, that is, in terms of the intentional action of an intelligent, supernatural agent."[13]

In short, a naturalistic causation is nowhere in sight as there are no natural causes that can kick-start this exotic universe with its well-defined atomic structures and its fine-tuned laws — nothing will always lead to nothing. The only candidate left is an intelligent Designer and Creator:

> "All things were made by him; and without him was not any thing made that was made."[14] (*Bible*)

> He was in the world, and the world was made by him, and the world knew him not."[15] (*Bible*)

The Fine-Tuning of the Universe points to a Creator God

As in our previous studies, we discovered that the universe is so exquisitely fine-tuned for intelligent life. The laws and matter, their existence and their relationship to each other, their almost infinitesimally fine-tuned constants in some cases, all point to an intelligent Designer. British physicist Sir James Jeans made this startling admission regarding the existence and attributes of a transcendent Creator for this universe:

> "There is a wide measure of agreement which, on the physical side of science approaches almost unanimity, that the stream of knowledge is heading towards a non-mechanical reality; the universe begins to look more like a great thought than a great machine. Mind no longer appears as an accidental intruder into the realm of matter. We are beginning to suspect that we ought rather to hail mind as the creator and governor of the realm of matter."[16]

Ed Harrison, adjunct Professor of Astronomy, Steward Observatory, University of Arizona, throws in his lot on the fine-tuning of the universe revealing a Fine-Tuner. He writes:

> "Here is the cosmological proof of the existence of God – the design argument of Paley – updated and refurbished. The fine tuning of the universe provides prima facie evidence of deistic design. Take your choice: blind chance that requires multitudes of universes or design that requires only one... Many scientists, when they admit their views, incline toward the teleological or design argument."[17]

The Scientific Prediction of the Bible on Cosmology points to a Creator God:

When you rule out the impersonal 'Nothing', you are left with only the personal 'Creator' who with intelligence and intention and is able to bring forth something from nothing. And let me have the privilege to introduce this Judeo-Christian Creator to you, this God of the Cosmos. You will find Him smarter and more satisfactory as an explanation than the ridiculous cosmological 'nothing'. And you will be amazed that the Bible is not an ancient story book as most simplistic atheists would imagine, but that it is capable of making accurate scientific predictions that are observable and testable.

1)   It predicted the earth is spherical:

> "It is he that sitteth upon the circle of the earth..."[18] (*Bible*)

2)   It predicted the earth is suspended in space:

> "He stretcheth out the north over the empty place, and hangeth the earth upon nothing."[19] (*Bible*)

3)   It predicted an expanding universe:

> "Who coverest thyself with light as with a garment: who stretchest out the heavens like a curtain."[20] (*Bible*) / "Thus saith God the Lord, he that created the heavens, and stretched them out..."[21] (*Bible*) / It is he that sitteth upon the circle of the earth, and the inhabitants thereof are as grasshoppers; that stretcheth out the heavens as a curtain, and spreadeth them out as a tent to dwell in."[22] (*Bible*) / "Which alone spreadeth out the heavens, and treadeth upon the waves of the sea."[23] (*Bible*)

17 times the Bible talks of the stretching of the cosmos - some in the past tense and others in the continuous tense. The Bible knew about the expansion of the universe way before Georges Lemaitre, Edwin Hubble and Albert Einstein had any inkling about it. The author believes in an expanding universe but not in the Big Bang cosmology. Today's cosmologists talk of the 'stretching of the fabric of space-time' and we see how close this comes to the Bible's equivalent of the 'stretching of the heavens like a curtain'. Again, the Bible is one step ahead of the secular cosmologists.

4)   It predicted the Two Laws of Thermodynamics:

"Of old hast thou laid the foundation of the earth: and the heavens are the work of thy hands (the First Law of Thermodynamics – after God's initial creation, the energy in the universe cannot be created or destroyed). They shall perish, but thou shalt endure: yea, all of them shall wax old like a garment (the Second Law of Thermodynamics – usable energy will decrease in entropy; the stars are burning out); as a vesture shalt thou change them, and they shall be changed: But thou art the same, and thy years shall have no end."[24] (Bible)

5)   It predicted the trillions of stars in the universe:

"That in blessing I will bless thee (Abraham), and in multiplying I will multiply thy seed (the Jews) as the stars of the heaven, and as the sand which is upon the sea shore..."[25] (Bible) / "As the host of heaven cannot be numbered, neither the sand of the sea measured: so will I multiply the seed of David my servant, and the Levites that minister unto me."[26] (Bible)

It is a known fact today that there are more stars in the universe than there are grains of sand on the sea shores in the world. The men of old who were inspired by God to pen this down could only see a few thousand stars at the most with their naked eyes. Yet, the Bible could dogmatically proclaim what science today has discovered – the trillions and trillions of stars embedded in the billions and billions of galaxies in this scintillating universe.

"According to astronomers, there are probably more than 170 billion galaxies in the observable Universe, stretching out into a region of space 13.8 billion light-years away from us in all directions. And so, if you multiply the number of stars in our galaxy by the number of galaxies in the Universe, you get approximately 10^{24} stars. That's a 1 followed by twenty-four zeros. That's a septillion stars."[27]

6) <u>It predicted the sun's ray will encompass the whole earth:</u>

"... In them hath he set a tabernacle for the sun... His going forth is from the end of the heaven (sky), and his circuit unto the ends of it: and there is nothing hid from the heat thereof."[28] (*Bible*)

How did these simple folks in ancient times know of the whole earth being heated up by the sun's rays? They don't. God revealed it to them.

7) <u>It predicted the universe was created by God from nothing:</u>

"Through faith we understand that the worlds were framed by the word of God, so that things which are seen were not made of things which do appear."[29] (*Bible*)

"The above brilliant modern day scientists (Einstein, Hawking, Heisenberg, Dirac, Schrodinger and Planck) were well accustomed at showing that invisible things were a reality. As Einstein predicted, the first atomic bomb released the huge amounts of invisible energy trapped in the atom and this was a reality!"[30] (Antony Flew)

8) <u>It predicted the simultaneous existence of day and night throughout the world:</u>

"Even thus shall it be in the day when the Son of man is revealed. *In that day*, he which shall be upon the housetop, and his stuff in the house, let him not come down to take it away: and he that is in the field, let him likewise not return back... I tell you, *in that night* there shall be two men in one bed; the one shall be taken, and the other shall be left."[31] (*Bible*)

When Jesus Christ returns to judge the world, some parts of the world will be day and others night.

9) <u>It predicted the creation of space-time and mass-energy from nothing:</u>

"In the beginning (time) God (the uncaused First Cause) created the heaven (space) and the earth (matter and energy)."[32] (*Bible*)

"The Hebrew word for create, bara, literally means to create matter from nothing. The word "beginning" has been understood by the rabbis to mean "at the beginning of time." So a literal rendering of Genesis 1:1 reads, "At the beginning of time, God created from nothing the heavens (space) and the earth (matter)."[33] (*Bible*)

It is for this reason the author believes in the Jehovah God of the Bible who knows what He is talking about and not in Thor, Zeus, the Flying Spaghetti Monster, the myriads of mythical gods, or the endless, speculative, naturalistic explanations of how the universe came into being. It is called 'the process of elimination'. The Bible is light years ahead of present-day science. And science today is just playing catch up with the Bible, huffing and puffing along the way. The Bible knew about cosmogony and cosmology long before man started tinkering with the telescope.

Above all, Science and Christianity are not adversaries – they are the best of friends. God is the source of objective science and the many discoveries of science point us back to Him. Science tells us how it is done, while the Bible tells us Who did it. Many men of science do not find their scientific discoveries contradicting God, but rather they complement Him. Faith in God gives them the confidence in the order of things governing the cosmos. And in this, they can truly do science. To them, every revelation of the natural world is a revelation of the mind of God. And every new discovery instils in them a sense of wonder and awe in the Almighty Creator and Sustainer of this Universe. They are always amazed and humbled by it. Let us hear from some of the Nobel Laureates who are unapologetically Christians in their faith in God:

"The first gulp from the glass of natural sciences will turn you into an atheist, but at the bottom of the glass God is waiting for you."[34] (Werner Heisenberg, Nobel Laureate in Physics, 1988)

"For myself, faith begins with the realization that a supreme intelligence brought the universe into being and created man. It is not difficult for me to have this faith, for it is incontrovertible that where there is a plan there is intelligence. An orderly, unfolding universe testifies to the truth of the most majestic statement ever uttered: 'In the beginning God...'"[35] (Arthur Compton, Nobel Laureate in Physics, 1936)

"There can never be any real opposition between religion and science; for the one is the complement of the other. Every serious and reflective person realizes, I think, that the religious element in his nature must be recognized and cultivated if all the powers of the human soul are to act together in perfect balance and harmony. And indeed it was not by accident that the greatest thinkers of all ages were deeply religious souls."[36] (Max Planck, Nobel Laureate in Physics, 1918)

"God is Truth. There is no incompatibility between science and religion. Both are seeking the same truth. Science shows that God exists."[37] (Sir Derek Barton, Nobel Laureate in Chemistry, 1997)

"A scientific discovery is also a religious discovery. There is no conflict between science and religion. Our knowledge of God is made larger with every discovery we make about the world."[38] (Joseph H. Taylor, Jr., Nobel Laureate in Physics, 1993)

Besides the many Christian Nobel Laureates, there are heaps of scientists who unapologetically believe in the God of the Bible. Their belief in God did not stop them from excelling in science, as men like Bill Nye would naively want us to believe. Theism is not a science-stopper and atheism is not a science-promoter. Both the theists and the atheists can be excellent or terrible scientists.

"I was reminded of this a few months ago when I saw a survey in the journal Nature. It revealed that 40% of American physicists, biologists and mathematicians believe in God — and not just some metaphysical abstraction, but a deity who takes an active interest in our affairs and hears our prayers: the God of Abraham, Isaac and Jacob."[39] (Jim Holt)

In conclusion, both the Big Bang and the Created Universe hypotheses have one thing in common — it is an inexplicable miracle that defies the laws of nature — how do you get something from nothing apart from a supernatural miracle? Even the Big Bangers cannot hide behind this silly demand: give me the first miracle and we will explain the rest. You still need to explain this 'mother of all miracles': the first miraculous 'Big Bang' that is capable of spawning this awesome Universe with all its exotic matter and finely-calibrated laws.

| The Big Bang Universe | = | A Miracle | = | From Nothing |
| The Created Universe | = | A Miracle | = | From God |

This is the materialist's story: Once, there was nothing, and then, there was a boom; after which, we have everything exquisite and fine-tuned. Take your pick – which sounds more like a fairy tale – a brilliant God who created everything from nothing or a booming Nothing?

Also, for (A) to create (B), (A) must first exist before it can create (B). Man must first exist before he can create a car. And if there were no (A), there will be no (B). If there were no man, there will be no car. And if there was once nothing, there can never be anything! It is inconceivable to comprehend why many respectable, secular scientists can convince themselves of an obvious impossibility – a cosmic lie – that a non-existing (A) is capable of creating itself (A) out of no existence! It is just mind-blogging. These cosmological lunatics must be suffering from some serious, cosmic, mental illness to believe in such an obvious, blatant impossibility.

Science goes where the evidence leads, and the evidence is pointing in the direction of the God hypothesis. The eternal universe never happened, and something from nothing is anti-science and a cosmic joke. The only candidate left is the eternal God of the Bible, the uncaused First Cause, that makes verifiable predictions of the cosmos that are testable.

> "The heavens declare the glory of God; and the firmament sheweth his handywork. Day unto day uttereth speech, and night unto night sheweth knowledge. There is no speech nor language, where their voice is not heard. Their line is gone out through all the earth, and their words to the end of the world."[40] (*Bible*)

> "From the perspective of the latest physical theories, Christianity is not a mere religion, but an experimentally testable science."[41] (Frank Tipler)

> "These findings, now available, make the idea that God created the universe a more respectable hypothesis today than at any time in the last 100 years."[42] (Frederick Burnham)

Science has created a world in which God has become a necessity.

References:

1.   Quotes by G. K. Chesterton

2.   Robert Charles Sproul, John Henry Gerstner, Arthur Lindsley, *Classical Apologetics: A Rational Defense of the Christian Faith and a Critique of Presuppositional Apologetics*, p. 118, Academic Books

3.   Missler, Chuck, Eastman, Mark, M.D. *The Creator Beyond Time and Space*, The Word for Today, 1996, p. 12-17

4.   Missler, Chuck, Eastman, Mark, M.D. *The Creator Beyond Time and Space*, The Word for Today, 1996, p. 12-17

5.   Paul Davies, *The Edge of Infinity*, New York: Simon and Schuster, 1981, p. 161

6.   Sir Arthur Eddington, *The Nature of the Physical World,* Cambridge University Press: Cambridge UK, 1933, p. 74-75

7.   Don Page, *Nature*, 1983

8.   Sir James Jeans, *The Mysterious Universe*, Cambridge Press, 1931, p. 146

9.   Isaac Asimov, *Science Digest*, May 1973, p. 76-77

10.   *Bible*, Genesis 1:1

11.   William Lane Craig, *The Existence of God and the Beginning of the Universe*

12.   Richard Swinburne, *The Existence of God,* rev. ed., Oxford: Clarendon Press, 1991, p. 32-48

13.   *Stanford Encyclopedia of Philosophy*, first published Jul 13, 2004; substantive revision, Oct 26, 2012

14.   *Bible*, John 1:3

15.   *Bible*, John 1:10

16.   Sir James Jeans, *The Mysterious Universe*, Cambridge Press, 1931, p. 137

17.   Harrison, E., *Masks of the Universe*, New York, Collier Books, 1985, Macmillan, p. 252, 263

18.   *Bible*, Isaiah 40:22

19.   *Bible*, Job 26:7

20.   *Bible*, Psalms 104:2

21.   *Bible*, Isaiah 42:5

22.   *Bible*, Isaiah 40:22

23.   *Bible*, Job 9:8

24.   *Bible*, Psalms 103:25-27

25.   *Bible*, Genesis 22:7

26.   *Bible*, Jeremiah 33:22

27.   Fraser Cain, *How Many Stars are There in the Universe*, June 3, 2013

28.   *Bible*, Psalms 19:4-6

29.   *Bible*, Hebrews 11:3

30.   Antony Flew, *There is a God – How the world's most notorious atheist changed his mind*

31.   *Bible*, Luke 17:30-34

32.   *Bible*, Genesis 1:1

33.   *Bible*, Genesis 1:1

34.   Werner Heisenberg, Nobel Laureate in Physics, *Hildebrand*, 1988, p. 10

35.   Arthur Compton, Nobel Laureate in Physics, *Chicago Daily News*, 1936

36.   Max Planck, Nobel Laureate in Physics, and founder of the Quantum Theory, *Where Is Science Going?* 1932, p. 168

37.   Sir Derek Barton, Nobel Laureate in Chemistry, as cited in *Margenau and Varghese*, *Cosmos, Bios, Theos*, 1997, p. 144

38.   Joseph H. Taylor, Jr., 1993 Nobel Prize in Physics, for the discovery of the first known binary pulsar, and for his work which supported the Big Bang theory of the creation of the universe

39.   Jim Holt, *Science Resurrects God*, The Wall Street Journal, December 24, 1997

40.   *Bible*, Psalms 19:1-4

41.   Frank Tipler, *The Physics Of Christianity*, New York, Doubleday, 2007

42.   Frederick Burnham, *The Los Angeles Times*, Saturday, 2nd May 1992

Who Created God?

"The postulate of a designer or creator only raises the
unanswerable question of who designed the designer...
Religion and theology... have consistently failed to
overcome this objection."[1] (Christopher Hitchens)

"... the designer himself (herself/itself) immediately raises
the bigger problem of his own origin... Far from
terminating the vicious regress, God aggravates it with a
vengeance."[2] (Richard Dawkins)

The triumph card of the atheist seems to center around this kindergarten question: "If God created everything, who created God?" And if Christians cannot answer that question, then God does not exist. In short, it doesn't matter even if there is the obvious miracle of 'something from nothing'; even if there is the mysterious 'fine-tuning' of the universe; even if there is the meticulous 'specified complexity' in the world of living things; even if there is the mind-boggling scientific predictions of the cosmos in the Bible – as long as Christians cannot answer the question, "If God created everything, who created God", they are reckoned to have lost the battle. And there has to be no Creator in this universe and, by default, the cosmos is the product of some yet-to-be-discovered naturalistic cause; end of story.

And even if the theist can answer the question, "Who created God?", the atheist would again demand from them, "Who created the Who, who created God", ad infinitum? And they would walk away seemingly triumph with their hands in the air in another trouncing victory over the Christians.

But, upon closer examination, such arguments are shown to be so naive and silly to be considered as arguments against the existence of God, much less, watertight proof of His non-existence. They are in the same category as: "Can God make a stone so heavy that He cannot carry, or can He make a round square or a married bachelor?" And to think that just because some Christians cannot answer the question, "Who created the Who, who created God", God is not allowed to exist. It is incredible to think the existence of the Almighty God is determined by the answer to that kindergarten question – plain silly isn't it? Can you imagine how ridiculous it would sound if a person made this conclusion about you: "If you do not know the names of all your ancestors, including the 'monkeys' in your family tree, you are not supposed to have existed!" What oxymoron?

What is good for the goose is also good for the gander – if the atheists cannot answer the question, "If the universe is created by the speculative Multiverse, what created the Multiverse", does their ignorance of the 'whatever' that caused the Multiverse to exist proves that there is no Multiverse? And, along the same line of argument, if the atheist has no answer to that question, a naturalistic causation to the existence of the universe does not exist then, by default, the cause has to be supernatural. And a Creator will be the most probable uncaused First Cause for the commencement of this cosmos.

And even if the atheist could answer the question, "What created the Multiverse", the theist would demand from him, "And what created the 'whatever' that created the Multiverse, ad infinitum." And the theist too can happily walk away with the same air of victory, snubbing the atheist for his ignorance and stupidity in asking such a question. In short, such a question, like a double-edged sword, will cut both ways. The atheist will bleed like the theist.

We do not need the 'explanation of the explanation' or the 'cause of the cause' to provide a reasonable explanation to a fair question. We do not need to explain 'Who created God' to best explain the existence of the cosmos. Whatever best explain the existence of the universe is the best explanation for its existence. There is no constraint for one to be historical to know the endless list of 'Who created the who' ad infinitum, to best explain the universe or anything. If that is the demand by these New Atheists, then there will be no explanation for anything if the 'cause of the cause' is not known. The universe created Richard Dawkins but what created the what that created the universe, ad infinitum? If Dawkins does not have the answer, then a naturalistic causality to the universe does not existed! Pretty silly right?

If one were to find the Rosetta Stone in some archaeological dig, and someone were to ask, "Do you know who carved it?" And if he were to demand, "Since you do not know who engraved those ancient writings on the Rosetta Stone, it is not supposed to be by design and, by default, it has to be some naturalistic, 'water and wind' phenomenon that penned down those intelligible inscriptions." Sometimes, the atheistic community does not seem to realize how patently silly they look to prove an obvious conclusion – intelligible writings point to an intelligent agency. You do not need to know the who wrote those ancient languages on the Rosetta Stone or his endless predecessors to prove that it was by design and not by chance.

And in a similar manner, we do not need to know all the 'God Makers', a trillion generations removed, to permit God to be the Creator of this universe. Once there was nothing, and now there is something. And an uncaused Someone is needed to explain how we get a physical something from an immaterial nothing, because in the physical world, 'ex nihilo nihil fit' (from nothing nothing comes), holds true every time and in every place.

Let us hear from Thomas Aquinas:

> "... that which does not exist begins to exist only through something already existing. Therefore if at one time nothing was in existence, it would have been impossible for anything to have begun to exist; and thus now nothing would be in existence – which is absurd...

> But every necessary thing has its necessity caused by another... Now it is impossible to go on to infinity in necessary things which have their necessity caused by another, as has already been proved in regard to efficient causes. Therefore, we cannot but admit the existence of some being having of itself its own necessity, and not receiving it from another, but rather causing in others their necessity. This all men speak of as God"[3]

Plato too, saw this obvious, logical cause-and-effect rationale in plain sight - anything that comes into existence from no existence needs a prior uncaused causality:

> "We must in my opinion begin by distinguishing between that which always is and never becomes and that which is always becoming and never is... everything that becomes or changes must do so owing to some cause; for nothing can come to be without a cause... As for the world – call it that or 'cosmos' or any other name acceptable to it – we must ask about it the question one is bound to ask to begin with about anything: whether it has always existed and had no beginning, or whether it has come into existence and started from some beginning. The answer is that it has come into being... And what comes into being or changes must do so, we said, owing to some cause."[4]

To paraphrase it, if the Universe exists, an uncaused Someone must have predated it. If not, there will be nothing and all that we are seeing is a cosmic illusion. According to the Bible, God is the uncaused First Cause, the self-existent One, and the eternal 'I am that I am'.

> "Look unto me, and be ye saved, all the ends of the earth: for I am God, and there is none else."[5] (*Bible*)

The Law of Causality does not require that everything needs a cause. A cause is needed only for anything that comes into being. The universe had a beginning in some finite past and therefore it needed a cause. And as God does not have a beginning, He doesn't need a cause. He created this physical structure called 'space-time' and not vice versa. He is eternal, spaceless, immaterial and omnipotent, and is not subjected to the laws of nature. He is the uncaused First Cause that gives rise to this visible creation we call the 'Universe'.

If there were no uncaused First Cause, there will be nothing thereafter, much less, an orderly, exquisite, fine-tuned universe with intelligent life. An uncaused First Cause will always be needed by the theists as well as by the atheists to justify why there is 'something rather than nothing'. Every vertical paper clip chain must terminate at the first clip - it cannot rise indefinitely without the first clip. And the long train of the cause-and-effect events must inevitably culminate in an uncaused First Cause. This physical universe is proven to be finite with a definite beginning in time, and there is no such thing as an infinite causation to the universe. The concept of infinity may exist in the abstract world of mathematics, but it does not exist in physical reality.

Peter S. Williams, in his article, *A Universe From Someone: Against Lawrence Krauss,* argues persuasively the same thought:

> "Suppose I ask you to loan me a certain book, but you say: 'I don't have a copy right now, but I'll ask my friend to lend me his copy and then I'll lend it to you.' Suppose your friend says the same thing to you, and so on. Two things are clear. First, if the process of asking to borrow the book goes on ad infinitum, I'll never get the book. Second, if I get the book, the process that led to me getting it can't have gone on ad infinitum. Somewhere down the line of requests to borrow the book, someone had the book without having to borrow it."[6]

Likewise, argues Richard Purtill:

> "... the same two principles apply. If the process of everything getting its existence from something else went on to infinity, then the thing in question would never [have] existence. And if the thing has... existence then the process hasn't gone on to infinity. There was something that had existence without having to receive it from something else..."[7]

For the theist, the explanation for having this 'something from nothing' is found in an uncaused God; for the atheist, he has to take the same leap of faith in an uncaused, naturalistic something that kick-started this cosmos. For Stephen Hawkins, that uncaused First Cause is gravity; for Carl Sagan, it is 'The Cosmos is all that is or was or ever will be'[5]; and for Lawrence Krauss, crazy as it may sound, it is 'nothing', the same unstable substance as in his head.

The theist and the atheist will have to travel this same, common path that ends in this cosmic cul-de-sac: the inexplicable, mystifying, uncaused First Cause that defies any explanation of 'why it exists' or 'what was before it'.

The buck will have to stop somewhere in the finite past with an ultimate, uncaused Someone or something. And, as we have previously seen, something cannot exist because something cannot creates itself out of nothing. There is no 'physics of nothingness' to bring something from nothing. Only an uncaused Someone with infinite power and wisdom can create this amazing Universe from nothing.

> "For by him were all things created, that are in heaven and that are in earth, visible and invisible... And he is before all things, and by him all things consist."[8] (*Bible*)

An uncaused First Cause is indispensable to both the atheist and the theist in explaining why there is something rather than nothing.

References:

1.   Christopher Hitchens, *God is not Great*, p. 71

2.   Richard Dawkins, *The God Delusion*, p. 120

3.   Thomas Aquinas, *Summa Theologica,* q. 3, art. 3

4.   Plato, *Timaeus*, p. 27-28

5.   *Bible*, Isaiah 45:22

6.   Peter S. Williams, in his article, '*A Universe From Someone: Against Lawrence Krauss*'

7.   Richard Purtill, quoted by Charles Taliaferro, *Contemporary Philosophy of Religion, Blackwell,* 2001, p. 358-359

8.   *Bible,* Colossians 1:16-17

Bang goes the Big Bang

"But if you were a scientist, I think you should ask yourself that same question... the Big Bang theory is different: The theory holds that billions of years ago, everything in the universe was contained in an area smaller than the head of a pin and that this minuscule speck of unbelievably dense and incredibly hot matter suddenly exploded violently. That sounds just plain nuts, right? But do you believe it? If so, how do you support your belief that the entire cosmos was once smaller than a polka dot? With a strong line of reasoning? Solid evidence? Anything at all? If you cannot, welcome to the world of faith: You're accepting what you've been told by those you respect."[1] (Marilyn Vos Savant)

The Big Bang hypothesis posits that the universe came into existence from nothing. Literally, nothing expanded exponentially and everything we now see - space, time, matter and energy - was suddenly brought into existence from no existence. And the initial hydrogen and helium molecules which, miraculously came from nowhere, and against all known laws of physics, managed to coalesce into stars and cluster into galaxies. And the heavier atoms like carbon from which we are made were by an infinitesimal big fluke forged in the furnace of the exploding stars and voila, here we are with all the amazing creatures in this cosmic Zoo we called 'Earth'. And against the backdrop, all the exquisitely fine-tuned laws of nature popped into existence inexplicably. One will find all these in the textbooks, parroted by the science teachers, and lapped up by the uninformed public.

But for those who are in the cutting-edge frontier of science will freely admit that they do not know how all these pieces of the cosmic puzzles come together – how do hydrogen molecules coalesce when they should expand like all the other gases; why the planets' composition differs so much from the sun and from one another when they all came from supposedly the same nebulous gas; and how can planets form when all the nearby boulders in space are vacuumed in a cosmic blink by the sun's gravity – just to name a few.

If the universe were the result of the Big Bang, we will see an epic, cosmic mess throughout the universe, like a bomb that went off in a room. Such a universe would be characterized by colossal, hazy, cosmic dusts and not by a well-ordered, exquisitely fine-tuned cosmos. But, if the universe were an act of creation, an awesome, beautiful, mosaic pattern would emerge, like the artist who paints unrestricted at will. Sometimes, I think God made a fool out of the

Big Bangers by the little quirks in the cosmos to confound them. He designed the universe in the way He desired and left it thereby to be governed by the laws of nature He had created. God is a God of variety and His amazing creation will always leave us with a sense of wonder and awe.

The Big Bang theory, under close scrutiny, looks more like a bewildered, shellshock, hospital patient with bandages all over his body. Whenever the secular cosmologist finds a cosmic 'wound' in the theory – an inexplicable conundrum – he would put a scientifically unsubstantiated 'bandage' over it. When he discovers the uniform temperature in every direction he looks in the universe, which should not be according to the theory, he plasters over it with the unobservable, flexible 'inflation' bandage (there are several models of the inflation theory to pick from to fit the observation – old, new and chaotic) to justify it; when he cannot explain the tight spin of the galaxies, he conveniently binds it with invisible 'dark matter'; and when he cannot account for the accelerating expansion of the universe, he quietly adds the dressing of religious 'dark energy' to make it look elegant. And on and on he goes on star formation, the nebular hypothesis, retrograde moons, planet formation, etc.

The Big Bang theory, with an ever-increasing numbers of cosmic bandages all over its body, now looks more like a putrefying Egyptian mummy from some ancient Pharaoh's tomb than an unassailable, scientific theory! And the smell of snake oil permeates the whole cosmological discussion with tooth fairies fluttering in the air – dark matter, dark energy, and the latest, dark flow (possibly due to some cosmic period). In reality, it is more of a dark mind, deliberately blinded to an obviously designed Universe. This is what some honest critics from the same evolutionary camp have to say about this mummified Big Bang. In *An Open Letter to the Scientific Community* by 33 scientists, published in New Scientist, May 22, 2004, it states:

> "The big bang today relies on a growing number of hypothetical entities, things that we have never observed – inflation, dark matter and dark energy are the most prominent examples. Without them, there would be a fatal contradiction between the observations made by astronomers and the predictions of the big bang theory. In no other field of physics would this continual recourse to new hypothetical objects be accepted as a way of bridging the gap between theory and observation. It would, at the least, raise serious questions about the validity of the underlying theory.

But the big bang theory can't survive without these fudge factors. Without the hypothetical inflation field, the big bang does not predict the smooth, isotropic cosmic background radiation that is observed, because there would be no way for parts of the universe that are now more than a few degrees away in the sky to come to the same temperature and thus emit the same amount of microwave radiation.

Without some kind of dark matter, unlike any that we have observed on Earth despite 20 years of experiments, big-bang theory makes contradictory predictions for the density of matter in the universe. Inflation requires a density 20 times larger than that implied by big bang nucleosynthesis, the theory's explanation of the origin of the light elements. And without dark energy, the theory predicts that the universe is only about 8 billion years old, which is billions of years younger than the age of many stars in our galaxy.

What is more, the big bang theory can boast of no quantitative predictions that have subsequently been validated by observation. The successes claimed by the theory's supporters consist of its ability to retrospectively fit observations with a steadily increasing array of adjustable parameters, just as the old Earth-centered cosmology of Ptolemy needed layer upon layer of epicycles...

Whereas Richard Feynman could say that "science is the culture of doubt," in cosmology today doubt and dissent are not tolerated, and young scientists learn to remain silent if they have something negative to say about the standard big bang model. Those who doubt the big bang fear that saying so will cost them their funding.

Even observations are now interpreted through this biased filter, judged right or wrong depending on whether or not they support the big bang. So discordant data on red shifts, lithium and helium abundances, and galaxy distribution, among other topics, are ignored or ridiculed. This reflects a growing dogmatic mindset that is alien to the spirit of free scientific enquiry."[2]

In *The Big Bang Theory – A Scientific Critique*, Branyon May, Bert Thompson and Brad Harrub write:

> "There is no mechanism known as yet that would allow the Universe to begin in an arbitrary state and then evolve to its present highly ordered state" (1983, 304:40). Three years after that, renowned cosmologist John Gribbin reiterated the point when he wrote of the Big Bang Theory that "many cosmologists now feel that the shortcomings of the standard theory outweigh its usefulness..." (1986, 110[1511]:30). A decade-and-a-half later, one scientist, writing under the title of *"The Bursting of the Big Bang,"* admitted that "while few people have seen the obituary... the reality is that the immensely popular Big Bang Theory is dead... The Big Bang cannot explain the nature of the universe as we know it" (Lindsay, 2001, emp. in orig.). Berlinski, in *"Was There a Big Bang?"* wrote: "If the evidence in favor of Big Bang cosmology is more suspect than generally imagined, its defects are far stronger than generally credited" (1998, p. 37)."[3]

The Big Bang theory is a tattered hypothesis. And the objections came largely from the same secular cosmological community.

1)   The Violation of the First Law

On one level, physicists would tell us that the laws of nature rule supreme in the universe and that science is superior to religion in that it is testable and checkable. But, on the other level, they would unashamedly violate the laws of nature in the very first instant of the birth of the universe – believing that something can come from nothing. They have no qualms about undermining the First Law of Thermodynamics or the conservation of energy – energy cannot be created or destroyed. And the total energy in the universe is not zero as commonly assumed by secular cosmologists. Here is what Lawrence Krauss has to say:

> "... there appears to be energy of empty space that isn't zero! This flies in the face of all conventional wisdom in theoretical particle physics. It is the most profound shift in thinking, perhaps the most profound puzzle, in the latter half of the 20th century. And it may be the first half of the 21st century, or maybe go all the way to the 22nd century. Because, unfortunately, I happen to think we won't be able to rely on experiment to resolve this problem."[4]

2)   The Horizon Problem

The Big Bang cannot account for the uniform temperature everywhere in the universe. And cosmic inflation was introduced to patch it up. There is so much adjustment made to fine-tune the shape of the potential function of the inflation 'theory' to fit the observation that it now looks really awkward, clumsy and contrived.

> "The universe as a whole has been cooling ever since it emerged from the fireball of the Big Bang. But there's a problem: For all of it to reach the same temperature, different regions of the universe would have to exchange heat, just as ice cubes and hot tea have to meet to reach the uniform temperature of iced tea. But as Einstein proved, nothing – including heat – can travel faster than the speed of light. In the conventional theory of the Big Bang, there simply hasn't been enough time since the universe was born for every part of the cosmos to have connected with every other part and cooled to the same temperature...
>
> Linde and other researchers knew that something was missing from the conventional theory of the Big Bang, because it couldn't explain a key puzzling fact about the universe: its remarkable uniformity. Strikingly, the temperature of space is everywhere the same, just 2.7 degrees Celsius above absolute zero. How could different regions of the universe, separated by such enormous distances, all have the same temperature?"[5] (Tim Folger)

3)   Star Formation

According to the Big Bang theory, the initial elements were mainly hydrogen and helium, and that stars came about because of the coalescing of the hydrogen gases. But hydrogen gases do not come together to form stars because the gravitational pull of the hydrogen molecules is far weaker than the outward pressure of the gases. Try spraying an aerosol mixture into the air and see if the gas molecules will come together. They will just disperse.

To have hydrogen gases coming together naturally to form stars is like leaving a cup of cold water in room temperature and seeing the water get heated up by itself. It can't. The best theory the present-day cosmologists have is that new stars are formed from explosions of dying stars, the supernovas, on the surrounding hydrogen gases. But where did the original stars come from? Let us acquaint ourselves with the frustration of these secular cosmologists.

"The universe we see when we look out to its furthest horizons contains a hundred billion galaxies. Each of these galaxies contains another hundred billion stars. That's 10^{22} stars all told. The silent embarrassment of modern astrophysics is that we do not know how even a single one of these stars managed to form."[6] (Martin Harwit)

"Stars are among the most fundamental building blocks of the universe, yet the processes by which they are formed are not understood."[7] (Derek Ward-Thompsom)

"We cannot even show convincingly how galaxies, stars, planets, and life arose in the present universe."[8] (Michael Rwan-Robinson)

"In its simplest form, the Big Bang scenario doesn't look like a good way to make galaxies. It allows too little time for the force of gravity by itself to gather ordinary matter – neutrons, protons and electrons – into the patterns of galaxies seen today. Yet the theory survives for want of a better idea."[9] (Ivars Peterson)

"There is general belief that stars are forming by gravitational collapse; in spite of vigorous efforts no one has yet found any observational indication of conformation. Thus the 'generally accepted' theory of stellar formation may be one of a hundred unsupported dogmas which constitute a large part of present-day astrophysics."[10] (Hannes Alfven, Nobel Laureate and Gustaf Arrhenius)

"The complete birth of a star has never been observed. The principles of physics demand some special conditions for star formation and also for a long time period. A cloud of hydrogen gas must be compressed to a sufficiently small size so that gravity dominates. In space, however, almost every gas cloud is light-years in size, hundreds of times greater than the critical size needed for a stable star. As a result, outward gas pressures cause these clouds to spread out farther, not contract."[11] (Don DeYong)

4) Galaxy Formation

If star formation seems improbable, what about galaxy formation? The candid astrophysicists are even more perplexed with regard to how galaxies came about.

> "It seems that the more we learn about the basic laws of nature, the more those laws seem to tell us that the visible matter – the stuff we can see – shouldn't be arranged the way it is. There shouldn't be galaxies out there at all, and even if there are galaxies, they shouldn't be grouped together the way they are... The problem of explaining the existence of galaxies has proved to be one of the thorniest in cosmology. By all rights, they just shouldn't be there, yet there they sit. It's hard to convey the frustration that this simple fact induces among scientist... Despite what you may read in the press, we still have no answer to the question of why the sky is full of galaxies..."[12] (James Trefil)

5) Planetary Formation

> "The conclusion of the world's experts on planetary formation is that they know nothing about the evolution and early history of the solar nebula... Despite volume after volume and year after year in solar system research, scientists have not made even a significant step in explaining how the solar system could have formed by natural processes. What they have done instead is to show the impossibility of natural formation and to leave special creation by the living God as the only explanation."[13] (Paul Steidl)

> "This [planet formation theories] has been a stumbling block for 30 years. The reason is that boulders tend to fall into the star in a celestial blink of an eye."[14] (Mordecai-Marc Low)

6) The Smoothness Problem

And then there is the smoothness problem. According to the Big Bang cosmology the universe is supposed to be isotropic (the same in all directions) and homogeneous (the same everywhere) on a large scale. But the universe is anything but 'smooth' with all the 'clumps' and 'voids', or 'walls' and 'bubbles', everywhere – from the gigantic Eridanus supervoid, about 1 billion light-years across consisting of empty space, to the sheets of galaxies like the amazing

'Great Wall' that is estimated to stretch across 500 million light-years of space and the Hercules–Corona Borealis Great Wall or the Great GRB Wall, which is about 10 billion light-years wide.

> "For more than a decade now, astronomers have been haunted by a sense that the universe is controlled by forces they don't understand. And now comes a striking confirmation: "The Great Wall."[15] (William R. Corliss)

> "The discovery of the Great Wall of galaxies and the regular clumping of galactic matter has greatly surprised astronomers, who have been emphasizing how uniformly distributed galactic matter should – according to theory, at least... M. Davis, an astrophysicist at Berkeley, admits that if the distribution of galaxies is truly so regular, "... it is safe to say we understand less than zero about the early universe."[16] (Wilford, John Noble)

In 2013, astronomers discovered something even bigger – the Hercules–Corona Borealis Great Wall or the Great GRB Wall, which is the biggest known galactic structure in the observable universe.

> "Astronomers used to think it was a "filament" of galaxies known as the Sloan Great Wall. But recent research suggests a different structure is even bigger – and its size has astronomers scratching their heads. Meet the Hercules-Corona Borealis Great Wall (Her-CrB GW)... "The Her-CrB GW is larger than the theoretical upper limit on how big universal structures can be," Dr. Jon Hakkila, an astrophysics professor at the College of Charleston in South Carolina and one of the astronomers who discovered the structure, told The Huffington Post in an email. "Thus, it is a conundrum: it shouldn't exist but apparently does."... Feast your eyes on the Hercules-Corona Borealis Great Wall measuring around 10 billion light-years across."[17] (Jacqueline Howard)

Besides the superclusters, there is the supervoid, a huge 'empty hole', in the universe that is too big to fit into the current Big Bang theory:

> "Astronomers have discovered what they say is the largest known structure in the universe: an incredibly big hole. The "supervoid", as it is known, is a spherical blob 1.8 billion light years across that is distinguished by its

unusual emptiness... The so-called Cold Spot was discovered 10 years ago and has proved a sticking point for the best current models for how the universe evolved following the Big Bang... The Cold Spot raised a lot of eyebrows. The real question was what was causing it and whether it was a challenge to orthodoxy... Even more perplexing, according to Frenk, is the fact that the supervoid can only account for about 10% of the Cold Spot's temperature dip."[18] (Hannah Devlin)

7) Early Universe with Old Galaxies

Why do galaxies in deep space share the same spiral formation as those that are nearer us? They are supposed to be closer to the initial moment of the Big Bang billions of light years back in deep time. Hubble Space Telescope reveals that instead of younger stars (metal-free) evolving into spiral galaxies billions of light years away in deep space, these early galaxies are matured just like those in our cosmic backyard. It is as one man puts it, "The cement mixer arriving to find the house already built."

"We expected to find basically zero massive galaxies beyond about 9 billion years ago, because theoretical models [based on the big bang] predict that massive galaxies form last. Instead we found highly developed galaxies that just shouldn't have been there, but are."[19] (De Nike)

"... over the past 18 months, several teams have found so many massive galaxies from this early epoch that the theory is being stretched to its breaking point, several astronomers say."[20] (Richard Cowen)

8) The 'Axis of Evil'

The Big Bangers would tell us that our planet earth, our pale blue dot, occupies no central or favored position in the universe. In short, we are nothing in the grand scheme of things in the universe. The Copernican principle is coined to convey this melancholic sentiment that we are just a cosmic accident in the backwater of the universe. Carl Sagan the pagan asserts:

"Who are we? We find that we live on an insignificant planet of a humdrum star lost in a galaxy tucked away in some forgotten corner of a universe in which there are far more galaxies than people."[21]

The only problem is that from the latest findings from the Planck satellite, it looks like we are in the center of the universe. From the satellite images of Planck, there appears to be an axis of minute temperature (1/100,000 degree) differences that is parallel to our ecliptic plane – the plane where the earth and all our planets orbit around the sun. Secular cosmologists hated this so much that they termed it *'The Axis of Evil'*. But why do they hate it so intensely? Isn't it obvious? It haunts them. Science is doing a U-turn and is heading back into the direction of the God hypothesis. We are more than a 'part of the dance of the stars', we occupy the centerstage. There is a good documentary, *The Principle*, by Rick DeLano and Robert Sungenis, that shows convincingly that we are located in the approximate center of the universe. But instead of celebrating the findings, the secular cosmological community despises it so passionately. Here is what Lawrence Krauss has to say in that documentary:

> "But when you look at CMB map, you also see that the structure that is observed, is in fact, in a weird way, correlated with the plane of the earth around the sun. Is this Copernicus coming back to haunt us? That's crazy. We're looking out at the whole universe. There's no way there should be a correlation of structure with our motion of the earth around the sun – the plane of the earth around the sun – the ecliptic. That would say we are truly the center of the universe.
>
> The new results are either telling us that all of science is wrong and we're the center of the universe, or maybe the data is imply incorrect, or maybe it's telling us there's something weird about the microwave background results and that maybe, maybe there's something wrong with our theories on the larger scales. And of course as a theorist I'm certainly hoping it's the latter, because I want the theory to be wrong, not right, because if it's wrong there's still work left for the rest of us."[22]

It is the author's conviction that God created the universe in 6 literal days and it is about 6,000 years or so despite the backdrop of 'billions of years'. God, being God, can create this universe in the 'middle of things' like when He first created Adam and Eve and the hosts of the living things. They were not formed at some embryonic stage and then grew into adulthood. They were created fully mature, functioning, and with an apparent age. And this mature universe is no different – He spoke it into existence. Instead of the 'Big Bang', it was the 'Big Word': "And God said, Let there be light: and there was light"[23] (*Bible*). And our universe can appear with a mature age in a cosmic instant. Humanly speaking, 6 days are a tad too long for an omnipotent God to create the universe. He could have done it in six seconds if He wanted to.

When all the different pieces of this vast cosmic jigsaw puzzle finally come together, a troubling picture will emerge – how do we get something from nothing? How can nothing create everything? How can nothing intelligently fine-tune the whole of the universe to permit intelligent life to exist? Why isn't there nothing – 'ex nihilo nihil fit' – from nothing nothing comes? And this thought will haunt the atheist to the grave – what if God exists? What is going to happen to me – a sinner in the hands of a Holy God – as I plunge over the cosmic cliff for all of eternity? Perhaps, this Universe was created; the Big Bang was just an article of faith.

> "I think however that we should go further than this and admit that the only accepted explanation is creation. I know that is anathema to physicists, as it is to me, but we must not reject a theory that we do not like if the experimental evidence supports it."[24] (H. J. Lipson)

> "Never has such a mighty edifice (*the Big Bang*) been built on such insubstantial foundations."[25]

References:

1. Marilyn Vos Savant, the lady with the world's highest IQ, in 'Ask Marilyn'

2. In *'An Open Letter to the Scientific Community'*, Published in New Scientist, May 22, 2004

3. Branyon May, Ph.D., Bert Thompson, Ph.D., and Brad Harrub, Ph.D., *The Big Bang Theory - A Scientific Critique, Part 1*

4. *The Energy of Empty Space that isn't Zero*, A Talk With Lawrence M. Krauss, Edge, [7.5.06]

5. Tim Folger, *Science's Alternative to an Intelligent Creator: the Multiverse Theory*, December 2008

6. Martin Harwit, Book Reviews, *Science*, Vol. 231, 7 March 1986, pp. 1201–1202

7. Derek Ward-Thompsom, Dept. Physics & Astronomy, Cardiff University, *Science*, V295, p. 76, 1/4/2002

8. Michael Rowan-Robinson, *Review of the Accidental Universe*, New Scientist, Vol. 97, 20 January 1983, p. 186

9. Ivars Peterson, *Seeding the Universe*, 24 March 1990, p. 184

10. Hannes Alfven, Nobel Laureate and Gustaf Arrhenius, *Evolution of the Solar System*, NASA, 1976, p. 480

11. Don DeYoung, Ph.D. in Physics, *Astronomy and the Bible,* 2000, p. 84

12. James Trefil, Prof. Physics, George Mason U., *Dark Side of the Universe*, 1988, pp. 2, 55

13. Paul Steidl, *The Earth, The Stars, and The Bible,* Grand Rapids, Baker Books, 1979, p. 123

14. Mordecai-Marc Low, Chair, Division of Physical Sciences American Museum of Natural History, Space.Com 8/29, 2007

15. William R. Corliss, *Astronomers up against the 'Great Wall'*, Science Frontier, No. 67: Jan-Feb 1990

16. Wilford, John Noble, *Unexpected Order in Universe Confuses Scientists*, Pittsburgh Post Gazette, May 28, 1990

17. Jacqueline Howard, *The Biggest Thing In The Universe Is So Gigantic It Shouldn't Exist At All,* The Huffington Post, Australia, 24 June 2014

18. Hannah Devlin, *Astronomers discover largest known structure in the universe is ... a big hole,* The Guardian, 20th April, 2015

19. De Nike, L., *Glimpse at early universe reveals surprisingly mature galaxies*, Johns Hopkins Gazette, 19 July 2004

20. Richard Cowen, University of California, *Science News*, Vol. 168, No. 15, October 8, 2005

21. Carl Sagan, *Cosmos*, 1980, p. 193

22. *The Energy of Empty Space that isn't Zero*, A Talk With Lawrence M. Krauss, Edge [7.5.06]

23. *Bible*, Genesis 1:3

24. H. J. Lipson, U. Of Manchester, Physics, Bulletin, Vol. 31, 1980, p. 138

25. Editorial comment in *New Scientist*, 21–28 December 1992, p. 3

Additional Resources:

1. *The Principle*, 2014, Rick DeLano and Robert Sungenis

2. *What You Aren't Being Told About Astronomy,* Vol. 1, Vol II, Vol III, YouTube

CHAPTER 2

By Nothing

Molecular Machines Dude

"We are all survival machines for the same kind of replicator – molecules called DNA – but there are many different ways of making a living in the world, and the replicators have built a vast range of machines to exploit them. A monkey is a machine that preserves genes up trees, a fish is a machine that preserves genes in the water; there is even a small worm that preserves genes in German beer mats. DNA works in mysterious ways."[1] (Richard Dawkins)

One of the most fascinating things the microscope reveals is the surreal world of molecular machines in every living thing. Living things are in reality 'living things', made up of molecular machines, robots, and factories – an eerie resemblance to the machines and factories that we are so accustomed to in the macroscopic world. Living organisms may look natural, but there is nothing natural about them – they are an amazing world of miniature machines, digital software, code-readers, switches, assembly lines, chemical pathways, firewalls, generators, recycling plants, etc., and all working in perfect unison.

If we were to peel away the skin of these 'natural' molecular machines, we will see that they are no different from the average machines we have built except that they are vastly more complex than ours. The only dissimilarity is that they look natural while ours look designed. But both, in essence, are machines with coordinated, functioning and moving parts designed for specified tasks.

With the arrival of the electron microscope and the advances made in microscopy, molecular biologists are astonished at the world of these incredible, miniature biological factories. What was once thought as a 'simple cell', a blob of jelly, turns out to be more complex than the whole of New York City put together with its road system, telephone connections, power lines, and sewerage system. A living cell has its control center (nucleus), digital software (DNA), highways (microtubules), powerhouse (mitochondrion), postal service (Golgi apparatus), gateway (nuclear pore), transporters (Kinesin proteins), etc. If you want to better understand how mind-bogglingly complex is a simple cell, just google for: 'The Inner Life of a Cell' (YouTube). You will be blown away by the intricacies you will see!

Molecular biologists are startled by the discoveries of the world of molecular machines beneath the veneer of living things. All over the world, the microscope is revealing a bizarre world of amazing molecular factories, robots and machineries. In his 1996 book *Darwin's Black Box: The Biochemical Challenge to Evolution*, biochemist Michael Behe reveals the world of molecular machineries in the biodiversity of life.

> "The cumulative results show with piercing clarity that life is based on machines – machines made of molecules! Molecular machines haul cargo from one place in the cell to another along "highways" made of other molecules, while still others act as cables, ropes, and pulleys to hold the cell in shape. Machines turn cellular switches on and off, sometimes killing the cell or causing it to grow. Solar-powered machines capture the energy of photons and store it in chemicals. Electrical machines allow current to flow through nerves. Manufacturing machines build other molecular machines, as well as themselves. Cells swim using machines, copy themselves with machinery, ingest food with machinery. In short, highly sophisticated molecular machines control every cellular process. Thus, the details of life are finely calibrated and the machinery of life enormously complex."[2]

Craig Venter, one of the first to decode the human genome and the first to transfect a cell with a synthetic genome is listed in the British magazine New Statesman as 14th in the list of "The World's 50 Most Influential Figures, 2010". He is also a member of the USA Science and Engineering Festival's Advisory Board. He states without ambiguity:

> "Life is machinery... which as we learn how to manipulate it, becomes a technology."[3]

The article *The Closest Look Ever At The Cell's Machines* reaffirms that living cells look more like factories bloated with machineries:

> "Today researchers in Germany announce they have finished the first complete analysis of the "molecular machines" in one of biology's most important model organisms: S. cerevisiae (baker's yeast)."

> It went on to say, "The study combined a method of extracting complete protein complexes from cells (tandem affinity purification, developed in 2001 by Bertrand Séraphin at EMBL), mass spectrometry and bioinformatics to investigate the entire protein household of yeast, turning up 257 machines that had never been observed. It also revealed new components of nearly every complex already known."[4]

Michael Denton, in his book *Evolution: A Theory in Crisis,* reinforces the concept that a living creature is a fascinating collection of molecular machines:

> "Although the tiniest living things known to science, bacterial cells, are incredibly small (10^{-12} grams), each is a veritable micro-miniaturized factory containing thousands of elegantly designed pieces of intricate molecular machinery, made up altogether of one hundred thousand million atoms, far more complicated than any machine built by man and absolutely without parallel in the non-living world."[5]

> "It has only been over the past twenty years with the molecular biological revolution and with the advances in cybernetic and computer technology that Hume's criticism has been finally invalidated and the analogy between organisms and machines has at last become convincing... In every direction the biochemist gazes, as he journeys through the weird molecular labyrinth, he sees devices and appliances reminiscent of our own twentieth-century world of advanced technology."[6]

Every component of a 3-dimension molecular machine has to be exactly pre-designed from a 2-dimension DNA software. It undergoes an extremely complicated process from transcription to translation assembling with the other molecular components to manufacture just one molecular machine. The cellular machinery is literally a molecular 3-D printer churning out a whole plethora of functioning proteins. And to top it all, there is no way to test a molecular machine except after its completion. And like the car, we can only know if it works at the final stage when all the precise and dissimilar parts are assembled and tested. All the intermediate parts have no purpose except upon completion. And evolution, as we are told, has no mind eyes to envision what the final product should be.

How did the Blind Watchmaker know the job scope of that one molecular machine in a vast array of other molecular machines in the whole biological system of just one living creature? And, this sounds even more bizarre – how did it know how to coordinate and work with the other molecular machines in a symbiotic relationship to turn photons and pineapples into digital signals and energy, to create factories to reproduce other molecular machines, to have molecular machines to transport, repair, and do a host of mind-boggling jobs necessary for life to exist? One has to be deliberately blind not to suspect that there is a great Mind and intelligence behind this whole process from the planning to the production of these molecular machineries.

Inorganic molecules can only align themselves chemically to form repetitive crystals, snowflakes, lipid vesicles, or the amino acids in the highly manipulated, Miller-Urey experiment, which is a far cry from the world of molecular factories. It is always more of the same – a repetitive pattern. But they cannot organize themselves into smart, self-replicating molecular machineries. Miller-Urey's amino acids were both-handed instead of only left-handed, of which life's proteins are strictly made of – the chirality problem. It takes only one right-handed amino acid to destroy a peptide chain of left-handed amino acids. Oxygen had to be removed from the apparatus as it would have destroyed the amino acids. But, according to geologists, the early earth had oxygen. And if there were no oxygen and no ozone, the cosmic rays from the sun would have destroyed the amino acids.

> "With oxygen in the air, the first amino acid would never
> have gotten started; without oxygen, it would have been
> wiped out by cosmic rays."[7] (Francis Hitching)

The Darwinists would often resort to the low-hanging fruits like snowflakes and crystals to convince themselves and others of an obvious impossibility – the turning of dead molecules into highly complex, symbiotically functioning, self-replicating, living machineries in the maelstrom of unrelenting hydrolysis in the water and oxidization in the biosphere. At the molecular level, it is chemically devastating – complex molecules are continuously and violently being ripped apart. Besides this, there is a host of other inextricable obstacles that have to be overcome for complex life to begin.

"Two amino acids do not spontaneously join in water. Rather, the opposite reaction is thermodynamically favored."[8]

"It is therefore hard to see how polymerization [linking together smaller molecules to form bigger ones] could have proceeded in the aqueous environment of the primitive ocean, since the presence of water favors depolymerization [*breaking up big molecules into simpler ones*] rather than polymerization."[9] (Richard E. Dickerson)

"We have failed in any continuous way to provide a recipe that gets from the simple molecules that we know were present on early Earth to RNA. There is a discontinuous model which has many pieces, many of which have experimental support, but we're up against these three or four paradoxes, which you and I have talked about in the past. The first paradox is the tendency of organic matter to devolve and to give tar. If you can avoid that, you can start to try to assemble things that are not tarry, but then you encounter the water problem, which is related to the fact that every interesting bond that you want to make is unstable, thermodynamically, with respect to water.

If you can solve that problem, you have the problem of entropy, that any of the building blocks are going to be present in a low concentration; therefore, to assemble a large number of those building blocks, you get a gene-like RNA — 100 nucleotides long — that fights entropy. And the fourth problem is that even if you can solve the entropy problem, you have a paradox that RNA enzymes, which are maybe catalytically active, are more likely to be active in the sense that destroys RNA rather than creates RNA."[10] (Suzan Mazur)

In the final analysis, we are not talking about the accidental coming together of some chemicals as the Darwinists would like us to believe, but the orderly organization of unrelated molecules through a carefully-executed, choreographed process before they can be synthesized step-by-step into amino acids, translated into peptides, folded into proteins, and on to the assembly of molecular parts, machines, robots, and factories. And above all, they are not just any molecular factories, but mind-boggling, highly complex, self-replicating biological factories that can reproduce identical copies of themselves.

"The living machine is clearly not just a mixture of chemicals, yet there seems to be widespread belief that, once the proper molecular compounds were there, life would appear, whether on the earth, on Mars, or elsewhere in the universe. This no more follows, I may point out at the risk of being thought overly facetious, than that an automobile, 1962 model, might spring spontaneously from a mixture of all the chemical species from which it is composed... And this machine is of a kind that is unique in our experience, for it is one that can replicate itself... "[11] (Blum H. F.)

The Blind Watchmaker (chance) is the illusory fantasy of men like Richard Dawkins. In the real world, living things can only be accounted for by the existence of an Intelligent Watchmaker. The only thing the Blind Watchmaker can produce naturally is a concoction of useless chemical compounds that keep breaking down into simpler chemicals over time. Does it dawn on you that every food, health and pharmaceutical product has an expiry date?

Let us study the complex processes of turning dirt into macroscopic machines naturally:

1) How did metal ores become pure or composite metal?

2) How are metallic 'building blocks' tooled to form exact machine parts?

3) How did it know how many different, specified, and limited parts are needed?

4) How did those components organize themselves to form just one machine?

5) How did it know what machine to produce and for what purpose?

6) How did it know what other machines are needed?

7) How did it get the blueprints to construct all the machines?

8) How were the machines tested, modified, and fine-tuned with the other tested, modified, and fine-tuned machines?

9) How did all these different, specified, and limited machines assemble themselves to form a factory?

10) How did that factory organize itself to procure raw materials and to churn out other identical, self-perpetuating factories?

The answer is patently obvious: it can't without an external, intelligent agency. It is for these reasons that we do not see machines or factories materializing naturally from the elements in the ground. Chance has no chance in this whole process of turning simple molecules into complex machines. And what is true in the macroscopic world is true in the microscopic world – the macroscopic world is mirrored in the microscopic world. If you cannot get a man-made machine by brute force, you cannot get a molecular machine by sheer chance too. The odds are even worse in the mind-boggling world of these highly complex, self-replicating, molecular factories.

Let us study the complex processes of turning mindless molecules into mind-boggling molecular machineries naturally:

1) How did dead chemicals bond together to form only linear chains of hundreds of exact, yet varied, left-handed amino acids? One right-handed amino acid would dismantle the whole peptide chain of left-handed amino acids – the chirality problem. And organic life uses only about 20 specific amino acids out of a hundred others available in nature.

2) How did the polypeptide chains fold together to create precise protein components?

3) How did it know how many different, exact, and limited proteins are needed?

4) How did the different proteins organize themselves to form a complex molecular machine?

5) How did it know what molecular machine to produce and for what purpose?

6) How did it know what other molecular machines are needed?

7) How did it get the exact, billion-worded, coded DNA to meticulously construct all the other precise molecular machines?

8) How were they tested, modified, and fine-tuned with the other tested, modified and fine-tuned molecular machines?

9) How did the different, specific, limited and complementary molecular machines assemble together in a symbiotic relationship to form the first biological factory - a living, self-replicating cell?

10) How did that molecular factory manage to feed upon the 'raw materials' through the processes of photosynthesis or metabolism, and to reproduce exact copies of itself that will, in turn, reproduce other molecular factories perpetually?

The overly simplistic Darwinist chemical-to-cell hypothesis is at least 10-steps removed from a living cell. In truth, it is light years away from reality when you take into consideration the numerous, mind-boggling, cellular processes, chemical pathways, gene expressions, genetic circuitry, layers of embedded codes in the DNA, epigenetics, et al. And every step is an exact, detailed, sequential process that requires intelligence, planning, coordination, assembly and testing.

If it is impossible for a simple man-made machine to be created by chance, it will be ridiculously even more impossible for a self-replicating, molecular machine, which is far more complex, to be the result of a chemical accident. And if chemical evolution (from non-life to life) is dead in the water from the start, biological evolution (from bacteria to man) is doomed forever. If the 'arrival of the fittest' never happened, the 'survival of the fittest' is a joke. The weakest link in the hypothesis of evolution has been indisputably identified and found irreparably broken. The so-called rocket science of biological evolution blew up before it could take off.

> Chemistry can never birth biology naturally just as bricks and mortar will never be assembled by chance into a house. And biology will die stillborn in unguided chemistry just as unorganized bricks and mortar will degrade over time.

Many cutting-edge evolutionists who are in the know realize the vastness of this chasm that cannot be crossed naturally and, in their desperation, they cling on to an even more feeble evolutionary straw called 'panspermia'. It posits that life on earth came from some other planets via extraterrestrial aliens or wandering meteorites. But this does not solve the problem of how life originated naturally; it simply pushes the problem one notch up the evolutionary ladder – how did complex, carbon-based life originate naturally from the other planets? They face the same impossible chemical and biological conundrum there as with us here on planet earth – how did dead molecules turn into highly complex, self-replicating, molecular factories naturally without the hand of an intelligent Designer?

Let us hear the conclusions of some of the men of science who have given some deep thoughts to this impossible chasm in chemical evolution:

"The likelihood of the formation of life from inanimate matter is one out of 10 to the power of 40,000 ($10^{40,000}$)... It is big enough to bury Darwin and the whole theory of evolution. There was no primeval soup, neither on this planet nor on any other, and if the beginnings of life were not random, they must therefore have been the product of purposeful intelligence."[12] (Sir Fredrick Hoyle)

"Many investigators feel uneasy about stating in public that the origin of life is a mystery, even though behind closed doors they freely admit that they are baffled. There are two reasons for their unease. First, they feel it opens the door to religious fundamentalism... Second, they worry that a frank admission of ignorance will undermine funding."[13] (Paul Davies)

"All of us who study the origin of life find that the more we look into it, the more we feel that it is too complex to have evolved anywhere. We believe as an article of faith that life evolved from dead matter on this planet. It is just that its complexity is so great, it is hard for us to imagine that it did."[14] (Harold Urey)

"More than 30 years of experimentation on the origin of life in the fields of chemical and molecular evolution have led to a better perception of the immensity of the problem of the origin of life on Earth rather than to its solution. At present all discussions on principal theories and experiments in the field either end in stalemate or in a confession of ignorance. New lines of thinking and experimentation must be tried."[15] (Dose, K.)

"If living matter is not, then, caused by the interplay of atoms, natural forces and radiation, how has it come into being... I think, however, that we must go further than this and admit that the only acceptable explanation is creation. I know that this is anathema to physicists, as indeed it is to me, but we must not reject a theory that we do not like if the experimental evidence supports it."[16] (H. J. Lipson)

"When it comes to the origin of life there are only two possibilities: creation or spontaneous generation. There is no third way. Spontaneous generation was disproved one hundred years ago, but that leads us to only one other conclusion, that of supernatural creation. We cannot accept that on philosophical grounds; therefore, we choose to believe the impossible: that life arose spontaneously by chance!"[17] (George Wald)

"The improbability involved in generating even one bacterium is so large that it reduces all considerations of time and space to nothingness. Given such odds, the time until the black holes evaporate and the space to the ends of the universe would make no difference at all. If we were to wait, we would truly be waiting for a miracle."[18] (Robert Shapiro)

"The Evolutionary model says that it is not necessary to assume the existence of anything, besides matter and energy, to produce life. That proposition is unscientific. We know perfectly well that if you leave matter to itself, it does not organize itself – in spite of all the efforts in recent years to prove that it does."[19] (Arthur E. Wilder-Smith)

"Instead of revealing a multitude of transitional forms through which the evolution of the cell might have occurred, molecular biology has served only to emphasize the enormity of the gap. We now know not only of the existence of a break between the living and non-living world, but also that it represents the most dramatic and fundamental of all the discontinuities of nature. Between a living cell and the most highly ordered non-biological system, such as a crystal or a snowflake, there is a chasm as vast and absolute as it is possible to conceive."[20] (Michael Denton)

One of the biggest jokes in the creation-evolution debate is this: Brilliant evolutionists hope to create life in the laboratory to prove that it requires no intelligence to do it!

"... Many of the experiments designed to explain one or other step in the origin of life are either of tenuous relevance to any believable prebiotic setting or involve an experimental rig in which the hand of the researcher becomes for all intents and purposes the hand of God."[21] (Simon Conway Morris)

And to top it all, the living cell has an amazing coordinated and operational functionality throughout the whole molecular machinery. A Designer is no longer the 'unwanted child' to the origin of life; a Designer now becomes the only viable explanation for the commencement of complex life. Even Dawkins, in his sane moments, recognized this basic truth:

> "The more statistically improbable a thing is, the less we can believe that it just happened by blind chance. Superficially the obvious alternative to chance is an intelligent Designer."[22] (Richard Dawkins)

> "And God said, Let the earth bring forth the living creature after his kind, cattle, and creeping thing, and beast of the earth after his kind: and it was so."[23] (*Bible*)

Evolutionism: Matter + Chance   =   Self-Replicating, Molecular Machines
Creationism: Matter + Intelligence =   Self-Replicating, Molecular Machines

It doesn't take much to see that evolutionism is just a mere religion without a leg to stand on while creationism is empirical science – we see machines being built top-down by design everywhere we look – from the humble car to the complex space shuttle. Accidents and deep time are no help to the making of man-made or biological machines naturally. In truth, they work against it. This is not an argument from ignorance – we don't know and therefore God did it. But, it is an argument from rationality – you need a brilliant Designer to build it top down. Goodbye Evolutionism; welcome Creationism.

> "From my earliest training as a scientist, I was very strongly brainwashed to believe that science cannot be consistent with any kind of deliberate creation. That notion has had to be painfully shed. At the moment, I can't find any rational argument to knock down the view which argues for conversion to God. We used to have an open mind; now we realize that the only logical answer to life is creation and not accidental random shuffling."[24] (Professor Chandra Wickramasinghe)

> Chemistry can never birth biology naturally,
> and biology will die stillborn in unguided chemistry.

References:

1.   Richard Dawkins, *The Selfish Gene,* Oxford University Press, 2006

2.   Michael Behe, *Darwin's Black Box: The Biochemical Challenge to Evolution*, 1996, Free Press, p. 4-5

3.   *Life: A Gene-Centric View*, 1/23/08, *Craig Venter & Richard Dawkins: A Conversation in Munich*

4.   *European Molecular Biology Laboratory*, Jan. 24, 2006

5.   Michael Denton, *Evolution: A Theory in Crisis*, 1986, p. 250

6.   Michael Denton, *Evolution: A Theory in Crisis*, 1985, p. 340

7.   Francis Hitching, *The Neck of the Giraffe*, 1982, p. 65

8.   Committee on the Limits of Organic Life in Planetary Systems, Committee on the Origins and Evolution of Life, National Research Council, *The Limits of Organic Life in Planetary Systems,* National Academy Press, 2007, p. 60, Washington D.C.

9.   Richard E. Dickerson, *Chemical Evolution and the Origin of Life*, Scientific American, September 1978, p. 75

10. Suzan Mazur, Steve Benner: *Origins Soufflé, Texas-Style*, The Huffington Post, 2014

11. Blum H.F., *Time's Arrow and Evolution*, 1951, Harper Torchbooks: New York NY, Second Edition, 1955, Revised, 1962, p. 178G-178H

12. Sir Fredrick Hoyle, professor of astronomy, Cambridge University, *Hoyle on Evolution,* Nature, Vol. 294, No. 5837, November 12, 1981, p. 148

13. Paul Davies, *The Fifth Miracle: The Search for the Origin and Meaning of Life*

14. Harold Urey, who conducted the Urey-Miller experiment to produce the first amino acid, *Christian Science Monitor*, January 4, 1962

15. Dose, K., *The Origin of Life: More Questions Than Answers*, Interdisciplinary Science Reviews, Vol. 13, No. 4, 1988, p. 348

16. H. J. Lipson, F.R.S., Professor of Physics, University of Manchester, UK, *"A physicist looks at evolution"* Physics Bulletin, 1980Vol. 31: 138

17. George Wald, *The Origin of Life,* Scientific American, 191:48, May 1954

18. Robert Shapiro, *Origins – A Skeptic's Guide to the Creation of Life on Earth*, 1986, p. 128

19. Arthur E. Wilder-Smith in Willem J. J. Glashouwer and Paul S. Taylor, *The Origin of the Universe,* Eden Communications and Standard Media, 1983

20. Michael Denton, *Evolution: A Theory in Crisis*, 1985, p. 249

21. Simon Conway Morris, *Life's Solution: Inevitable humans in a Lonely Planet*, Cambridge University Press, p. 41

22. Richard Dawkins, *The Necessity of Darwinism*, New Scientist, Vol. 94, April 15, 1982, p. 130

23. *Bible*, Genesis 1:24

24. Chandra Wickramasinghe, Interview in London Daily Express, August 14, 1981

Additional Resources:

1. *The Nano Robots Inside You* (YouTube)

2. *The Workhorse of the Cell: Kinesin* (YouTube)

3. *ATP Synthase: The power plant of the cell* (YouTube)

4. *Mind-blowing Animations of Molecular Machines inside Your Body!* (YouTube)

5. Michael Behe, *Darwin's Blackbox*

6. Stephen c. Meyer, *Signature in the Cell*

Darwin's Worst Nightmare

"If it could be demonstrated that any complex organ existed, which could not possibly have been formed by numerous, successive, slight modifications, my theory would absolutely break down."[1] (Charles Darwin)

The first hurdle to chemistry evolving into biology is that living things are complex molecular factories and machines, and not a potpourri of random chemical compounds. And the first living cell does not consist of just one molecular machine but a whole factory of specific and dissimilar molecular machines that 'talk' to each other, metabolize its raw materials, and is able to replicate itself.

And like all machines, every major component of that biological machine must be present before it can work. In this inception of life, the necessary requirement of 'irreducible complexity' cannot be dispensed with – either every necessary molecular component, software, signal, and switch is present or, the creature, the biological machine, dies from the first moment. There are no 'secondary functions' for that early cell – unlike Michael Behe's mousetrap being used for a tiepin in a parody by the Darwinists. In this initial stage, the cell is reduced to the bare minimum working components for life to exist.

Irreducible and specified complexity may be conveniently 'explained away' when life has begun, but it cannot be argued away for life to commence. The machinery of life has only one precarious attempt to take off when all of its varied and necessary molecular machineries are in place and functioning in a symbiotic relationship to live and reproduce. Try taking away the DNA, RNA, cell membrane, mitochondrion, kinesin protein, ATP, or some other major components from the first cell, and it will die stillborn. In this biological genesis, it is either all or nothing. There are no 'hopeful prototypes' – the delicate, unstable amino acids, RNA, or lipid vesicles.

Irreducible and specified complexities are non-negotiable in the inception of life. Anything less than that will return the emerging cell back into its previous lifeless chemical compounds that will keep breaking down into the simpler basic elements. A spontaneous degeneration will take place the moment life ceases to exist. Every corpse will turn into fertilizer, and so will every incomplete cell. The RNA world, deep-sea hydrothermal vents, crystals-as-genes, lipid vesicles, and 'biochemical predestination' origin-of-life hypotheses are light years away from this minimum demand for life to take off. But, the Darwinist would want us to religiously believe that given enough time, all things will evolve 'upward'.

> "Time is in fact the hero of the plot... Given so much time, the 'impossible' becomes possible, the possible probable, and the probable virtually certain. One has only to wait; time itself performs the miracles."[2] (George Wald)

But long periods of time are no friends to chemical evolution or abiogenesis. In this inception of life, deep time is its worst enemy. It is not the 'hero of the plot' but the 'villain of the plot'. It is either all from the beginning or nothing subsequently. If the first cell cannot live, eat and replicate itself, it dies a most certain death. It has only a brief moment to get all its acts together. Degradation will always outpace synthesis in incomplete biological systems.

> "Time is no help. Bio-molecules outside a living system tend to degrade with time, not build up. In most cases, a few days is all they would last. Time decomposes complex systems. If a large 'word' (a protein) or even a paragraph is generated by chance, time will operate to degrade it. The more time you allow, the less chance there is that fragmentary 'sense' will survive the chemical maelstrom of matter."[3] (Michael Pitman)

> "Yet, under ordinary conditions, no complex organic molecule can ever form spontaneously, but will rather disintegrate, in agreement with the second law. Indeed, the more complex it is, the more unstable it will be, and the more assured, sooner or later, its disintegration. Photosynthesis and all life processes, and even life itself, cannot yet be understood in terms of thermodynamics or any other exact science, despite the use of confused or deliberately confusing language."[4] (George P. Stravropoulos)

In addition, to evolve from dead chemicals to the first, mind-boggling, living cell is like a man trying to jump over a mile-long chasm in the Grand Canyon. He either does it in one jump or he dies trying. There are no series of small jumps to talk about in this biological genesis. Amino acids, polypeptides, DNA and RNA are just the tip of the iceberg of a vast array of necessary cellular components for life to begin. And they are highly unstable and fragile by nature. They have only a brief moment of existence - at times, only days or weeks, before certain decomposition.

This NETTEAS Chasm (Not Enough Time To Evolve And Survive) is too ridiculously wide to cross for a brainless evolution. Deep time works against it. It is for this reason that we do not see new forms of life emerging from the warm ponds of dead molecules. And there are no hopeful 'Second Genesis' with repeats of life coming from non-life.

Likewise, when a man's heart stops beating, the rest of his approximately 75-100 trillion cells in his body will die; none of them will evolve into a higher order. This is despite the fact they are all perfectly functioning cells with all the biological components – DNA, RNA, ribosome, et al. – the evolutionists could ever dream of for life to begin. And yet, despite all these biological freebies, they degrade instead of evolving into something fitter. No donkey will ever crawl out from a decomposing dog.

In a similar manner, if a living cell is punctured, all the functioning molecular machines within will degrade. They will not evolve into something fitter – they simply break down. You cannot put this Humpty Dumpty together again naturally. And you can never build a living cell with segmental DNA, RNA, or ATP through dumb luck. And yet, our evolutionary friends would unashamedly believe with a sincere, childlike faith in the self-organization of these critical components when all empirical observations prove otherwise.

> "Even if all the essential proteins for life were collected and put in a test tube, these efforts would not result in producing a living cell. All the experiments conducted on this subject have proved to be unsuccessful. All observations and experiments indicate that life can originate only from life. The assertion that life evolved from non-living things, in other words, "abiogenesis," is a tale existing only in the dreams of the evolutionists and completely at variance with the results of every experiment and observation."[5] (Professor Chandra Wickramasinghe)

Now, this is deep thinking. You have got to be very smart to understand it. Darwinists are racing furiously to create piecemeal biological components like the RNA, DNA, amino acids, or cell membrane, and pray that they will somehow magically synthesize into the first functioning cell. They could have gotten all these biological freebies from a punctured cell and observed the probability or improbability of self-organization thereafter. They could have first pricked a living cell, let all the molecular machineries ooze out onto a sterile dish, and then documented how they could have self-organized into a living cell again. This would have saved millions of taxpayers' dollars for the obviously unnecessary and hopeless attempts in creating these biological constituents from scratch.

And if perfectly functioning biological freebies cannot synthesize naturally, the synthesis of the meagerly accidental cellular components is kaput! Darwinists have been hopelessly banging their heads against this biological wall and have been working on the wrong end of the equation – if these biological freebies cannot synthesize naturally, why waste time on the accidental appearance of these individual cellular components? They could have jumpstarted the whole process by using all the biological components that come from a living cell.

There seems to be some kind of caveman mentality in these cutting-edge scientists in wanting to prove something that is blatantly impossible to the man in the street – scattered car parts or piles of building materials can never in a billion, billion years organize itself into a Ferrari or the Empire State Building. You will need the input of able agencies, specified information, and precise, sequential assemblies to build such things. And it is no different with biological factories, molecular machineries, biochemical systems, DNA software, and what we call 'living things'.

There are only two possibilities of how a car factory is built – one, naturally, and two, by design. Naturalism boasts of everything possible – from the inception of dead atoms in the universe to the arrival of complex living things on earth – that they can and will have a naturalistic explanation. But from all observation and rationality, a simple wind mill or a complex car factory can never in a billion, billion years be built by chance or necessity – it needs an intelligent designer. Watching for it to happen naturally is no different from waiting for a miracle to happen.

The Darwinist can see that such a factory will never be built without a designer but, at the same time, he believes that a far more complex, self-replicating, molecular factory can organize itself by chance or necessity. Talk about faith, I have to give it to the Darwinists that they have more faith than the average believer in God. They need this faith and irrationality to deny their observation. A car factory needs a designer, not chance or necessity, period! A biological factory, which exceeds in complexity by a magnitude of many orders, is no different.

This is why Spontaneous Generation, where life comes from non-life, was decisively disavowed and discarded by the scientific community since 1859 after the experiments of Louis Pasteur and others before him. Why the attempt to resurrect this rotting corpse of an impossible chemical evolution? Perhaps, it has nothing to do with science, but a deep-seated faith in scientism. Science says it can't be done!

There are heaps of origin-of-life (OOL) conferences by eminent scientists. They would generally commence with a pyrotechnic display of some esoteric construct and processes of how life could have begun, and inevitably end with the usual let down - we don't know beyond that. And the 'beyond that' is arguably the other 99.99% of the whole cellular machinery.

And the results they present before their audience are so ridiculously meager in comparison to the colossal demands for the first complex life to emerge. Without exaggeration, it is like finding a few bolts and nuts here and there, and extrapolating the discovery to eventually include a Boeing 747 being built through chance or necessity. Any thinking person could see these emperors seem terribly comfortable in parading around naked. And the display of their ignorance is spectacular!

Esoteric ingredients like unobservable 'cosmic imperative', religious 'deterministic laws', or Calvinistic 'chemical predestination', are usually added to their primordial soup to make it savory. But they kept forgetting that the final product is not a chemical accident but a functioning, self-replicating biological machine. You will need an intelligent Watchmaker and not a blind Watchmaker!

In an article entitled: *"Pssst! Don't tell the creationists, but scientists don't have a clue how life began",* John Horgan states:

> "Exactly 20 years ago, I wrote an article for Scientific American that, in draft form, had the headline above. My editor nixed it, so we went with something less dramatic: "In the Beginning..." Scientists are having a hard time agreeing on when, where and – most important – how life first emerged on the earth. That editor is gone now, so I get to use my old headline, which is even more apt today."[6]

As the truth of this vast chasm of irreducible complexity begins to sink into the minds of many honest scientists, some have become open to the possibility of the existence of a divine Creator. All the evidence is pointing in that direction – how can the demand for the complexity of life begin without the aid of a Designer? How can you get an intricate and functioning car or an airplane without a maker? Or, how do you build a complex, molecular or man-made machine bottom-up naturally? Waiting for that to happen is, in essence, waiting for a miracle. And a Creator is brought back into the equation again.

This is not a 'thinking stopper' but a 'thinking arrival'. This is not an argument from incredulity but an argument from rationality – now it makes perfect sense. A building, a car, or the granite busts of the four US presidents in Mount Rushmore, all demand a designer. No one would claim that it is a thinking stopper or an argument from ignorance to explain how we get all these structures and machines with the help of a designer.

In fact, it is an evolutionary comatose to attribute them to random chance. Chance and necessity have no part in it. Someone intelligent has to build this whole mind-boggling, chemical factory called 'life' for life to get started.

Accident produces rubbish, and infinite number of accidents produce infinite rubbish, not the machinery of life. The evidence to the contrary is this indisputable Creator of the Universe. No man, no machine; no Designer, no biological factory! And all intricate machines have been observed to be built top-down by intelligence.

The bottom-up approach where a complex biological machine can evolve naturally through dumb luck is anti-science, anti-commonsense and insane. Can any Darwinist show us just one such complex molecular machine occurring naturally in real life instead of telling us just-so stories? Empirical science demands it. Evolution says it can be done. Science says it can be observed, falsified and repeated. Prove it! Repeat it! Publish it! Don't hide behind the lame, sacerdotal excuse: 'we don't know', or 'we are still working on it', or 'someday science will figure it out'. Even a five-year-old kid knows that it is a blatant cop-out. Can a highly complex, molecular factory with machines within machines, supercomputers and microprocessors, codes upon codes, lumbering robots of all stripes, and intricate chemical pathways, be built by chance or necessity? Honest Science knows when it runs out of options and turns to Design and Creation. But Scientism will stubbornly and ridiculously carry on to an obvious and impossible dead end.

Let those who are in the frontier of cutting-edge science tell us why abiogenesis, where life comes from non-life, is nothing more than an evolutionary rubbish. Ilya Prigogine, chemist-physicist, and recipient of two Nobel Prizes in chemistry, unapologetically debunks chemical evolution:

> "The statistical probability that organic structures and the most precisely harmonized reactions that typify living organisms would be generated by accident, is zero."[7]

Sir Fred Hoyle, the man who unwittingly coined the term 'Big Bang', openly denounces abiogenesis as nonsense:

> "The notion that not only the biopolymer but the operating program of a living cell could be arrived at by chance in a primordial organic soup here on the Earth is evidently nonsense of a high order."[8]

Francis Crick, the co-discoverer of the structure of the DNA molecule in 1953 with James Watson, frankly admits:

> "An honest man, armed with all the knowledge available to us now, could only state that in some sense, the origin of life appears at the moment to be almost a miracle, so many are the conditions which would have had to have been satisfied to get it going."[9]

In the beginning of a biological course, the students will be told that spontaneous generation (chemical evolution) is dead. But somewhere downstream, it will be resurrected without any empirical proof of its possibility. Religious fairy tales, disguised as science, will be enthusiastically weaved in the classroom to show that life did come from non-life. But, they are just religious folklores.

> "Cell Theory [*life comes from life*] is a well-known and fundamental theory of biology... This theory replaced one known as "Spontaneous Generation" [*life comes from non-life*]. For around 400 years it was believed by the majority of scientists that life spontaneously arose from non-living matter... It was not until the experiments of Redi in the 17th century and Pasteur in the 18th century that this was conclusively disproven. It is now defined as a theory now abandoned.

> However, when one comes to the issue of evolution, the question must be asked, "how did life begin without God?" Current evolutionary thought requires the existence of "pools of chemicals" with natural energy sources, such as the sun, lightning, or geo-thermal vents of water, etc., that gave birth to the first cell. Experiments by evolutionists through the ages have tried to duplicate this feat, but all have failed. Regardless of the initial conditions the evolutionists use, no life is formed.

> The incredible thing is that this idea is exactly the same as "Spontaneous Generation". But both Cell theory and Spontaneous Generation cannot be true. Since Cell theory has much empirical evidence and the evolutionary beginning of life has none, which one should we believe? Why would people believe in evolution in spite of the evidence?"[10] (John Curtis)

For years, the evolutionary pot has been calling the creationist kettle black; but it seems to be terribly ignorant of its own blackness.

> "With the failure of these many efforts [to explain the origin of life] science was left in the somewhat embarrassing position of having to postulate theories of living origins which it could not demonstrate. After having chided the theologian for his reliance on myth and miracle, science found itself in the unenviable position of having

to create a mythology of its own: namely, the assumption that what, after long effort, could not be proved to take place today had, in truth, taken place in the primeval past."[11] (Loren C. Eiseley)

"In accepting the "primeval soup theory" of the origin of life, scientists have replaced religious mysteries which shrouded this question with equally mysterious scientific dogmas. The implied scientific dogmas are just as inaccessible to the empirical approach."[12] (Sir Fred Hoyle and Chandra Wickramasinghe)

"The irony is devastating. The main purpose of Darwinism was to drive every last trace of an incredible God from biology. But the theory replaces God with an even more incredible deity – omnipotent chance."[13] (T. Rosazak)

Evolutionary scientists have long left science and ventured deep into philosophy and religion unknowingly when they made those unreasonable demands for scientifically-proven miracles. It is like demanding bricks from thin air (something from nothing) and buildings (complexity from simplicity) through some dumb luck called 'evolution'. Something from nothing and a self-replicating molecular factory by nothing are unnatural or rather, supernatural. But the evolutionary ostrich would prefer to bury its head in the sand and not go where the evidence leads.

"I do not want to believe in God. Therefore, I chose to believe in that which I know is scientifically impossible: spontaneous generation arising to evolution."[14] (George Ward)

Evolution demands gradualism and, in this first instant of life, Darwin's worst nightmare is finally and fully realized.

"If it could be demonstrated that any complex organ existed, which could not possibly have been formed by numerous, successive, slight modifications, my theory would absolutely break down."[15] (Charles Darwin)

"Without gradualness in these cases, we are back to miracle..."[16] (Richard Dawkins)

What Darwin did not reckon with was that the first self-replicating cell was his dreaded 'complex organ' that could not be built through numerous, slight modifications! Unlike a building which you can build step-by-step, a self-replicating cell, with its myriads of highly complex and highly unstable, molecular components and its intricate biochemical systems, either comes complete or comes dead. If it cannot feed, fend or replicate itself from the beginning, it is history – it will undergo an irreversible, spontaneous, chemical meltdown. Darwin's theory of evolution has been irreparably falsified in this inception of life. If the 'arrival of the fittest' did not occur, the 'survival of the fittest' is nothing more than a myth. The Theory of Evolution is, in essence, the religiosity of unrestraint imagination! And that leaves us with the only viable option – an intelligent Designer!

> "Once you eliminate the impossible, whatever remains,
> no matter how improbable, must be the truth."[17]
> (Arthur Conan Doyle)

> "And God said, Let the earth bring forth the living creature
> after his kind, cattle, and creeping thing, and beast of the
> earth after his kind: and it was so."[18] (*Bible*)

And design is the evolutionist's worst nightmare for it points to the awesome Designer whom they must one day give an account of themselves. Darwin's worst nightmare has finally been identified and realized – it is either all at the beginning or nothing subsequently. And the 'all' points to a special creation by a spectacular Creator.

Darwin's book *The Origin of Species* is about everything except the 'Origin' of Species – of how dead molecules first turned into a living cell. And the first living cell is Darwin's dreaded 'complex organ', which can never be built by 'numerous, successive, slight modifications', and his theory has absolutely broken down. But, the myth lives on!

> "To have a functioning cell by chance is quite a miracle;
> to have a self-replicating functioning cell by chance requires
> a quantum miracle."[19]

References:

1. Charles Darwin, *The Origin of Species,* Harvard University Press, 1964, p. 189

2. George Wald, late professor of biology, Harvard University, *The Origin of Life,* Scientific American, August, 1954, p. 48

3. Michael Pitman, *Adam and Evolution*, p. 233

4. George P. Stravropoulos, *The Frontiers and Limits of Science*, American Scientist, vol. 65, November-December 1977, p. 674

5. Professor Chandra Wickramasinghe, Cardiff University, *Interview in London Daily Express*, 14 August 1981

6. John Horgan, *Scientific American*, Feb 28, 2011

7. I. Prigogine, N. Gregair, A. Babbyabtz, Physics Today, p. 23-28

8. Sir Fred Hoyle, *The Big Bang in Astronomy*, New Scientist, Vol. 92, No. 1280, 1981, p. 527

9. Francis Crick, *Life Itself*, 1981, p. 88

10. John Curtis, *Evolution Exposed, How do the Bible and Science both refute evolution?*

11. Loren C. Eiseley, Professor of Anthropology, University of Pennsylvania, *The Immense Journey*, p. 199, 1957 reprint, New York, NY: Vintage, 1946

12. Hoyle, Fred and Chandra Wickramasinghe, *Life cloud,* New York: Harper & Row, 1978, p. 26

13. T. Rosazak, *Unfinished Animal* (1975), p. 101-102

14. George Ward, Nobel Laureate for Biology in 1971, Harvard University, *The Origin of Life*, Scientific American, August, 1954

15. Charles Darwin, *The Origin of Species*, Harvard University Press, 1964, p. 189

16. Richard Dawkins, *River Out Of Eden,* 2015, p. 83

17. Arthur Conan Doyle

18. *Bible*, Genesis 1:24

19. Source Unknown

Additional Resource: *James Tour: The Mystery of the Origin of Life* (YouTube)

In the Beginning was Information

"The problem of the origin of life is clearly basically equivalent to the problem of the origin of biological information."[1]

The double helix DNA (deoxyribonucleic acid), first identified and isolated in the 1860s by Swiss chemist Friedrich Miescher, and was later 'discovered' by James Watson and Francis Crick in 1953. It is the 'language of life', the biological software, that determines the construct of every living thing – from bacterium to man. For a human being, it is approximately six-foot long when unwound, consisting of about 3.1 billions base pairs or nucleotides of 4 chemical letters (A, T, C, G). Every living thing has its unique, signature DNA, and it is a volume of exact digital information to construct the creature from birth to death. This two-dimension code will generate all the three-dimension proteins that will, in turn, create all the molecular machinery in the critter. Above all, this genetic information is transferable and can be stored in a computer hard disk, paper or in any encrypting medium. It can be sent via an email attachment and be stored in iCloud or Dropbox.

The amazing thing is that this information is independent of the medium it is being housed – just as in Shakespeare's book Macbeth – the information is independent of the paper and ink. The storyline, the information, is in Shakespeare's head, but the paper and ink are the materials he uses to pen it down. Not only is information independent from matter, but there is a real distinction between tangible matter and intangible information. The DNA language or code is not the same as the DNA molecules. And unless this distinction is acknowledged, the Darwinist will be forever hopelessly clinging on to his 'lucky chance' and 'chemical accident' for life to emerge. The emergence of life is not about the chemicals only, just as the construction of a building is not about the raw materials per se – it is more about information.

"One of the things I do in my classes, to get this idea across to students, is I hold up two computer disks. One is loaded with software, and the other one is blank. And I ask them, 'what is the difference in mass between these two computer disks, as a result of the difference in the information content that they possess'? And of course the answer is, 'Zero! None!' There is no difference as a result of the information. And that's because information is a mass-less quantity. Now, if information is not a material entity, then how can any materialistic explanation account for its origin? How can any material cause explain its origin?

And this is the real and fundamental problem that the presence of information in biology has posed. It creates a fundamental challenge to the materialistic, evolutionary scenarios because information is a different kind of entity that matter and energy cannot produce.

In the nineteenth century we thought that there were two fundamental entities in science; matter, and energy. At the beginning of the twenty first century, we now recognize that there's a third fundamental entity; and it's 'information'. It's not reducible to matter. It's not reducible to energy. But it's still a very important thing that is real; we buy it, we sell it, we send it down wires.

Now, what do we make of the fact, that information is present at the very root of all biological function? In biology, we have matter, we have energy, but we also have this third, very important entity; information. I think the biology of the information age, poses a fundamental challenge to any materialistic approach to the origin of life."[2] (Dr. Stephen C. Meyer)

Without specified information, buildings cannot be built; aircrafts cannot be crafted; and living things cannot be constructed. There is neither luck nor chance for dead molecules to blossom into the amazing world of complex biological machines we called 'living things'. In a word, no information means no biological machines, and no biological machines means no life, period. The problem of biological evolution is the exact problem of the origin of software – how can computer software be written on its own without any external help? The origin of life is about the origin of specified information, not the origin of chemical accidents. There is no word to describe this incredibly complex information in a single DNA strand. Let us hear from the many eminent scientists on this informational conundrum in living things:

"DNA is like a computer program but far, far more advanced than any software ever created."[3] (Bill Gates)

"Life is just bytes and bytes and bytes of digital information."[4] (Richard Dawkins)

"... The machine code of the genes is uncannily computer-like. Apart from differences in jargon, the pages of a molecular biology journal might be interchanged with those of a computer engineering journal... What has happened is that genetics has become a branch of information technology. The genetic code is truly digital, in exactly the same sense as computer codes. This is not some vague analogy, it is the literal truth."[5] (Richard Dawkins)

"... there is enough information capacity in a single human cell to store the Encyclopaedia Britannica, all 30 volumes of it, three or four times over... There is enough storage capacity in the DNA of a single lily seed or a single salamander sperm to store the Encyclopaedia Britannica 60 times over. Some species of the unjustly called 'primitive' amoebas have as much information in their DNA as 1,000 Encyclopaedia Britannicas."[6] (Richard Dawkins)

"... The capacity of DNA to store information vastly exceeds that of any other known system: it is so efficient that all the information needed to specify an organism as complex as man weighs less than a few thousand millionths of a gram. The information necessary to specify the design of all the species of organisms which have ever existed on the planet... could be held in a teaspoon and there would still be room left for all the information in every book ever written..."[7] (Michael Denton)

"The coding system used for living beings is optimal from an engineering standpoint. This fact strengthens the argument that it was a case of purposeful design rather that a [lucky] chance."[8] (Werner Gitt)

If all that is mentioned is not bad enough for the Darwinist, there is the intractable symbiosis between the DNA (digital code) and the genetic code (code reader). Which came first – the DNA or its code translator? The DNA is useless without the means to decode it. One cannot exist without the other. The proteins for the code reader are constructed by the information in the code (DNA). But the DNA cannot build the proteins for the code reader without first having the code reader decode the DNA. It is like trying to build a DVD code reader by just having a DVD!

In short, the DNA cannot build the code reader without first having an existing code reader. Both must be present simultaneously for the translation of a two-dimension DNA into a three-dimension protein – the biological 3-D printing. And both are highly complex proteins in themselves. This tops the chart of the myriads of 'chicken and egg' conundrums displayed all over the biodiversity of life. And to make matter worse for the Darwinist, Craig Ventor, the 'Genome

Guru', has discovered there are more than one genetic code or code reader in the ecosystem of life.[9] Irreducible complexity is replayed time and again in every direction you look in the universe of living organism.

> "But the most sweeping evolutionary questions at the level of biochemical genetics are still unanswered. How the genetic code first appeared and then evolved and, earlier even than that, how life itself originated on earth remain for the future to resolve... Did the code and the means of translating it appear simultaneously in evolution? It seems almost incredible that any such coincidence could have occurred, given the extraordinary complexities of both sides and the requirement that they be coordinated accurately for survival. By a pre-Darwinian (or a skeptic of evolution after Darwin), this puzzle would surely have been interpreted as the most powerful sort of evidence for special creation."[10] (Caryl P. Haskins)

> "The code is meaningless unless translated. The modern cell's translating machinery consists of at least 50 macromolecular components, which are themselves coded in DNA: the code cannot be translated otherwise than by products of translation themselves. It is the modern expression of omne vivum ex ovo [all life from eggs, or idiomatically, what came first, the chicken or the egg?]. When and how did this circle become closed? It is exceedingly difficult to imagine."[11] (Jacques Monod)

DNA + Translation = Digital Code + Code Reader
= Intelligent Design + Intelligent Designer

(PS: There is more than one genetic code!)

To sum it up, first and foremost, life is about information – no information, no life. And it is not just any information, but specified, optimal, complex, functional information that can be read forward, backward, or recombined with the non-coding 'junk DNA' to organize the amino-acids, string them into polypeptide chains, fold them into proteins, direct them to specified locations, and organize them into functioning cellular machineries. And it can replicate itself in hours through cell division, and have checkers to ensure its duplication is done with the highest degree of fidelity; unheard of in the macroscopic world. It is for this reason that many thinking people just cannot see how this information residing in the DNA is just the outcome of a lucky chance. Software programmers ensure that chance is out of the way through their intelligent inputs.

"A code system is always the result of a mental process (it requires an intelligent origin or inventor). It should be emphasized that matter as such is unable to generate any code. All experiences indicate that a thinking being voluntarily exercising his own free will, cognition, and creativity, is required... there is no known law of nature and no known sequence of events which can cause information to originate by itself in matter."[12] (Dr. Werner Gitt)

"Instead, the living cell is best thought of as a supercomputer – an information processing and replicating system of astonishing complexity. DNA is not a special life-giving molecule, but a genetic databank that transmits its information using a mathematical code. Most of the workings of the cell are best described, not in terms of material stuff – hardware – but as information, or software. Trying to make life by mixing chemicals in a test tube is like soldering switches and wires in an attempt to produce Windows 98. It won't work because it addresses the problem at the wrong conceptual level."[13] (Paul Davies)

"To the skeptic, the proposition that the genetic programmes of higher organisms, consisting of something close to a thousand million bits of information, equivalent to the sequence of letters in a small library of one thousand volumes, containing in encoded form countless thousands of intricate algorithms controlling, specifying and ordering the growth and development of billions and billions of cells into the form of a complex organism, were composed by a purely random process is simply an affront to reason. But to the Darwinist the idea is accepted without a ripple of doubt – the paradigm takes precedence!"[14] (Michael Denton)

"From an organizational point of view... the whole genome is a single integrated system, regulated both in cis and trans-by networks employing DNA repeats."[15] (James A. Shapiro)

"How did stupid atoms spontaneously write their own software?"[16]

131

References:

1. Bernd-Olaf Kuppers, *Information and the Origin of Life*, 1990

2. Dr. Stephen C. Meyer

3. Bill Gates, *The Road Ahead*

4. Dawkins, *River Out of Eden: A Darwinian View of Life*, New York: Basic Books, R. 1995, p. 19

5. Richard Dawkins, *River Out of Eden: A Darwinian View of Life*

6. Richard Dawkins, *The Blind Watchmaker*, p. 116–117

7. Michael Denton, *Evolution: A Theory in Crisis*, p. 334

8. Werner Gitt, *In the Beginning was Information*, 1997, p. 95

9. *The Great Debate: What is Life*, February 12, 2011, (YouTube)

10. Caryl P. Haskins, *Advances and Challenges in Science in 1970*, American Scientist, Vol. 59, May-June, 1971, p. 305

11. Jacques Monod, *Chance and Necessity,* New York: 1971, p. 143

12. Dr. Werner Gitt, *In The Beginning Was Information*, 1997 p. 64-67, 79, 107

13. Davies, P., *How we could create life — The key to existence will be found not in primordial sludge, but in the nanotechnology of the living cell,* The Guardian, 11 December 2002

14. Michael Denton, *Evolution: A Theory in Crisis*, London: Burnett Books, 1985, p. 351

15. James A. Shapiro, *A 21st century view of evolution: genome system architecture, repetitive DNA, and natural genetic engineering*, Department of Biochemistry and Molecular Biology, University of Chicago, 9 November 2004

16. Paul Davies, *New Scientist,* 163(2204): 27-30, 18 Sept 1999

The Car with No Engine

"Do we, therefore, ever see mutations going about the business of producing new structures for selection to work on? No nascent organ has ever been observed emerging, though their origin in pre-functional form is basic to evolutionary theory. Some should be visible today, occurring in organisms at various stages up to integration of a functional new system, but we don't see them: There is no sign at all of this kind of radical novelty. Neither observation nor controlled experiments has shown natural selection manipulating mutations so as to produce a new gene, hormone, enzyme system, or organ."[1] (Michael Pitman)

Darwinian Evolution is like a car without an engine. And a car with no engine is not going anywhere. The engine of Darwinian Evolution is encased in the chassis of natural selection and random mutation. And if it is proven to be unworkable and impossible, there is no engine to drive the vehicle of biological evolution – no bacterium has ever evolved into a man and the Darwinian tree of life is just a figment of a grand imagination. And the fossil record, geologic column, and homology – the touted 'evidence' of the Darwinian theory of evolution – are all about connecting the wrong dots. They are the products of a Common Designer (divine creation) instead of a Common Descent (dumb evolution).

Most scientific theories are contingent on one or a handful of core propositions upon which all the other ancillary predictions depend. If the foundational proposition is falsified, the rest of the supporting hypotheses and predictions will inadvertently fall apart. The mechanism of natural selection and random mutation is the central dogma in the theory of biological evolution. This is the heart and soul of evolution, the rest are peripherals. And if the foundation of biological evolution is demolished, the evolutionary house of cards will eventually come crashing down. Let us now place Natural Selection and Random Mutation in the crosshairs, magnify their exaggerated claims, and dispatch them.

Natural Selection: Natural Selection or the 'survival of the fittest' is empirical science. The creationists are in total agreement with it. But natural selection is destructive, not creative. Its only purpose is to remove the weaker creatures from the scene – sheep with thicker wool survive the harsher winters while sheep with little wool die. And sheep with thicker wool do not evolve into non-sheep, they just simply multiply and dominate the landscape. Likewise, finches with thicker beaks will survive the severe weathers better than their weaker cousins, but they will always be finches with thicker beaks and nothing more. And so it is with bacteria that survive the antibiotics. There are just more bacteria that are immune to antibiotics. No bacterium is on its way to become a non-bacterium with evolving eyes or ears despite the supposedly 'millions of years' to their existence. This is observational science.

The survival of the fittest simply means: whatever survives is the fittest, and the fittest survives – an impressive but useless evolutionary tautology. The 'survival of the fittest' is neither identical with nor equivalent to the 'evolution of the fittest'. It seems to have been implanted in the mind and lingo of the Darwinist that 'fittest equals evolved'.

But the myriads of living fossils before us show no such things. The blue-green algae (3.5 billion years), horseshoe crab (445 million years), coelacanth (360 million years), cockroach (350 million years), squid (160 million years), dragonfly (150 million years), and hundreds of other examples have survived for 'millions of years' without evolving. The survival of the fittest is, in reality, the preservation of the species – it eliminates the weakest and preserves the fittest within its kind. Natural selection may permit hybridization and variation but it ensures stasis – that every living critter and plant does not stray into another kind but remains within the confines of its created genome.

Evolutionists are generally embarrassed by the 'living fossils' – why they did not evolve over the 'millions of years'? Why the hiatus? Why the stasis? Maybe there was no evolution, just creation! As evolutionist Niles Eldredge once remarked:

> "In the context of Darwin's own founding conceptions, and certainly from the perspective of the modern synthesis, living fossils are something of an enigma, if not an embarrassment."[2]

The world-renowned evolutionist Stephen J. Gould, like many other honest Darwinists, acknowledges this stubborn stasis in the fossil record:

> "Every paleontologist knows that most species don't change. That's bothersome... brings terrible distress... They may get a little bigger or bumpier but they remain the same species and that's not due to imperfection and gaps but stasis. And yet this remarkable stasis has generally been ignored as no data. If they don't change, it's not evolution so you don't talk about it."[3]

Also, natural selection has a culling effect. It does not create new genetic information for the mechanism of evolution. It merely sorts out and kills. At times, natural selection simply selects out whole species and sends them into extinction as can be seen in extinct creatures like the dinosaurs in the fossil record. There is no evolutionary obligation for natural selection to improve the fitness of any species. And what is designed to kill cannot be the mechanism for improvement. The selector is a destroyer of genetic information and not a contributor, just as the butcher kills but does not nurture. Natural selection is the *Blind Gunman* that decimates and not the *Blind Watchmaker* (chance) that supposedly improves. Roger Lewin, winner of the Royal Society Prizes for Science Books for *Bones of Contention,* writes:

> "Natural selection, a central feature of Neo-Darwinism... can weed out some of the complexity and so slow down the information decay that results in speciation. It may have a stabilizing effect, but it does not promote speciation. It is not a creative force as many people have suggested."[4]

In addition, natural selection is the 'quality control' department that removes faulty merchandise; it is not the 'research and development' unit that creates new products. And natural selection is not even a mechanism or an agent – it is just a process, a process of killing and eliminating – it is a kind of biological terrorism. It is all about the subtraction and not the addition of gain-of-function, genetic information despite a host of evolutionary jargons attached to it – stabilizing, purifying, disrupting or balancing natural selection. And the end results are always less than the beginning.

> "The very name "selection" implies that you're choosing between two or more variants. So that means that the end result is extinction of one in favour of the other. Natural selection never increases the number of variants; it only decreases them. So my problem with it was, "how does a mechanism that makes less and less end up making more and more?"[5] (Dr. Walter J. Veith)

> "No one has ever produced a species by the mechanisms of natural selection. No one has ever got near it, and most of the current argument in Neo-Darwinism is about this question."[6] (Colin Patterson)

> "Oh sure natural selection's been demonstrated... the interesting point, however, is that it has rarely if ever been demonstrated to have anything to do with evolution in the sense of long-term changes in populations...

Summing up we can see that the import of the Darwinian theory of evolution is just unexplainable caprice from top to bottom. What evolves is just what happens to happen [ellipsis in original]."[7] (Stanley Salthe)

Above all, natural selection can only kick in if there is more than one self-replicating life form to select from. Even Charles Darwin foresaw the impossibility of natural selection alone to provide the raw materials for evolution:

> "Natural selection can do nothing until favourable individual differences or variations occur."[8]

Charlie is right. Natural selection can do nothing if there are no variants to select from. Natural selection is a downstream process. If there were no preexisting variants, there will be nothing to select from subsequently. And the term 'pre-biotic natural selection' is an oxymoron as there is nothing to select from at the inception of life. No replicator, no selection. In the end, natural selection is all about the destruction of pre-existing genetic information.

<u>Natural Selection = Destruction of pre-existing, functional, genetic information</u>

Random Mutation: Mutation is nothing more than copying errors in DNA duplication. Sporadically, in cell duplication, copying errors are made resulting in faulty copies of the original cells. Mutation is the only game in town for biological evolution to take place. The evolutionary gun is out of ammunition except for this one last bullet – mutation.

> "The process of mutation is the only known source of the raw materials of genetic variability, and hence of evolution."[9] (Theodosius Dobzhansky)

> "By far the most important way in which chance influences evolution is the process of mutation. Mutation is, ultimately, the source of new genetic variations, and without genetic variation there cannot be genetic change. Mutation is therefore necessary for evolution."[10] (Futuyma, Douglas J.)

Evolutionists believe random copying errors can give rise to new, prescriptive, genetic information and biochemistry to eventually produce new body plans and new creatures – from dogs to non-dogs. They have a sincere, child-like faith, believing that copying mistakes in the DNA can produce survivable creatures unbeknown – creatures with never-before-seen, highly complex lungs, gills, legs, wings, or fins. Now, isn't that quite a stretch of faith? And it sounds pretty religious!

Biological evolution is the only pseudo-science that thrives on random mistakes. You will never find that in the fields of engineering, medicine, or construction. No computers, pharmaceutical drugs, or skyscrapers came about or progressed through random errors. They are always the products of intelligent design. Sometimes, all it takes is just 3 copying mistakes in a gene to kill a person.

> "The recent decoding of the human genome has allowed scientists to determine that cystic fibrosis is caused by a random change of three nucleotides in a gene that codes for a 1480-amino acid-long ion transport protein. The human genome has three billion nucleotides, or base pairs, in the DNA. Since a random change of three nucleotides in a three-billion-part genome is fatal (0.0000001%), how is it remotely possibly that a chimp could be the evolutionary cousin of a human? The lowest estimate of the genetic differences between our DNA and that of chimps is at least 50 million nucleotides (some estimates of the disparity are much higher). Quantitative information in genetics today is proving evolutionary theory as simply a man-made and irrational philosophical belief."[11] (Maddox, B)

It blows our minds that these men in white coats have this strange, esoteric, child-like, religious faith to believe that you can get a future bestseller by getting a monkey to type randomly. But mutation is all about the messing up of specified complexity; the degrading of intricate functionality; and the deletion of precise information. It has scant little to do with the creation of new specified, prescriptive, and functional information. That is why it is called 'copying errors'! Even the high priest of New Atheism Richard Dawkins recognizes that. He writes:

> "Mutation is not an increase in true information content, rather the reverse, for mutation, in the Shannon analogy, contributes to increasing the prior uncertainty."[12]

Over 99% of mutations is either fatal or neutral. The other less than 1% degrades the intrinsic genetic information of the creature, even in the so-called 'beneficial mutations' – like the sickle cells in the blood that cause one to be immune to malaria, or the 'damaged pumps' in the bacteria that cannot not take in the antibiotics and thus help them to be resistant to it. These 'beneficial mutations', like harmful mutations, are going downwards, not upwards. They all suffered from a loss of genetic information. Folks with sickle cells are sick, and bacteria with damaged receptors cannot survive long in the wild. Mutation is down, not up. One of the most feared words for any would-be mother is 'mutation'. No dad or mum looks forward to a mutated baby.

"Literally thousands of human diseases associated with genetic mutations have been catalogued in recent years, with more being described continually. A recent reference book of medical genetics listed some 4,500 different genetic diseases. Some of the inherited syndromes characterized clinically in the days before molecular genetic analysis (such as Marfan's syndrome) are now being shown to be heterogeneous; that is, associated with many different mutations.

With this array of human diseases that are caused by mutations, what of positive effects? With thousands of examples of harmful mutations readily available, surely it should be possible to describe some positive mutations if macroevolution is true. These would be needed not only for evolution to greater complexity, but also to offset the downward pull of the many harmful mutations. But, when it comes to identifying positive mutations, evolutionary scientists are strangely silent."[13] (David Demick)

"However, although geneticists know of some mutations which cause fairly drastic changes, they have entirely failed to discover the kind of macromutations required by the saltation theory — the kind of mutation which would take a group of organisms from one order to another. Moreover, the large-effect mutations which are known are usually just those mutations which are the most crippling to their carrier... Of course, one might argue that the failure to find the right kind of macromutations does not necessarily prove their nonexistence; but, like unicorns, there is a difference between saying that logically they might exist or that it is reasonable to suppose that they exist."[14] (Michael Ruse)

"The occurrence of genetic monstrosities by mutation... is well substantiated, but they are such evident freaks that these monsters can be designated only as 'hopeless.' They are so utterly unbalanced that they would not have the slightest chance of escaping elimination through stabilizing selection... the more drastically a mutation affects the phenotype, the more likely it is to reduce fitness. To believe that such a drastic mutation would produce a viable new type, capable of occupying a new

138

adaptive zone, is equivalent to believing in miracles... The finding of a suitable mate for the 'hopeless monster' and the establishment of reproductive isolation from the normal members of the parental population seem to me insurmountable difficulties."[15] (Ernst Mayr)

In the book *Acquiring Genomes: A Theory of the Origins of Species,* evolutionists Lynn Margulis and Dorion Sagan, the son of Carl Sagan, explain:

"... many ways to induce mutations are known but none leads to new organisms. Mutation accumulation does not lead to new species or even to new organs or new tissues... even professional evolutionary biologists are hard put to find mutations, experimentally induced or spontaneous, that lead in a positive way to evolutionary change."[16]

Professor Murray Eden, a specialist in information theory and formal languages at the Massachusetts Institute of Technology, makes no bones about the impossibility, from a mathematical standpoint, of natural selection acting upon random mutation to drive the engine of evolution. The DNA is an exact, single-sentence, billion-character, digital code that cannot tolerate random perturbations without messing up its functionality. He states:

"No currently existing formal language can tolerate random changes in the symbol sequence which expresses its sentences. Meaning is almost invariably destroyed. Any changes must be syntactically lawful ones. I would conjecture that what one might call 'genetic grammaticality' has a deterministic explanation and does not owe its stability to selection pressure acting on random variation."[17]

Grasse Pierre-Paul was a French zoologist and the author of over 300 publications including the influential 52-volume Traité de Zoologie. He saw the impossibility of evolution through natural selection and mutation, and relegated this ridiculous hypothesis to the religious dustbin.

"Some contemporary biologists, as soon as they observe a mutation, talk about evolution. They are implicitly supporting the following syllogism: mutations are the only evolutionary variations, all living beings undergo mutations, therefore all living beings evolve. This logical scheme is, however, unacceptable: first, because its major premise is neither obvious nor general; second, because its conclusion does not agree with the facts. No matter how numerous they may be, mutations do not produce any kind of evolution... [*With regard to mutations in bacteria*]... merely hereditary fluctuations around a median position; a swing to the right, a swing to the left, but no final evolutionary effect...

Mutations, in time, occur incoherently. They are not complementary to one another, nor are they cumulative in successive generations toward a given direction. They modify what preexists, but they do so in disorder, no matter how... As soon as some disorder, even slight, appears in an organized being, sickness, then death follow. There is no possible compromise between the phenomenon of life and anarchy... Mutations have a very limited 'constructive capacity'; this is why the formation of hair by mutation of reptilian scales seems to be a phenomenon of infinitesimal probability.

The opportune appearance of mutations permitting animals and plants to meet their needs seems hard to believe. Yet the Darwinian theory is even more demanding: a single plant, a single animal would require thousands and thousands of lucky, appropriate events. Thus, miracles would become the rule: events with an infinitesimal probability could not fail to occur.... There is no law against daydreaming, but science must not indulge in it.

Directed by all-powerful selection, chance becomes a sort of providence, which, under the cover of atheism, is not named but which is secretly worshipped."[18]

Lynn Margulis, Carl Sagan's first wife, and a member of the US National Academy of Sciences until her recent demise, in a 2011 interview, commented:

"Natural selection eliminates and maybe maintains, but it doesn't create... Neo-Darwinists say that new species emerge when mutations occur and modify an organism. I was taught over and over again that the accumulation of random mutations led to evolutionary change [which] led to new species. I believed it until I looked for evidence."[19]

Above all, the multi-layered 'codes within codes' in the DNA will guarantee the impossibility of evolution via natural selection and random mutation. It was initially thought that the DNA was decoded in a simple, linear fashion but, with the latest findings, scientists are stunned by the multi-layered codes within the DNA – it is literally 'codes intertwined with codes'. About 20,000 coding genes in our human genome produce more than 100,000 different proteins.

The DNA can be read forward and backward to produce different proteins; the same gene can produce two entirely different proteins due to the duons; the mythical 98% 'junk DNA' in the human genome turns out to be the 'operating system' in modifying gene expressions to churn out a diversity of necessary proteins; the alternate splicing in which different segments of the DNA is 'cut and recombined' to generate other proteins; and then there is the epigenetics which influences how the cell reads the DNA without changing it.

To put it bluntly, a few mutated chemical letters in the DNA can have an amplified, deleterious effect upon the whole, bundled up, intertwined, and interdependent coding system. Even if it is beneficial to one function, it tends to unsettle the others. And that spells disaster for the creature. Cancers and debilitating diseases are without fail the outcome of such messed up, random mutations in the original, specified and functioning DNA. This 'developmental constraint', well known in the biology community, accounts for the stasis in the creature – there is only so much its biochemical system can tolerate before the critter dies. It may account for the variation of the same critter but it cannot account for the 'jump' from one taxon to another – like the fish to land tetrapod where the gill is transformed into lung, or the reptile to bird where the lung system changes from tidal to circulatory. Half and half of these morphological changes would have long killed the creature.

> "… organisms are so complex that it is very hard to change
> one aspect without wrecking everything else."[20] (Dicks, L.)

Dr. John Stamatoyannopoulos, University of Washington associate professor of genome sciences, and his research team, have discovered this 'second language' in the DNA through the ENCODE program:

> "Since the genetic code was deciphered in the 1960s,
> scientists have assumed that it was used exclusively to
> write information about proteins. UW scientists were
> stunned to discover that genomes use the genetic code to
> write two separate languages. One describes how
> proteins are made, and the other instructs the cell on how
> genes are controlled. One language is written on top of
> the other, which is why the second language remained
> hidden for so long.

"For over 40 years we have assumed that DNA changes affecting the genetic code solely impact how proteins are made," said Stamatoyannopoulos. "Now we know that this basic assumption about reading the human genome missed half of the picture. These new findings highlight that DNA is an incredibly powerful information storage device, which nature has fully exploited in unexpected ways."

The genetic code uses a 64-letter alphabet called codons. The UW team discovered that some codons, which they called duons, can have two meanings, one related to protein sequence, and one related to gene control. These two meanings seem to have evolved in concert with each other. The gene control instructions appear to help stabilize certain beneficial features of proteins and how they are made."[21] (Stephanie Seiler)

Random Mutation = Degradation of pre-existing, functional, genetic information

Variation: Variation is nothing more than the reshuffling, duplication or degradation of genetic information within the genome. When you crossbreed dogs and isolate them, you can produce a wide variety of dogs from the Chihuahua to the Great Dane. But they are still the dog kind. And variation can only go as far as its genome would permit. In short, it will eventually hit an impassable, genetic brick wall, run out of teleonomic (literally purpose-law, or end-directed) information, and return to its original design. All the years of artificial breeding of dogs could never increase its genomic information and produce a non-dog.

"From a teacup-size Chihuahua to a Great Dane, there is an incredible amount of variety among dog breeds. But all breeds belong to a single species, so scientists have studied the breeds to better understand the workings of evolution, and how such great variation could have arisen within one group.

The dog (*Canis lupus familiaris*) is far more variable in size, shape and behavior than any other living mammal, but most experts now believe that all dogs, no matter how different, originated exclusively from a single species: the gray wolf..."[22] (Remy Melina)

142

The possible variants for us human beings are larger than all the estimated stars in the night sky.

> "With humans, both the mother's and father's halves have 100,000 genes, the information equivalent to a thousand 500-page books (3 billion base pairs, as *Teaching about Evolution* correctly states on page 42). The ardent Neo-Darwinist Francisco Ayala points out that humans today have an "average heterozygosity of 6.7 percent." This means that for every thousand gene pairs coding for any trait, 67 of the pairs have different alleles, meaning 6,700 heterozygous loci overall. Thus, any single human could produce a vast number of different possible sperm or egg cells — 2^{6700} or 10^{2017}.
>
> The number of atoms in the whole known universe is "only" 10^{80}, extremely tiny by comparison. So there is no problem for creationists explaining that the original created kinds could each give rise to many different varieties. In fact, the original created kinds would have had much more heterozygosity than their modern, more specialized descendants. No wonder Ayala pointed out that most of the variation in populations arises from reshuffling of previously existing genes, not from mutations... However, Ayala believes the genetic information came ultimately from mutations, not creation."[23] (Jonathan Sarfati)

<u>Variation = Reshuffling of pre-existing, functional, genetic information</u>

Adaptation: The very last bastion the Darwinist can retreat to is 'adaptation'. But adaptation is of no help to the Darwinist as it still does not provide for the new, gain-of-function, genetic information for evolution. Adaptation, as defined by Theodosius Dobzhansky, is:

> "... the evolutionary process whereby an organism becomes better able to live in its habitat or habitats."[24]

Adaptation is the critter's ability to adjust to its habitat to survive. But all observable adaptive plasticity comes from the genetic information within its genome. It is simply a reorganization of existing genetic information, or the switching on or off of the genetic switches, or the loss of genetic information. There is no new, gain-of-function, genetic information created in adaptation.

E-coli bacteria have 'turned on' their genetic switch to feed on citrate instead of glucose, while blind cave fishes have 'turned off' their genetic switch for the eyes to better adapt to the dark caves. The stickleback fishes in the oceans have 'turned on' their genetic switches for the spines in their dorsal fins, while the spineless sticklebacks in the fresh water lakes have 'turned off' the same genetic switch. The 'clicking' of genetic switches does not amount to a net increase in specified, genetic information.

"When E. coli finds itself in the absence of oxygen, it switches on a gene called citT. Like other species (including us), E. coli turns genes on and off by attaching proteins to short stretches of DNA nearby. When E. coli senses a lack of oxygen, proteins clamp onto one of these genetic switches near citT. Once they turn the gene on, it produces proteins that get delivered to the surface of the cell. There they poke one end out into the environment and pull in citrate, while also pumping out succinate. After the citrate gets inside the microbe, the bacteria can chop it up to harvest its energy."[25] (Carl Zimmer)

Antibiotic resistance in bacteria and arthropods are often touted as evidence for evolution, but their ability to overcome antibiotics is not due to evolution but to the pre-existing, genetic information already present in their genomes. It is not a case of an increase in gain-of-function, genetic information, but rather occasionally, a loss of prescriptive information or a turning on of a genetic switch.

"Many bacteria possessed resistance genes even before commercial antibiotics came into use. Scientists do not know exactly why these genes evolved and were maintained."[26] (Stuart B. Levy)

"In 1845, sailors on an Arctic expedition were buried in the permafrost and remained deeply frozen until their bodies were exhumed in 1986. Preservation was so complete that six strains of nineteenth-century bacteria found dormant in the contents of the sailors' intestines were able to be revived! When tested, these bacteria were found to possess resistance to several modern-day antibiotics, including penicillin."[27] (Medical Tribune)

"Insect resistance to a pesticide was first reported in 1947 for the housefly (Musca domestica) with respect to DDT. Since then the resistance to one or more pesticides has been reported in at least 225 species of insects and other arthropods. The genetic variants required for resistance to the most diverse kinds of pesticides were apparently present in every one of the populations exposed to these man-made compounds."[28] (Francisco J. Ayala)

In 2011, a paper was published by Nature entitled: *Antibiotic resistance is ancient.* In it, a group of researchers from McMaster University studied the DNA of the bacteria extracted from the permafrost of the Yukon Territories which also encased the extinct mammoths. These researchers were amazed to find these primitive bacteria were able to resist present-day antibiotics.

"These results show conclusively that antibiotic resistance is a natural phenomenon that predates the modern selective pressure of clinical antibiotic use."[29] (Vanessa M. D'Costa, et al.)

However, there is no net increase in gain-of-function, genetic information in this adaptive process for the creature to better survive in its ecological niche. It has been always a domestic rearrangement of the genetic furniture within its genome.

<u>Adaptation = Recalibration of pre-existing, functional, genetic information</u>

Many evolutionists will attempt to hoodwink the public with their mesmerizing display of evolutionary jargons to bypass this embarrassing conundrum, and hope that nobody will notice this glaring glitch in their tattered hypothesis. But this observable absence of new, gain-of-function, genetic information in mutation is so damning that those who have given this conundrum their full attention, and have understood the depth of this dilemma, know that biological evolution is dead in the water and is a proven impossibility. And the shocker is this: no new, gain-of-function, genetic information means no new kinds! No new kinds mean no biological evolution! And no biological evolution means plenty of deluded evolutionists!

Natural Selection =	Destruction of pre-existing, functional, genetic information
Mutation =	Degradation of pre-existing, functional, genetic information
Variation =	Reshuffling of pre-existing, functional, genetic information
Adaptation =	Recalibration of pre-existing, functional, genetic information

Darwinism	=	Natural Selection + Mutation + Variation + Adaptation
	=	Destruction + Degradation + Reshuffling + Recalibration
	=	No new, gain-of-function, genetic information
	=	No new organelles, organisms, or organs
	=	No biological evolution

Natural selection and random mutations are going the wrong way – from a fitter organism to a degraded one, or just drifting sideways with variants of the same kind. There is no Darwinian Evolution, only Darwinian Devolution. This is true despite all the genetic variations, genetic drift, bottleneck effect, Lamarckism, et al., in the evolutionary literature. They will always remain within the boundaries of their unique and created genome. Dr. Stanley Salthe writes:

> "Darwinian evolutionary theory was my field of specialization in biology. Among other things, I wrote a textbook on the subject thirty years ago. Meanwhile, however I have become an apostate from Darwinian theory and have described it as part of modernism's origination myth. Consequently, I certainly agree that biology students at least should have the opportunity to learn about the flaws and limits of Darwin's theory while they are learning about the theory's strongest claims."[30]

Above all, the theory of biological evolution is the butt of the joke for the well-informed mathematicians that deal with mathematical probability.

> "The fact that systems [such as advanced computers], in every way analogous to the living organism, cannot undergo evolution by pure trial and error [by mutation and natural selection] and that their functional distribution invariably conforms to an improbable discontinuum comes, in my opinion, very close to a formal disproof of the whole Darwinian paradigm of nature. By what strange capacity do living organisms defy the laws of chance which are apparently obeyed by all analogous complex systems?"[31] (Michael Denton)

> "To propose and argue that mutations even in tandem with 'natural selection' are the root-causes for 6,000,000 viable, enormously complex species, is to mock logic, deny the weight of evidence, and reject the fundamentals of mathematical probability."[32] (Cohen, I. L.)

When the cheetah attacks its preys, it usually goes for the jugular. Once the jugular vein is punctured, that creature will inevitably die despite the rest of its body being intact for a while. Biological evolution has an exposed jugular – natural selection acting on random mutation. If this jugular vein of evolution is ripped out, the theory of biological evolution will bleed to death in due time. Natural selection cannot provide for new, gain-of-function, genetic information, and mutation keeps degrading existing, functional information. The jugular of biological evolution has now been punctured. Now, we are waiting for Darwinian Evolution to slowly bleed to death.

> "What you'd like to see is a good case for gradual change from one species to another in the field, in the laboratory, or in the fossil record—and preferably in all three. Darwin's big mystery was why there was no record at all before a specific point [dated to 542 million years ago by modern researchers], and then all of a sudden in the fossil record you get nearly all the major types of animals. The paleontologists Niles Eldredge and Stephen Jay Gould studied lakes in East Africa and on Caribbean islands looking for Darwin's gradual change from one species of trilobite or snail to another. What they found was lots of back-and-forth variation in the population and then— whoop—a whole new species. There is no gradualism in the fossil record."[33] (Lynn Margulis)

Biological evolution has been falsified and it is for this reason that we do not see the greatest proof of evolution before us – the observable, living transitions. The creationists can go to bed and have a restful sleep. Natural Selection and Random Mutation are a proven double negative that is of no help to Evolution – one destroys and the other degrades. Biological evolution did not happen in the past and will not happen anytime presently or in the future. The car with no engine is not going anywhere. Good night!

> "It is not the duty of science to defend the theory of evolution, and stick by it to the bitter end no matter which illogical and unsupported conclusions it offers. On the contrary, it is expected that scientists recognize the patently obvious impossibility of Darwin's pronouncements and predictions... Let's cut the umbilical cord that tied us down to Darwin for such a long time. It is choking us and holding us back."[34] (I. L. Cohen)

Natural Selection destroys, not designs.
Random Mutation degrades, not creates.

References:

1. Michael Pitman, *Adam and Evolution*, 1984, pp. 67-68

2. Nile Eldredge and Steven M. Stanley, *Living Fossils*, p. 272

3. Stephen J. Gould, Harvard, Lecture at Hobart & William Smith College, 14/2/1980

4. Roger Lewin, Science, 217:1239-1240, 1982

5. Dr. Walter J. Veith, Professor at the University of the Western Cape, Republic of South Africa, where he holds the chair of Zoology, *A distinguished zoologist 'tells it like it is' about evolution*, by Carl Wieland and Jonathan Sarfati

6. Colin Patterson, senior paleontologist at the British Museum of Natural History in London, Cladistics, Interview by Brian Leek, interviewer Peter Franz, March 4, 1982, BBC

7. Stanley Salthe in *The Altenberg 16: An Exposé of the Evolution Industry*, by Suzan Mazur, 2010, p. 21

8. Charles Darwin, *The Origin of Species by Means of Natural Selection*, The Modern Library, New York, p. 127

9. Theodosius Dobzhansky, *On Methods of Evolutionary Biology and Anthropology,* American Scientist, 1957, 45, 385

10. Futuyma, Douglas J., *Science on Trial*, New York: Pantheon Books, 1983, p. 136

11. Maddox, B, *Mutations: The Raw Material for Evolution?* Acts & Facts, 36 (9): 10, 2007

12. Richard Dawkins, *The Information Challenge*

13. David Demick, *The Blind Gunman*, Impact, No. 308, February 1999

14. Michael Ruse, *Philosophy of Biology*, 1973, p. 111

15. Ernst Mayr, *Populations, Species, and Evolution*, p. 235

16. Lynn Margulis, Dorion Sagan, *Acquiring Genomes: A Theory of the Origins of Species,* 2002

17. M. Eden, *"Inadequacies of Neo-Darwinian Evolution as a Scientific Theory,"* in Mathematical Challenges to the Neo-Darwinian Interpretation of Evolution, P. S. Moorhead and M. M. Kaplan, eds., Wistar Institute Press, Philadelphia, p. 11, 1967

18. Pierre-Paul, Grasse, *Evolution of Living Organisms*, Academic Press, New York, N.Y., 1977, p. 88, 87, 97, 98, 103, 107

19.   Quoted in Lynn Margulis: Q & A, Discover Magazine, April 2011, p. 68

20.   Dicks, L., *The Creatures time Forgot*, New Scientist, 164(2209):36–39, 1999

21.   Stephanie Seiler, *Scientists discover double meaning in genetic code*, UW Today, University of Washington, December 12, 2013, italics mine

22.   Remy Melina, *The Incredible Explosion of Dog Breeds*, Live Science, 2010

23.   Jonathan Sarfati, *Refuting Evolution*, 2008

24.   Theodosius Dobzhansky, Hecht, MK; Steere, WC, 1968, *On some fundamental concepts of evolutionary biology*, Evolutionary Biology volume 2 (1st ed.), New York: Appleton-Century-Crofts. p. 1–34

25.   Carl Zimmer, *The Birth of the New, The Rewiring of the Old*, The Loom, Sept 19, 2012

26.   Stuart B. Levy, *The Challenge of Antibiotic Resistance*, Scientific American, March 1998, p. 35

27.   Medical Tribune, 29 December 1988, p. 1

28.   Francisco J. Ayala, *The Mechanisms of Evolution*, Scientific American 239(3): 56–69, 1978; p. 65

29.   Vanessa M. D'Costa, et. al., *Antibiotic Resistance is Ancient*, Nature, doi: 10.1038 / nature 10388, 2011

30.   Dr. Stanley Salthe, Professor Emeritus, Brooklyn College of the City University of New York

31.   Michael Denton, *Evolution: A Theory in Crisis*, 1985, p. 342

32.   Cohen, I. L., *Darwin Was Wrong: A Study in Probabilities*, New York: New Research Publications, Inc., 1984, p. 81

33.   Quoted in Lynn Margulis: Q & A, Discover Magazine, April 2011, p. 68

34.   Dr. I. L. Cohen, *"Darwin Was Wrong:" A Study in Probabilities*, 1985

Magic Did It

"I suppose that nobody will deny that it is a great misfortune if an entire branch of science becomes addicted to a false theory. But this is what has happened in biology... One day the Darwinian myth will be ranked the greatest deceit in the history of science."[1] (Dr. Seren Levtrup)

One of the laziest definitions of evolution is 'change over time'. The bar is sometime intentionally lowered to help qualify the theory of evolution as empirical science. But the complete ideology of biological evolution includes the theory of common descent in which all living things are related to a common ancestor – the first living cell. No creationist would dispute the lazy notion of 'change over time' in evolution – we change all the time – from growing thinner to growing fatter. We have different looking kids. And there are varieties of plants and animals within their kinds.

But to theorize that one kind of animal can morph into another requires a great deal of faith and imagination as not a single creature or plant has been observed to evolve into something different – from a dog to a non-dog or a cat to a non-cat. Although there are speculative fossil record, geologic column, homology, and DNA similarity, but like Ripley's *Believe It or Not*, to date, no dog has turned into a non-dog. In fact, no new, observable, emerging organs or body plans have been documented to have arisen.

As it is wont to say, "Evolution is something the Darwinist often wish for but cannot demonstrate." No creature has been observed to have evolved into something else, something different, and something unlike its previous design – from fish to amphibian, or tetrapod to mammal, or reptile to bird. Biological evolution is the strangest 'scientific theory' that is unobservable, untestable and unrepeatable, unlike all the other demonstrable sciences, and yet it blatantly lays claims to be an unassailable scientific theory. Big joke! Nobody fights over the testable, falsifiable and repeatable scientific law of gravity or the theory of quantum mechanics because we can observe it and repeat it with rigorous consistency.

However, it is not so with evolution. Evolution is 'data-poor and imagination-rich' – a phrase borrowed from Michael Lemonick. For the general populace, evolution is about turning bacterium into man, or a leg into a wing; but for the Darwinists, it is usually about antibiotic resistance, or the fluctuating sizes of the beaks of finches, or the fraudulent peppered moth observation. Anything beyond that, like a new organelle or organism, is unobservable!

Horizontal Variation or Microevolution within a given kind of animal or plant is empirical science. We do observe that the cross-breeding of dogs produces a variety of dogs – from the chihuahua to the great Dane. But they are still the 'dog kind'. There are hybrids of dogs, cats, peas, roses, and whales, but they are all restricted to their genomes. And all these variations come from the genetic information within the gene pool of that plant or critter. It is nothing more than the reshuffling of the genes, or the 'switching on or off' of existing genetic switches, or the loss of genetic information. There is no net increase in specified, gain-of-function, genetic information to produce new kinds of animals.

If biological evolution is nothing more than 'changes within limits' or 'changes within kinds', the creationists would have no quarrel with this definition. No creationist will quibble with the fact that variations and hybrids have been observed. Bacteria can mutate to feed on citrate instead of sugar; the beaks of the finches in the Galapagos Islands have been observed to change their shapes depending on their food supplies; there are hybrids of creatures and plants of every stripe; and folks that do weight lifting have more muscles than the rest of us. But none of these can or has been observed to change from one animal kind to another – no dog has ever produce a non-dog. It is just the reorganization of the genes within its gene pool. And its ability to vary and adapt is always constrained by its original, genetic blueprint. It cannot produce what it does not have within its genome.

Both horizontal variation (dogs birthing different kinds of dogs) and stasis (the dog kind remaining as dog kind) are observational science. They mark the limits of biological evolution. And creationists have absolutely no issues with this definition of biological evolution – changes within limits or just common, genetic 'mix and match'.

Vertical Evolution, Macroevolution or Transmutation, on the other hand, is vastly different. It is the belief of 'unrestricted genetic changes' – positing that the first, living cell can transmutate up the evolutionary ladder from the bacterium to man. In a word, one animal kind can leap over its genetic barrier and morph into another of a different kind – like the fish to amphibian, or the reptile to bird. This is the universally-accepted definition of biological evolution today – that the diversity of living creatures are descended from a common ancestor, and one creature kind can transmutate into another through the 'millions of years' of deep time and the process of gradualism.

To extrapolate microevolution to macroevolution is like getting a man to add one kilogram to his weight-lifting exercise every day and he will eventually be able to lift an elephant. Or, if he keeps swimming, he will someday develop gills. Or, if he keeps stretching his neck, he will, in due course, have the neck of a giraffe. Or, if he keeps jumping off the tree tops, he will eventually evolve complex wings under his sinking armpits. In the kindergarten, it is called 'just-so stories'. In biological evolution, it is called 'science'.

Many biological evolutionists attempt to hoodwink the uninformed public by erasing the distinction between microevolution (bacteria to more mutated bacteria, or dogs to more variants of dogs) and macroevolution (bacterium to Batman, or fish to amphibian), and lump them together, muddy the water, and define biological evolution as 'change with time'. But microevolution and macroevolution are not terminologies conjured by creationists, but are established scientific definitions used by Darwinists themselves to describe changes below or above the species level. In the text book *Biology*, it states:

> "Macroevolution: Evolutionary change above the species level, including the appearance of major evolutionary developments, such as flight, that we use to define higher taxa.
>
> Microevolution: Evolutionary change below the species level; change in the genetic makeup of a population from generation to generation."[2]

This is where the great divide takes place – young earth creationists do not subscribe to this definition of evolution where a dog can evolve to a non-dog or a cat to a non-cat. It is not being observed today and, as we have seen before, it has never occurred in time past. Horizontal Variation (dogs birthing different kinds of dogs) is empirical science. Vertical Evolution (dogs morphing into non-dog) via accumulative microevolutions or punctuated equilibrium and saltation (the hopeful monster hypothesis – a reptile lays an egg and a bird is hatched) is pseudo-science and science fiction. Neither of these has been observed, because for a dog to morph into a non-dog, it requires additional new, prescriptive, gain-of-function, genetic information and specified biochemistry, which all observable mutations could not provide.

In a conference in Chicago, the hypothesis of macroevolution was mooted and booted:

> "The central question of the Chicago conference was whether the mechanisms underlying microevolution can be extrapolated to explain the phenomena of macroevolution. At the risk of doing violence to the positions of some of the people at the meeting, the answer can be given as a clear, No."[3] (Lewin, R.)

Some evolutionists believe that hox (homeobox) genes are the solutions to punctuated equilibrium because of their abilities to effect an organism in a big way. A little change in the hox gene can have a magnified effect on the organism. But, as Dr. Christian Schwabe from the Medical University of South Carolina has shown, this 'hopeful monster' scenario is a hopeless cause because its downline amplified effects is horribly deleterious. He writes:

> "Control genes like homeotic genes may be the target of mutations that would conceivably change phenotypes, but one must remember that, the more central one makes changes in a complex system, the more severe the peripheral consequences become... Homeotic changes induced in Drosophila (fruit fly) genes have led only to monstrosities, and most experimenters do not expect to see a bee arise from their Drosophila constructs."[4]

Without exaggeration, the hypothesis of evolution is equivalent to a single-engine, Cessna propeller plane taking off and transforming into the state-of-the-art F-22 Raptor on route to the next airport. We know it can't for obvious reasons. And it is for this reason we do not see fishes coming out of the water and turning into some land animals, or mammalian critters transforming into some kind of aquatic creatures, or crawling reptiles on their way to become airborne birds. A semi-evolved leg, wing, or fin has never been observed in any form of adaption or pre-adaption to another order of life. Natural selection would have long decimated these sickly, 'transitional modifications' before they could be fully realized. This developmental constraint is the ultimate brick wall in the path of biological evolution.

Microevolution or horizontal variation can never lead to macroevolution or vertical evolution. The biochemical chasm is so ridiculously wide that no amount of evolutionary imagination or hollering is going to get the Darwinist across. To get a foot from a fin, or a wing from a hand, is never about deep-time 'slight modifications' but instant 'massive biochemistry overhaul'. One cannot help but to think the way the many evolutionists theorize about the evolution of whale from Pakicetus, or man from fish, is like children playing Lego – they would change the 'animals' by rearranging the pieces to shape them. It is just so amateurish and childish the way they describe this mind-boggling, biochemical complexity at the molecular level.

A common evolutionary, just-so story would go something like this: The predators in the ocean would chase the Tiktaalik and it would attempt to escape to land. In the process, the Tiktaalik's gills would later turn into lungs and its fins to legs. And through this 'flight to escape' or rather 'flight of fancy', the Tiktaalik would eventually evolve into a tetrapod, and on to all the four-legged, mammalian critters we have today. You see my point? Another evolutionary Lego playtime! Another just-so story! Have they ever meticulously examined the mind-blowing biochemistry between a fin and a leg, or a gill and a lung? Are they in some kind of 'Darwinian Delusion' to believe that such incredible transformations are possible? Why are no present-day 'Tiktaalik' found crawling onto our shores with semi-evolved lungs and legs despite being pursued by their predators? The chase is still on. Trillions of fishes are constantly and violently being displaced from their aqueous environment every day and none have been observed to be evolving with a recognizable lung or leg to live on land.

Are they blind to the fact that natural selection would have first eliminated these sickly, evolving creatures long before they could have adapted to their new ecological niche? How did they transmutate and survive from feeding in the water to feeding on land; or from aquatic eyes to aerial eyes; or from sex in the water to sex on land; and a host of other necessary, mind-boggling, instant changes to survive in their new environment? Slight, random modifications would have long killed them with hunger, blinded their eyes, rendered them impotent, handicapped them in a million ways, and ensured their certain demise in quick time.

You can never get from a working car to a functioning submarine through slight modifications, or a moving vehicle to an airborne fighter plane through 'gradualism'. You will sink the sub and crash the plane in the process. Massive and complete systemic transformations will be required to change from one mechanical vehicle to another. What is true of man-made machines is also true of biological machines.

If one is incapable of jumping a certain height, one is tempted to lower the bar. When biological evolution cannot be observed to have happened, then the logical thing is to lower the bar for the definition of evolution. Instead of 'change in kind', it is now 'change with time', and any wee little change will do. If macroevolution cannot be observed, Darwinists would latch on to microevolution, and pray that it will lead to a massive 'change in kind' eventually.

Evolutionists like Richard Dawkins would have no qualms in accusing creationists of 'Magic' with regard to an unobservable God creating the world of living things. But he could not see the same 'Magic' when he boasted of an unobservable evolution creating the whole realm of highly complex, living creatures from molecule to man.

154

"Evolution can be thought of as sort of a magical religion. Magic is simply an effect without a cause, or at least a competent cause. 'Chance', 'time', and 'nature', are the small gods enshrined at evolutionary temples. Yet these gods cannot explain the origin of life. These gods are impotent. Thus, evolution is left without competent cause and is, therefore, only a magical explanation for the existence of life..."[5] (Dr. Randy L. Wysong)

In truth, horizontal variation is not evolution and vertical evolution is not science. There are varieties of dogs, but no dog has been observed on its way to become a non-dog.

"... we must concede that there are presently no detailed Darwinian accounts of the evolution of any biochemical or cellular system, only a variety of wishful speculations."[6] (Franklin M. Harold)

"We have had enough of the Darwinian fallacy.
It is time that we cry: 'The emperor has no clothes.'"[7]

References:

1.   Dr. Seren Levtrup, famed Swedish evolutionist, *Darwinism: The Refutation of a Myth*, 1987, p. 422

2.   *Biology*, 7th ed. Neil A. Campbell & Jane B. Reece

3.   Lewin, R., *Evolutionary Theory Under Fire*, Science, vol. 210, 21 November, 1980, p. 883

4.   Mini Review: Schwabe, C., 1994, *Theoretical limitations of molecular phylogenetics and the evolution of relaxins*, Comp. Biochem. Physiol.107B: 167–177

5.   Dr. Randy L. Wysong, *The Creation-Evolution Controversy*, p. 418

6.   Franklin M. Harold, *The way of the cell: molecules, organisms and the order of life*, Oxford University Press, New York, 2001, p. 205

7.   K. Hsu, geologist at the Geological Institute at Zurich; *Darwin's Three Mistakes,* Geology, vol. 14, 1986, p. 534

Evolution's Voodoo Science

"A growing number of respectable scientists are defecting from the evolutionist camp... moreover, for the most part these 'experts' have abandoned Darwinism, not on the basis of religious faith or biblical persuasions, but on strictly scientific grounds, and in some instances, regretfully."[1] (Wolfgang Smith)

Observational science is what we can observe, falsify and repeat. This is the definition of a scientific theory. Biological Evolution is never a scientific theory and will never be a scientific theory because it has never been observed, tested or repeated, period. No dog has ever changed into a non-dog inside or outside of the laboratory. There are no observable, transitional creatures - from dogs to non-dogs. And what is true of the dog kind is true of every other critter – nothing has changed or morphed into something other than their original, intrinsic kind.

Historical science, on the other hand, is unobservable presently and the conclusion is derived from the clues left behind. It has to do with the past – something has happened – and we need to figure out what had happened. It is like doing a detective work – a murder has been committed and we are here to find who did it by studying the evidence left behind. Evolutionary biology does not fall under observational or empirical science, and this may come as a shock to many. It comes under forensic or historical science – it cannot be observed today despite the thousands of years of observable human history that have passed.

All the evolutionists are doing today is to attempt to prove that evolution has taken place based on the evidence left behind – the fossil record (the attempts to string up similar sets of bones to prove the links between them); or homology (the similarities of appearances between man and apelike creatures to prove that man came from some kind of primates); or DNA similarities (man and chimp have supposedly about 98% similarity in DNA).

There is no better person to confirm that biological evolution is a historical science than the renowned high priest of New Atheism Richard Dawkins. He is reputed to be the most intelligent person in the world, the leader of the pack for New Atheism, and a T.V. evangelist for anti-theism. The following is from an interview by Bill Moyers in the PBS network:

MOYERS:	Is evolution a theory, not a fact?
DAWKINS:	Evolution has been observed. *It's just that it hasn't been observed while it's happening.*
MOYERS:	What do you mean it's been observed.
DAWKINS:	The consequences of. It is rather like a detective coming on a murder after the scene. And you... the detective hasn't actually seen the murder take place, of course. But what you do see is a massive clue.
MOYERS:	Circumstantial evidence.
DAWKINS:	Circumstantial evidence, but masses of circumstantial evidence. Huge quantities of circumstantial evidence. It might as well be spelled out in words of English. Evolution is true. I mean it's as circumstantial as that, but it's as true as that.[2]

In another place, Richard Dawkins reaffirms that evolution has never been observed:

> "*Nobody has actually seen evolution take place over a long period* but they have seen the after effects, and the after effects are massively supported. It is like a case in a court of law where nobody can actually stand up and say I saw the murder happen and yet you have got millions and millions of pieces of evidence which no reasonable person can possibly dispute."[3]

Few realize how devastating that statement is to the average student of evolution – *evolution has never been observed while it is happening!* What? Say that again? I thought Richard Dawkins would state emphatically that evolution is observable and checkable. Well, you just heard it from the horse's mouth. Our friend Richie has just said before millions of enthusiastic viewers that *evolution has never been observed while it is happening.* I am sure many evolutionary jaws just dropped in shock. It is based on circumstantial evidence. It is about historical speculations, not observational or empirical science.

This is a 9.5 earthquake on the evolutionary Richter scale. I am sure that many diehard evolutionists are shaken to the core because this places evolution on the same playing field as creation – they are both historical and not empirical science. Both are trying to figure out who or what did it – God or Evolution. All that the theists and the evolutionists are doing is second-guessing what really took place in the past – who or what brought about this world teeming with all kinds of mind-boggling, complex, self-replicating, living things? The truth has to be deduced from the circumstantial evidence left behind. Dawkins' admission has just degraded evolution one notch down and put it on par with creation – both are attempting to make an educated guess. It is a probability argument – which is a more likely candidate for the biodiversity of life?

Many thought it is a done deal with regard to the 'theory of evolution'. It must have been observed, tested and repeated in the laboratory; there is a plethora of scientific papers on biological evolution subjected to peer reviews; the biologists, geneticists, molecular biologists, paleontologists and scientists of all stripes have vouched for its veracity; the biology textbooks are plastered with convincing pictures of the evolution of man, whale, horse, bird and a host of other creatures, and not to mention PBS, NOVA and National Geographic have been relentlessly promoting it. Besides, there are millions in the educated populace worldwide who have embraced it. How can it not be science and a scientific theory? It is supposed to be 'as good as cash'.

When sentiments are set aside, and objectivity is brought into focus, one will have to go where the evidence leads – *evolution never was, is not, and never will be, an empirical or observational science*. We don't see any creature diversifying into something different from its original kind naturally or artificially. And evolution does not qualify to be a scientific theory based on the ironclad definition of a scientific theory. A scientific theory is one that is observable, falsifiable, and repeatable. And the results hold true every time. The Theory of General Relativity and the Law of Gravity are empirical science – we can see it happening and repeat it with consistent outcomes. And hardly anyone quarrels with them. But it is not so with biological evolution. The National Academy of Science defines a scientific theory as:

> "A scientific theory is a well-substantiated explanation of some aspect of the natural world that is acquired through the scientific method and repeatedly tested and confirmed through observation and experimentation."[4]

But, the theory of evolution is vastly different. It makes predictions – chemical to cell and bacterium to man – that cannot be observed. And if you cannot see it happening, how do you test it? And this just blows our mind into oblivion – if you cannot test it, how did it evolve into a scientific theory? A scientific theory is observable, falsifiable and reproducible. Wow! This is pretty scary. It is turning into a horror movie. Millions are told that evolution is a scientific theory, as good as gravity, while empirical science unequivocally labels it a speculative hypothesis because it cannot be observed and repeated. The so-called 'theory of evolution' is, in reality, the 'hypothesis of evolution'. Unrepeatable history is history, and repeatable science is science. How did a speculative hypothesis manage to slip past the peer review committee and emerge as a 'scientific theory' when it cannot be observed, falsified and repeated?

"It is inherent in any definition of science that statements that cannot be checked by observation are not really saying anything - or at least they are not science."[5] (George G. Simpson)

"For example, Darwin introduced historicity into science. Evolutionary biology, in contrast with physics and chemistry, is a historical science - the evolutionist attempts to explain events and processes that have already taken place. Laws and experiments are inappropriate techniques for the explication of such events and processes. Instead one constructs a historical narrative, consisting of a tentative reconstruction of the particular scenario that led to the events one is trying to explain."[6] (Mayr, Ernst)

"We must ask first whether the theory of evolution by natural selection is scientific or pseudoscientific... Taking the first part of the theory, that evolution has occurred, it says that the history of life is a single process of species-splitting and progression. This process must be unique and unrepeatable, like the history of England. This part of the theory is therefore a historical theory, about unique events, and unique events are, by definition, not part of science, for they are unrepeatable and so not subject to test."[7] (Colin Patterson)

"The history of organic life is indemonstrable; we cannot prove a whole lot in evolutionary biology, and our findings will always be hypothesis. There is one true evolutionary history of life, and whether we will actually ever know it is not likely."[8] (Jeffrey Schwartz)

Empirical Science = Present + Observable + Repeatable
Historical Science = Past + Unobservable + Unrepeatable

"The pathetic thing about it is that many scientists are trying to prove the doctrine of evolution, which no science can do."[9] (Dr. Robert A. Milikan)

There are no scientific frameworks to test the theory of evolution. And unbeknown to many, there is no watertight, foolproof, scientific framework or mechanism to verify the evolutionary past – it has been, and will always be, nothing more than an educated guess, and that leaves open the possibility that it may turn out to be horribly wrong. And it is for this reason that many of the past findings turn out later to be such a painful embarrassment to the evolutionary community – like the Piltdown Man, which for 40 years, was the postal boy for the evolution of ape to man, and which later turned out to be a fraud. The jaw of an ape was joined to the skull of a man. Or, the famous Nebraska Man constructed from a single tooth, and the tooth turned out to be the tooth of a peccary. And to add insult to injury, the peccary was later discovered to be alive and kicking. The Nebraska Man was used as an exhibit in the Scope Monkey Trial in 1925 to introduce biological evolution into the classroom.

Now you understand why many would call evolution a voodoo science. There is nothing in the evolutionary construct that one can call 'scientific' to verify the past. If there were, the Piltdown Man, Nebraska Man, Ida, Rodhocetus, Archaeoraptor and heaps of homologous, fossilized bones would never have slipped through the peer-review safety net and fooled the world, in some cases, for donkey years.

Religious jargons like: 'probably', 'most likely', 'it looks like', 'it should have been', 'it anticipates', 'it bursts onto the scene', and the likes permeate the bulk of the evolutionary literature and lingo. This is a classic evidence that there are no evidence for evolution – just untestable speculations of an unobservable past. Hardly anyone would quarrel with gravity or quantum mechanics as they are testable and reproducible, but biological evolution generates so much controversy by both the creationists and the unconvinced atheists. Why? It is because biological evolution cannot be observed and repeated – a demand by empirical science! If it is observable and reproducible, all debates will cease immediately, like the veracity of general relativity or quantum mechanics.

And the appeals to authorities, credentials, charts, artistic drawings, and just-so stories are legendary. Very often, it is only 'true' because 'it looks right to me'. Looking right to you or me, but not able to observe it happening, is not empirical science – it is as good as mass hysteria. Is it testable, falsifiable and reproducible? If not, it is as Max Planck puts it: nothing more than poetry and imagination.

> "Experiments are the only means of knowledge at our disposal. The rest is poetry, imagination."[10]

There is no empirical evidence for evolution. What is often touted as the 'evidence for evolution' is just the 'interpretation of the expert', and not the evidence for evolution. There is no evidence for evolution; there is only the interpretation of the experts on evolution. You cannot see biological evolution (bacterium to man) taking place presently; you are only second-guessing what might have happened. And you have no way of knowing if it happened – of how one fossilized bone is linked to the next in chronological order. And what cannot be observed and repeated cannot be taken as the indisputable 'evidence for evolution'.

One of the fatal flaws in biological evolution is that Darwinists cannot and, very often, will not differentiate between a fallible interpretation of an unrepeatable past event and an infallible observation of a present, testable experimentation. Creationists are behind testable science and are dead against untestable Darwinism. Science and Darwinism are two different disciplines – one, observable, testable and repeatable, while the other, unobservable, untestable and unrepeatable. Darwinism is not observational science!

> "My attempts to demonstrate Evolution by an experiment carried on for more than 40 years have completely failed. At least, I should hardly be accused of having started from a preconceived antievolutionary standpoint...
>
> It may be firmly maintained that it is not even possible to make a caricature of an evolution out of paleo-biological facts. The fossil material is now so complete that it has been possible to construct new classes, and the lack of transitional series cannot be explained as being due to the scarcity of material. The deficiencies are real, they will never be filled."[11] (Dr. Heribert Nilsson)

And peer reviews in biological evolution is not a surefire science. Oftentimes, it is just the sharing of fallible prejudices and facetious ignorance. *All the peer reviews on biological evolution are about untestable interpretations of unobservable and unrepeatable past events, and not empirical, observational science!* They will always be guesswork and guesstimates. Remember, 'it sure looks right to me' is not empirical science; it is no different from a caveman's approach in second-guessing the superstitious explanation behind a violent thunderstorm. Can you see it, test it, and repeat it? If not, all the evolutionary hollering and foot stomping would not help. And the piles of mistaken 'perfect missing links' keep piling up.

"To take a line of fossils and claim that they represent a lineage is not a scientific hypothesis that can be tested, but an assertion that carries the same validity as a bedtime story – amusing, perhaps even instructive, but not scientific."[12] (Henry Gee)

"Is Archaeopteryx the ancestor of all birds? Perhaps yes, perhaps no: there is no way of answering the question. It is easy enough to make up stories of how one form gave rise to another, and to find reasons why the stages should be favoured by natural selection. But such stories are not part of science, for there is no way to put them to the test."[13] (Dr. Colin Patterson)

And unlike a murder case in forensic science where we sometimes have a face or a DNA to begin with and to compare notes, and to nail the culprit with a high degree of certainty, biological evolution commences with a 'if I did not believe it, I would not have seen it' religious approach.

Doubtful findings are compared with doubtful findings in the hope of finding the truth. Questionable discoveries are piled on questionable discoveries to prove something that cannot be observed in real life and time. Conjectures are used to support hunches, and hunches are used to support conjectures. Fossils are used to date rock strata, and rock strata are used to date fossils. Some index fossils like the Coelacanth turn out to be an embarrassing 'living fossil' instead. Unobservable, past 'lookalikes' are compared with past, unobservable 'lookalikes' to prove they have to be alike. And how many of these fossilized 'lookalikes' turn out to be horribly unlike upon further investigation.

And how many of these uncorrected 'lookalikes' are still embedded in the biology textbooks today – Haeckel's fraudulent embryo drawings, the Horse series, Archaeopteryx (reptile to bird), Titaalik (fish to tetrapod), or Lucy and Ida (primate to man). The problem with these 'lookalikes' in the fossil record is that they turn out to be different species altogether and not the missing links as in numerous proven instances like the Archaeopteryx, Coelacanth, Titaalik, Ida, or Lucy, which for years were showcased as the perfect missing links and the indisputable proofs for evolution.

Evolutionism and Creationism are forever locked in some kind of 'quantum entanglement' – you cannot redefine one without affecting the other. When Darwinists redefine the universally accepted definition of a scientific theory to include the unobservable past, they have unwittingly made the wrong move and are checkmated by the creationists – they have just legitimized the 'God hypothesis'. Unobservable, past creationism now becomes another plausible scientific theory rivaling biological evolution. If evolutionists stick strictly to the definition of observational, empirical science, biological evolution ceases to be a scientific theory – it is unobservable and is relegated to a hypothesis – just like creationism. So, take your pick, whichever way, it is 'head I win, tail you lose' – to the creationists.

The evolutionists would often accuse the creationists that their belief in God is non-science – it is faith-based, unobservable, untestable and unrepeatable. And it is ironical the 'theory of evolution', when examined critically, finds itself in the same realm as the 'God hypothesis' – it is forensic or historical science – it too, cannot be observed to have happened. And yet, it is religiously believed and promoted as empirical science. Evolution is a hypothesis at best and a voodoo science at worst.

> "The fact of evolution is the backbone of biology, and biology is thus in the peculiar position of being a science founded on an improved theory – is it then a science or faith? Belief in the theory of evolution is thus exactly parallel to belief in special creation – both are concepts which believers know to be true but neither, up to the present, has been capable of proof."[14] (L. Harrison Matthews)

> "At present, science has no satisfactory answer to the question of the origin of life on the earth. Perhaps the appearance of life on the earth is a miracle. Scientists are reluctant to accept that view, but their choices are limited; either life was created on the earth by the will of a being outside the grasp of scientific understanding, or it evolved on our planet spontaneously, through chemical reactions occurring in nonliving matter lying on the surface of the planet.

> The first theory places the question of the origin of life beyond the reach of scientific inquiry. It is a statement of faith in the power of a Supreme Being not subject to the laws of science. The second theory is also an act of faith. The act of faith consists in assuming that the scientific view of the origin of life is correct, without having concrete evidence to support that belief."[15] (Robert Jastrow)

Evolution is a non-science in a cheap tuxedo attempting to pass off as science.

References:

1. Wolfgang Smith, cited from Ian Taylor, *Origins Answer Book*, p. 107

2. Richard Dawkins, *Battle over Evolution*, Bill Moyers interviews Richard Dawkins, 3 December 2004, PBS Network

3. Richard Dawkins, *The Genius of Charles Darwin (Episode 3),* Channel 4 (UK), 18th Aug 2008

4. The National Academy of Sciences, 1999

5. George G. Simpson, *The Non-prevalence of Humanoids*, in Science, 143, 1964, p. 770

6. Mayr, Ernst, *Darwin's Influence on Modern Thought*, Scientific American, 24 November 2009

7. Patterson, Colin, *Evolution*, 1978, London: British Museum of Natural History, p. 145-146

8. Jeffrey Schwartz, U-Pitt anthropology professor, on his paper *'Do Molecular Clocks Run at All?'* Biological Theory, 2/9/2007

9. Dr. Robert A. Milikan, physicist and Nobel Prize winner, in a speech before the American Chemical Society

10. Max Planck, *Advances in Biochemical Psychopharmacology*, Vol. 25, 1980, p. 3

11. Dr. Heribert Nilsson, *Synthetische Artbildung*, Verlag CWK Gleerup, Lund, Sweden, 1953, p. 1185 and 1212

12. Henry Gee, *In Search of Deep Time - Beyond the Fossil Record to a New History of Life*, p. 116-117

13. A letter from Dr. Colin Patterson to creationist Luther D. Sunderland

14. L. Harrison Matthews, *Introduction to Origin of the Species, by Charles Darwin*, 1971 edition, p. 10-11, 1971 edition

15. Robert Jastrow, *Until the Sun Dies*, New York: W.W. Norton, 1977, p. 62-63

The Greatest Poof of Evolution

"Firstly, why, if species have descended from other species by insensibly fine gradations, do we not everywhere see innumerable transitional forms? Why is not all nature in confusion instead of the species being, as we see them, well defined?"[1] (Charles Darwin)

If there is one proof that will forever end the debate between evolutionism and creationism, it will be the proof of living transitions. Our terrestrial landscape would be populated with 'half and half' of every living creature imaginable – there will be literally millions of transitional forms of evolving organisms and body plans – of apelike man; half gill and half lung; or half leg and half wing.

The theory of evolution predicted there will be a continuum of intermediates. They would be observable. This will make biological evolution empirical science where it is now demonstrable, falsifiable and reproducible. The plethora of living transitions would have put paid to the theory of creationism. We can now see it happening. And creationism would be a thing of the past and forever entombed in the annals of human history. And the mouths of the theists would be forever shut up. But, we cannot see it happening.

And like the observable and demonstrable law of gravity, biological evolution will be 'as good as cash'. But looking around, instead of the proof of evolution, we see only the 'poof' of evolution. Instead of witnessing a plethora of living transitions, we see the conspicuous absence of it. And in its place, there are unmistakable, genetic barriers erected that separate every imaginable taxon of critters. Every living thing is frozen in its designated kind and nothing is evolving into a different kind. There are variations and subspecies within its kind, but there are no observable transmutations into another kind! There are varieties of dogs, but no dog is on its way to become a non-dog.

If biological evolution did take place in time past, it would have taken place right now before our very eyes. It should never be a 'start-stop' process. Our textbooks would be filled with millions of snapshots of evolving creatures. It cannot be that large scale evolution did take place in the past but not now. And if the millions of transitional forms were 'survivable' in the past, they will be very 'survivable' today – semi-evolved creatures would still be crawling, burrowing, running, and flying everywhere. If evolving creatures were a dime a dozen in yesteryears, why do we not have them presently? Can any evolutionist provide an empirical reason for its hiatus? We should be in the middle of an unending continuum of observable intermediates. The proofs for evolution would have been plentiful and irrefutable. Evolutionists would emerge triumphant and creationists would be fossilized in quick time.

165

In addition, the men in white coats have verified that natural selection and random mutation have never ceased and are ever ongoing. Bacteria are still mutating and the beaks of finches are still changing. Our climate is still plagued with erratic weather, and predators still roam the savannas and prey in the oceans. And adaptation and exaptation to changing environments are ever ongoing. And the evolutionary arm race has never ceased. But what we observe today is a stasis where every animal and plant is stuck in their specified kinds – there are variants of dog, cat, and mouse, but they are still the dog, cat and mouse kinds.

And this stasis has been observed for 'millions of years' even in the 'living fossils' like the 'millions-of-years-old' fossilized blue-green algae (3.4 billion years), coelacanths (360 million years), horseshoe crabs (445 million years), squids (160 million years), or dragonflies (150 million years). These creatures and scores of others did not change into another kind despite the 'millions of years' of deep time. They look just like their present-day counterparts. Why? It is because there is an impassable genetic barrier called 'developmental constraint' that prevents one creature from evolving into another kind.

> "Both blue-green algae and bacteria fossils dating back 3.4 billion years have been found in rocks from S. Africa. Even more intriguing, the pleurocapsalean algae turned out to be almost identical to modern pleurocapsalean algae at the family and possibly even at the generic level."[2] (Science News)

> "... that is the potential mutations of a given biotype are normally limited, else we should have been able to observe drastic evolutionary changes in laboratory studies with bacteria. Despite the rapid rate of propagation and the enormous size of attainable populations, changes within initially homogeneous bacterial populations apparently do not progress beyond certain boundaries under experimental conditions."[3] (W. Braun)

This stasis is the 800-pound gorilla the Darwinists wish was never there. But there it sits, unmovable, in the path of an imaginary and illusory evolution. In case you have not noticed, this 'gorilla' is empirical science. There is nothing changing into something else presently and the fossil record favors creation – sudden appearance, stasis, and extinction, rather than evolution, even in deep time. Every distinct creature may drift 'sideway' but not evolve 'upward' – there are observable hybrids but there are no observable hopeful monsters which the theory of evolution predicts and fails.

There is a subtle evolutionary distraction today. The evolutionists would want us to focus on the 'dead transitions' instead of the 'living transitions' – the dead, untestable 'missing links' in the fossil record instead of the observable, living 'connecting links' everywhere. They attempt to prove that evolution did take place in the past through the 'fossil record' but not in the 'living record'. But why little is said about the living transitions? The answer has been staring at us in the face all this while dude – there are no living transitions to prove the theory of evolution, and stasis is the norm instead. Every creature or plant is frozen in its evolutionary 'stratum'. The present, living 'missing links' are not only missing, they are not even there despite the myriads of distinct plants and critters all around us.

The fact that we can practice taxonomy and classify all living things today into 'kinds' proves that there never was any evolution. Instead, it points to creationism. If evolution is true and ongoing, all living critters and plants will be unclassifiable – they will be just one vast, goofy continuum of gradualistic transitions. The biological demarcation between every living thing would be blurry and largely erased. How do you classify millions of evolving creatures with minutely, almost imperceptible, slightly modified, transitional scale to feather, fin to leg, or invertebrate to vertebrate?

This gradualism in evolution is what Darwin had posited: *natura non facit saltum* or 'nature takes no leaps'. But what we observe presently are largely classifiable species, genera, phyla, families and domains, instead of a continuum of confusion.

Darwinists would often tell us in a reassuring, calming, religious tone that it takes 'millions of years' for evolution to happen, and that we cannot observe it today because of the brevity of time. But the argument here is not about the 'millions of years' but the 'middle of things' – it is about the continuum of intermediates regardless of the time factor.

It is like how one American pilot, during the surprise attack on Pearl Harbor by the Japanese in World War II, thought he was chasing a single Jap Zero fighter but soon discovered that he was in the middle of a long line of enemy planes. And so it is with biological evolution – we are in the middle of an unending evolutionary transition independent of deep time. The paradigm of evolution includes the present time and is not exclusive to the past time. It is about 'every time' – the past, present, and future.

We should not be stuck 'at the end of a queue' but right 'in the thick of actions' – of one long, ongoing, relentless process of evolution that has never ceased since the first living cell supposedly emerged from some prehistoric warm pond. And we should still be part of the 'millions of years' of deep time, albeit, in the latter stage with potentially a far greater number of living, intermediary, transitional forms. There should be a spectacular display of evolving creatures of all stages. But none of this is observed today. Why the no show? It is because there never was any evolution dude! Not only are there no new kinds, but massive extinctions of species both now and before are expected as predicted by the creationists – critters may vary, go extinct, but not evolve!

Naturally or artificially, no creature presently has transmutated into something else. Richard Lenski's E-coli bacteria feeding on citrate are still bacteria despite more than 30 years of experimentation and more than 68,000 generations of selective breeding (it has to be a government project). And countless generations of fruit flies subjected to all kinds of 'tortures' and 'nukes' in the laboratory are still fruit flies with mutated dead ends – fruit flies with small wings, an extra pair of useless wings, curly wings, or bulging eyes. Nothing has transmutated into something else despite all human attempts to make them evolve.

This stubborn stasis is a consistent witness to the fact that evolution has never occurred. Around us, we don't see evolution happening naturally, and in the laboratory, we cannot make it happen artificially. Are your neurons starting to wake up?

> "After observing mutations in fruit flies for many years, Professor Goldschmidt fell into despair. The changes, he lamented, were so hopelessly micro [insignificant] that if a thousand mutations were combined in one specimen there would still be no new species."[4] (Norman Macbeth)

> "It is a striking, but not much mentioned fact that, though geneticists have been breeding fruit flies for sixty years or more in labs all round the world – flies which produce a new generation every eleven days – they have never yet seen the emergence of a new species or even a new enzyme."[5] (Gordon R. Taylor)

The principle of gradualism is a relentless and an unending process. The evolutionary arms race has never ceased. Some creatures are still chasing and chewing up other critters. The evolutionary show does not start and stop. It should be just one continuous, mesmerizing, evolving display of millions of living, transitional intermediates in adaptation to survive. Dawkins' *Mount Improbable* would be crawling with all kinds of creepy, goofy, continuum of confusion of all imaginations – half legs and half wings, incipient eyes and ears; or emerging organelles and organs. But today, his *Mount Improbable* is denuded of all the evolutionary foliage and scientific evidence.

Mount Improbable turns out to be *Mount Mission Impossible* with unscalable, vertical cliffs on all sides. Mutation cannot climb mountains and natural selection forces the unfit off the cliffs. There are no gentle slopes for one creature to evolve into another through gradualism or saltation. Nothing is evolving into something else before our very eyes. Stasis is the established rule and biological evolution is an observable joke.

There is a built-in genome that only permits variation and hybridization, but not evolution to a different kind. There is an impossible biological chasm, commonly known as 'developmental constraint', that will send any creature back to its gene pool if it attempts to alter its biochemical systems to switch from a gill to a lung or turn a leg into a wing. Can any Darwinist lay before us an evolving lung or wing from the fossil record or the 'living record'? This is science. All we see are fully developed gills and lungs, or legs and wings. There are no 'half and half' of any evolving organisms. Our 800-pound gorilla, stasis, is not only having the last laugh, but has been hysterically rolling on its sides since Charles Darwin penned down his book *On the Origin of Species* in 1859.

> "Biology has no proof at all of the spontaneous origin of life, or rather biology has proved its impossibility. There is no such thing as a gradation of life from elementary to complex. From a bacterium to a butterfly to man the biochemical complexity is substantially the same."[6] (Giuseppe Sermonti)

The heaps of 'living fossils' in the fossil record reveal that there was no transmutation into another kind despite the 'millions of years' of deep time. These deep time snapshots put paid to the idea of evolving creatures in time past. These are data; these are evidence.

And the absence of 'living transitions' — the continuum of present intermediates — reveals there is no biological evolution before us. The only thing left are the few, miserable pieces of fossilized bones — the questionable and speculative missing links — to lend support to this flimsy, bedtime story of evolution. These 'bones of contention' are quickly pulverized by the fact they are not testable in the laboratory to prove conclusively that they are the 'missing links' of the whole show. They are all about lookalikes, speculations, interpretations, just-so stories, and connecting the wrong dots. They are neither the indisputable evidence of evolution nor are they testable science! 'Now you see it, now you don't', is characteristic of the fifteen minutes of fame for these mistaken links. One day, they are touted as the 'missing link', the next, they are classified as the 'mistaken link' — from Piltdown Man to Ida, Tiktaalik, Archaeopteryx, Archaeoraptor, Lucy, Neanderthal, et al..

Biological evolution has never been observed both now in the living transitions and, in time past, in the living fossils. The 'poof of evolution' from the heaps of 'living fossils' in the fossil record and the lack of 'living transitions' before us – two very massive domains with millions of observable species – are now beyond dispute! The theory of common descent never happens!

"Evolution is data-poor and imagination-rich."[7]

References:

1. Charles Darwin, *The Origin of Species*

2. *Ancient Alga Fossil Most Complex Yet,* Science News, Vol. 108, 20 September 1975, p. 181

3. W. Braun, *Bacteria Genetics*

4. Norman Macbeth, *Darwin Retried,* 1971, p. 33

5. Gordon R. Taylor, *The Great Evolution Mystery,* 1983, p. 48

6. Giuseppe Sermonti, renowned geneticist, University of Perugia, Italy, *After Darwin – A Critique of Evolutionism,* Rusconi, 1980

7. A phrase borrowed from Michael Lemonick

Timber! There goes Darwin's Tree of Life

"The tree of life, one of the iconic concepts of evolution, has turned out to be a figment of our imagination."[1] (Graham Lawton)

"There isn't a tree of life. The tree of life is an artifact of some early scientific studies that aren't really holding up... So there is not a tree of life... there may be a bush of life."[2] (Craig Venter)

"We've just annihilated the tree of life. It's not a tree any more, it's a different topology entirely," says Syvanen. "What would Darwin have made of that?""[3] (Michael Syvanen)

"For a long time the holy grail was to build a tree of life," says Eric Bapteste, an evolutionary biologist at the Pierre and Marie Curie University in Paris, France. A few years ago it looked as though the grail was within reach. But today the project lies in tatters, torn to pieces by an onslaught of negative evidence. Many biologists now argue that the tree concept is obsolete and needs to be discarded. "We have no evidence at all that the tree of life is a reality," says Bapteste."[4] (Graham Lawton)

Evolutionists posit that the Darwinian Tree of Life in which a single, living, replicating entity – the mythical LUCA (last universal common ancestor) – somehow managed to blossom into the evolutionary tree with the different branches representing the different phyla. However, many today, both in the evolutionist and creationist camps, do not buy this TOL (Tree of Life). Instead, they see a BOL (Bush of Life) where individual phylum sprouts up separately from the Cambrian era onwards with no links to one another.

First, there are different genetic codes.

The DNA has a code reader that reads the four chemical letters (A, C, G, T) to translate the amino acids into proteins. Darwinists, like Richard Dawkins, believe there is only one universal genetic code for all living things, and any change in that will render the creature inoperative. If the genetic code is different, the same DNA sequence will produce largely rubbish or nothing at all. It will not produce functional proteins and that will most certainly kill the critter. For example, the same English alphabets with different codes (languages) will read differently:

> English: "For God so loved the world, that he gave his only begotten Son, that whosoever believeth in him should not perish, but have everlasting life." (*Bible*, John 3:16)
>
> Dutch: "Want alzo lief heeft God de wereld gehad, dat Hij Zijn eniggeboren Zoon gegeven heeft, opdat een iegelijk die in Hem gelooft, niet verderve, maar het eeuwige leven hebbe." (*Bible*, John 3:16)
>
> German: "Denn also hat Gott die Welt geliebt, daß er seinen eingeboren Sohn gab, auf daß alle, die an ihn glauben, nicht verloren werden, sondern das ewige Leben haben." (*Bible*, John 3:16)

Dawkins believes there is only one genetic code that defines life and if there is more than one genetic code, then it will spell disaster for evolution.

> "... the genetic code is universal, all but identical across animals, plants, fungi, bacteria, archaea and viruses. The 64-word dictionary, by which three letter DNA words are translated into 20 amino acids and one punctuation mark, which means 'start reading here' or 'stop reading here,' is the same 64-word dictionary wherever you look in the living kingdoms (with one or two exceptions too minor to undermine the generalization)...
>
> Any mutation in the genetic code itself (as opposed to mutations in the genes that it encodes) would have an instantly catastrophic effect, not just in one place but throughout the whole organism. If any word in the 64-word dictionary changed its meaning, so that it came to specify a different amino acid, just about every protein in the body would instantaneously change, probably in many places along its length. Unlike an ordinary mutation... this would spell disaster."[5]

Yes Richie, if there is more than one, it sure spells disaster for the theory of evolution. Craig Venter, the genome guru, and no friend to creationists, begs to differ. In *The Great Debate: What is Life,* February 12, 2011, (YouTube, about the 9th minute), Venter, an American biologist, who is one of the first to sequence the human genome shocked the whole panel of speakers by dropping the bombshell that there is more than one genetic code in the world of living things. And if there is more than one genetic code, there goes the mythical Darwinian Tree of Life. Instead, it points to the Designer's Bush of Life.

Craig Venter: "I'm not so sanguine as some of my colleagues here that there's only one life form on this planet. We have a lot of different types of metabolism, different organisms. I wouldn't call you [with reference to physicist Paul Davies] the same life form as the one we have that lives in pH 12 base, that would dissolve your skin if we dropped you in it."

Paul Davis: "Well, I've got the same genetic code. We all have a common ancestor."

Craig Venter: "You don't have the same genetic code. In fact, the Mycoplasmas [a group of bacteria Venter and his team have used to engineer synthetic chromosomes] use a different genetic code that would not work in your cells. So there are a lot of variations on the theme..."

Paul Davies: "But you're not saying it [i.e., Mycoplasma] belongs to a different tree of life from me, are you?"

Craig Venter: "There isn't a tree of life. The tree of life is an artifact of some early scientific studies that aren't really holding up... So there is not a tree of life... there may be a bush of life."

Lawrence Krauss: "I don't like that word." [*Well, facts are facts Lawrence. One needs to go where the evidence leads. There is no one universal genetic code to construct the mythical tree of life. It looks like another 'put up' job and the Creator is having the last laugh.*]

Richard Dawkins: "I'm intrigued at Craig saying that the tree of life is a fiction. I mean... the DNA code of all creatures that have ever been looked at is all but identical. Surely that means that they're all related? Doesn't it?"

There were lots of laughter following Dawkins' timid response to Venter's revelation and Venter could only smile at Dawkins' redundant question. He had earlier stated that there was never a universal genetic code for the entire biodiversity of life and there was never a single Darwinian Tree. There are many other genetic codes identified and the theory of common descent is just another bedtime story. Well, there goes Darwin's mythical tree – TIMBER! And great was the fall of it. The old Darwinian theory of common descent finally gives way to the new creative theory of uncommon descent.

"And God made the beast of the earth after his kind... and God saw that it was good."[6] (*Bible*)

DNA + Translation = Digital Code + Code Reader
= Intelligent Design + Intelligent Designer

(PS: There is more than one genetic code!)

Secondly, homologous (similar) structures are not necessarily produced by similar genes, and they do not consistently follow similar developmental pathways.

It is a taken by the Darwinists that homologous structures of different animals are produced by similar genes and they go through the same developmental pathways. Similar genes of different critters should produce the same eyes, guts or some other body plans. They are, after all, parts of the Darwinian Tree of Life. But the shocker is this: they don't! And that points to creation!

"But biologists have known for a hundred years that homologous [similar] structures are often not produced by similar developmental pathways. And they have known for thirty years that they are often not produced by similar genes, either. So there is no empirically demonstrated mechanism to establish that homologies are due to common ancestry rather than common design."[7] (Jonathan Wells)

"Therefore, homologous structures need not be controlled by identical genes, and homology of phenotypes does not imply similarity of genotypes. It is now clear that the pride with which it was assumed that the inheritance of homologous structures from a common ancestor explained homology was misplaced; for such inheritance cannot be ascribed to identity of genes...

But if it is true that through the genetic code, genes code for enzymes that synthesize proteins which are responsible (in a manner still unknown in embryology) for the differentiation of the various parts in their normal manner, what mechanism can it be that results in the production of homologous organs, the same 'patterns', in spite of their not being controlled by the same genes? I asked this question in 1938, and it has not been answered."[8] (Gavin R. DeBeer) [*Nor has it been answered today*, emphasis mine]

"Therefore, I do not understand the mechanisms needed to change body plans or the mechanisms along the descent pathway between the australopithecine brain and modern human brains if we were indeed commonly descended as predicted by the theory of universal common descent. Nobody else understands the mechanisms either. Nobody... Recall, evolution is both about the mechanism by which change occurs over time, and the theory of universal common descent. But the mechanisms are unknown and the theory of universal common descent is confronted by issues of uncommonness through ENCODE and orphan gene research. And each year the evidence for uncommonness is escalating."[9] (James Tour)

Thirdly, the Cambrian Explosion contradicts the Darwinian theory of common descent.

The oldest rock strata in the Cambrian Period, which is supposed to be about 570 – 500-million-year-old, is claimed to house the very first forms of life. It is the era in which the earliest living creatures were supposed to have their origins. In that first moment of life, one would expect to see the gradual evolution of the first living cell – from the single cell animals to the multicellular creatures. But instead, we see the instant appearance of almost all the major phyla in the animal kingdom. It is like, in Richard Dawkins' own words, "as though they were planted there". Sometimes, this epoch is known as the biological 'Big Bang' – an explosion of almost every phylum of living things without any traces of their origins.

Charles Darwin recognized that the Cambrian Explosion could potentially destroy his theory of evolution:

"There is another and allied difficulty, which is much more serious. I allude to the manner in which species belonging to several of the main divisions of the animal kingdom suddenly appear in the lowest known fossiliferous rocks."[10]

Renowned evolutionist Stephen J. Gould came to the same conclusion that the Cambrian Explosion speaks of uncommon descent:

"Modern multicellular animals make their first uncontested appearance in the fossil record some 570 million years ago – and with a bang, not a protracted crescendo. This 'Cambrian explosion' marks the advent (at least into direct evidence) of virtually all major groups of modern animals – and all within the minuscule span, geologically speaking, of a few million years."[11]

Even Richard Dawkins acknowledged that the Cambrian Explosion reveals creation rather than progressive gradualism:

"And we find many of them [Cambrian fossils] already in an advanced state of evolution, the very first time they appear. It is as though they were just planted there, without any evolutionary history. Needless to say, this appearance of sudden planting has delighted creationists."[12]

Of course, Dawkins believes the Cambrian critters were evolved, not created. He has to bend the evidence (sudden appearances) to fit a tattered theory (progressive evolution) even though the earlier Precambrian strata reveal no traces of copious slight modifications of body plans. There were fossilized soft body sponges, pollens, spores and bacteria, but there were no evolving body plans in the older, Precambrian record.

"The most famous such burst, the Cambrian explosion, marks the inception of modern multicellular life. Within just a few million years, nearly every major kind of animal anatomy appears in the fossil record for the first time... The Precambrian record is now sufficiently good that the old rationale about undiscovered sequences of smoothly transitional forms will no longer wash."[13] (Stephen Jay Gould)

"Granted an evolutionary origin of the main groups of animals, and not an act of special creation, the absence of any record whatsoever of a single member of any of the phyla in the Pre-Cambrian rocks remains as inexplicable on orthodox grounds as it was to Darwin."[14] (T. Neville George)

"The introduction of a variety of organisms in the early Cambrian, including such complex forms of the arthropods as the trilobites, is surprising... The introduction of abundant organisms in the record would not be so surprising if they were simple. Why should such complex organic forms be in rocks about six hundred million years old and be absent or unrecognized in the records of the preceding two billion years... If there has been evolution of life, the absence of the requisite fossils in the rocks older than the Cambrian is puzzling."[15] (Kay, Marshall, and Edwin H. Colbert)

As the mystery of this Cambrian explosion deepens, it is now known that there are hardly any more new phyla appearing thereafter. Instead of the predicted increase of phyla by the Darwinists, we have less today. Some phyla have gone extinct. It looks like biological evolution is going the wrong way – from more in the Cambrian era to less today. The evidence not only does not fit the prediction, it is fatal to the theory of evolution.

"A simple way of putting it is that currently we have about 38 phyla of different groups of animals, but the total number of phyla discovered during that period of time (including those in China, Canada, and elsewhere) adds up to over 50 phyla. That means [there are] more phyla in the very, very beginning, where we found the first fossils [of animal life], than exist now. Stephen J. Gould, [a Harvard University evolutionary biologist], has referred to this as the reverse cone of diversity. The theory of evolution implies that things get more and more complex and get more and more diverse from one single origin. But the whole thing turns out to be reversed. We have more diverse groups in the very beginning, and in fact more and more of them die off over time, and we have less and less now."[16] (Dr. Paul Chien)

"The paleontological data is consistent with the view that all of the currently recognized phyla had evolved by about 525 Ma. Despite half a billion years of evolutionary

177

exploration generated in Cambrian time, no new phylum level designs have appeared since then."[17] (Valentine, Erwin, and Jablonski)

"Evolutionary biology's deepest paradox concerns this strange discontinuity. Why haven't new animal body plans continued to crawl out of the evolutionary cauldron during the past hundreds of millions of years? Why are the ancient body plans so stable?"[18] (Jeffrey S. Levinton)

"It is considered likely that all the animal phyla became distinct before or during the Cambrian, for they all appear fully formed, without intermediates connecting one form to another."[19] (Douglas Futuyma)

There are less evidence of biological evolution today in this inceptive Cambrian period than in Darwin's day – the evolutionary time frame for this 'explosion' has become shorter (from 75 million years previously to less than 5 million years as agreed by most evolutionists today) and the diversities of phyla have literally exploded from the recent discoveries stretching from the Burgess Shale in the Canadian Rockies of British Columbia, Canada, to the Chengsjiang region in Yunnan, in Southern China. In short, the length of time of the 'explosion' has been shortened and the breath of the varieties of phyla of the 'explosion' is augmented tremendously. And that spells disaster for the theory of evolution. It is like everything was there in a brief geologic moment in the beginning. Biological evolution demands a simple root with a long period of time for the branches to gradually radiate out into upward complexity. Without that, you would need a miracle:

"Without gradualness in these cases, we are back to miracle..."[20] (Richard Dawkins)

Yes, Richie, you finally got it right! There was a miracle called 'creation'. And even soft-bodied parts were preserved in the Cambrian and Precambrian strata. And there were no evolving body plans to prove Darwin's theory of evolution.

"The long-held notion that Precambrian organisms must have been too small or too delicate to have been preserved in geologic materials... [is] now recognized to be incorrect."[21] (J. William Schopf)

In the final analysis, the explosion of life is not only limited to the Cambrian era, but in every taxon of living things – the explosion of practically every kind of critters and plants without any ancestors – from the ferns to the dinosaurs.

Fourthly, the discovery of the pervasive Horizontal Gene Transfer (HGT).

Molecular taxonomy, which is based upon a comparison of similarity in genes, has constructed a supposedly more precise, phylogenetic tree. It seems now a done deal with regard to this traditional, Darwinian tree. Every creature can now be hung on that tree with 'indisputable exactness' at the molecular level. But with the discovery of Horizontal Gene Transfer (HGT) in genomics, where parts of the gene can migrate or jump from creature to creature via the Bacteria, Archaea, and Eukarya, that Darwin's Tree is being chopped down. The solid branches in the Darwinian Tree now look more like dried up twigs ready to drop off.

The *New Scientists* published an honest admission on this mythical Darwinian Tree:

> "For a long time the holy grail was to build a tree of life," says Eric Bapteste, an evolutionary biologist at the Pierre and Marie Curie University in Paris, France. A few years ago it looked as though the grail was within reach. But today the project lies in Darwin's first sketch of an evolutionary tree of life tatters, torn to pieces by an onslaught of negative evidence. Many biologists now argue that the tree concept is obsolete and needs to be discarded. "We have no evidence at all that the tree of life is a reality," says Bapteste. That bombshell has even persuaded some that our fundamental view of biology needs to change. So what happened? In a nutshell, DNA...

> The true extent of HGT in bacteria and archaea (collectively known as prokaryotes) has now been firmly established. Last year, Dagan and colleagues examined more than half a million genes from 181 prokaryotes and found that 80 per cent of them showed signs of horizontal transfer (Proceedings of the National Academy of Sciences, vol 105, p 10039). Surprisingly, HGT also turns out to be the rule rather than the exception in the third great domain of life, the eukaryotes...

> The neat picture of a branching tree is further blurred by a process called endosymbiosis... These "endosymbionts" later transferred large chunks of their genomes into those of their eukaryote hosts, creating hybrid genomes. As if

that weren't complicated enough, some early eukaryotic lineages apparently swallowed one another and amalgamated their genomes, creating yet another layer of horizontal transfer...

Rose goes even further. "The tree of life is being politely buried, we all know that," he says. "What's less accepted is that our whole fundamental view of biology needs to change." Biology is vastly more complex than we thought... "The tree of life was useful," says Bapteste. "It helped us to understand that evolution was real. But now we know more about evolution, it's time to move on."[22] (Graham Lawton)

Others too, have studied and concluded that the Darwinian Tree of Life is more of a myth than a reality:

"A molecular palaeobiologist at nearby Dartmouth College, Peterson has been reshaping phylogenetic trees for the past few years, ever since he pioneered a technique that uses short molecules called microRNAs to work out evolutionary branchings. He has now sketched out a radically different diagram for mammals: one that aligns humans more closely with elephants than with rodents.

I've looked at thousands of microRNA genes, and I can't find a single example that would support the traditional tree," he says. The technique "just changes everything about our understanding of mammal evolution."[23] (Elie Dolgin)

"The edifice of the Modern Synthesis has crumbled, apparently, beyond repair... The discovery of pervasive HGT and the overall dynamics of the genetic universe destroys not only the Tree of Life as we knew it but also another central tenet of the Modern Synthesis inherited from Darwin, gradualism. In a world dominated by HGT, gene duplication, gene loss, and such momentous events as endosymbiosis, the idea of evolution being driven primarily by infinitesimal heritable changes in the Darwinian tradition has become untenable...

The summary of the state of affairs on the 150th anniversary of the Origin is somewhat shocking: in the post-genomic era, all major tenets of the Modern Synthesis are, if not outright overturned, replaced by a new and incomparably more complex vision of the key aspects of evolution (Box 1). So, not to mince words, the Modern Synthesis is gone. What's next? The answer... a postmodern synthesis."[24] (Eugene V. Koonin)

Even among the higher organisms where gene-swapping does not take place, the same story is true – the Darwinian tree is just a figment of a grand imagination.

"Syvanen recently compared 2000 genes that are common to humans, frogs, sea squirts, sea urchins, fruit flies and nematodes. In theory, he should have been able to use the gene sequences to construct an evolutionary tree showing the relationships between the six animals. He failed. The problem was that different genes told contradictory evolutionary stories. This was especially true of sea-squirt genes. Conventionally, sea squirts – also known as tunicates – are lumped together with frogs, humans and other vertebrates in the phylum Chordata, but the genes were sending mixed signals. Some genes did indeed cluster within the chordates, but others indicated that tunicates should be placed with sea urchins, which aren't chordates. "Roughly 50 per cent of its genes have one evolutionary history and 50 per cent another," Syvanen says."[25] (Graham Lawton)

"Phylogenetic incongruities can be seen everywhere in the universal tree, from its root to the major branchings within and among the various taxa to the makeup of the primary groupings themselves."[26] (Carl Woese)

J. CRAIG VENTER is no creationist but is one of leading scientists of the 21st century in genomic research. He is the founder and the president of the J. Craig Venter Institute. The Venter Institute conducts basic research that advances the science of genomics, specializes in human genome based medicine, and synthetic genomics, besides the many other fields. He is the author of *A Life Decoded: My Genome: My Life*. He writes:

> "One question is, can we extrapolate back from this data set to describe the most recent common ancestor. I don't necessarily buy that there is a single ancestor. It's counterintuitive to me. I think we may have thousands of recent common ancestors and they are not necessarily so common."[27] (J. Craig Venter)

In the end, it is not the creationist that brought down Darwin's tree of life; it is empirical science and honest Darwinists that toppled it. There never was a Darwinian tree. Empirical science is now revealing a created forest of life from the beginning instead. Every kind is a biological 'Big Bang' in its own right without ancestors. One modest man in yesteryear recognized the fatality of this discovery to the theory of evolution more than many other superficial evolutionists today; and strangely enough, that man was Charles Darwin himself, the progenitor of the Theory of Evolution.

> "The abrupt manner in which whole groups of species suddenly appear in certain formations, has been urged by several paleontologists – for instance, by Agassiz, Pictet, and Sedgwick – as a fatal objection to the belief in the transmutation of species. If numerous species, belonging to the same genera or families, have really started into life at once, the fact would be fatal to the theory of evolution through natural selection."[28]

And so it is Charlie! And so it is! There goes your bedtime story on evolution and your mythical tree of life – timber! God will always have the last laugh Charlie. No wonder you are feeling even more depressed these days.

> "The fossil record had caused Darwin more grief than joy. Nothing distressed him more than the Cambrian explosion, the coincident appearance of almost all complex organic designs..."[29] (Stephen Jay Gould)

If the biodiversity of life was never the outcome of a tree but a bush, then the Bible will return to haunt the Darwinists – "In the beginning God created..."[30] (*Bible*)

> "Most biologists now accept that the tree is not a fact of nature
> – it is something we impose on nature."[31]

References:

1. Graham Lawton, features editor of New Scientist, *Uprooting Darwin's Tree*, 24 January 2009

2. Craig Venter, *'The Great Debate: What is Life'*, Feb 12, 2011

3. Michael Syvanen, quoted in Graham Lawton, *Why Darwin was wrong about the tree of life*, New Scientist, 21 January 2009

4. Graham Lawton, *"Why Darwin was wrong about the tree of life,"* New Scientist, January 21, 2009 (emphasis added)

5. Richard Dawkins, *The Greatest Show On Earth*, 2009, p. 409

6. *Bible*, Genesis 1:25

7. Jonathan Wells, *Survival of the Fakest*, The American Spectator, January 2001, p. 22

8. Gavin R. DeBeer, formerly Professor of Embryology at the University of London and Director of the British Museum, Natural History, *Homology, An Unsolved Problem*, London: Oxford University Press, 1971, p. 16

9. James Tour, *Origin of Life, Intelligent Design, Evolution, Creation and Faith*, Rice University, Updated August 2017

10. Charles Darwin, *The Origin of Species*, p. 348

11. Gould, Stephen J., *Wonderful Life: The Burgess Shale and the Nature of History*, 1989, p. 23-24

12. Richard Dawkins, *The Blind Watchmaker*, London: W.W. Norton & Company, 1987, p. 229

13. Stephen Jay Gould, *An Asteroid to Die For, Discover*, October 1989, p. 65

14. T. Neville George, Professor of Geology at the University of Glasgow, *Fossils in Evolutionary Perspective, Science Progress,* Vol. 48, No. 189, January 1960, p. 5

15. Kay, Marshall, and Edwin H. Colbert, *Stratigraphy and Life History*, 1965, 736 p. 102-103, as cited in Morris, 1974

16. Dr. Paul Chien, chairman of the biology department at the University of San Francisco, *The Explosion of Life,* in an interview with Real Issue, 30 June 1997

17. Valentine, Erwin, and Jablonski, *Developmental Evolution of Metazoan Body Plans: The Fossil Evidence, Developmental Biology 173*, Article No. 0033, 1996, p. 376

18. Jeffrey S. Levinton, *The Big Bang of Animal Evolution*, Scientific American, Vol. 267, November 1992, p. 84

19. Douglas Futuyma, *Evolutionary Biology*, 1985, p. 325

20. Richard Dawkins, *River Out Of Eden* p. 83

21. J. William Schopf, *Trends in Ecology and Evolution*, 1994

22. Graham Lawton, *Uprooting Darwin's Tree*, New Scientist, 24 January 2009

23. Elie Dolgin, *Phylogeny: Rewriting evolution, Tiny molecules called microRNAs are tearing apart traditional ideas about the animal family tree*, 27 June 2012

24. Eugene V. Koonin, *The Origin at 150: Is a new evolutionary synthesis in sight?* 2009

25. Graham Lawton, *"Why Darwin was wrong about the tree of life,"* New Scientist (January 21, 2009

26. Carl Woese, *The Universal Ancestor*, Proceedings of the National Academy of Sciences USA, 95:6854-9859, June, 1998

27. J. Craig Venter, Craig Venter, *Life: What a Concept!* An Edge Special Event at Eastover Farm, 8.27.07

28. Charles Darwin, *The Origin of Species*, p. 344

29. Gould, Stephen Jay, *The Panda's Thumb*, 1980, p. 238-239

30. *Bible*, Genesis 1:1

31. *Editorial: Uprooting Darwin's Tree*, New Scientist, 21 January 2009

Bones of Contention

"Why is not every geological formation and every stratum full of such intermediate links? Geology assuredly does not reveal any such finely graduated organic chain; and this is the most obvious and serious objection which can be urged against the theory."[1] (Charles Darwin)

Evolutionary biologists postulate that evolution did take place but paleontologists are hard pressed to find the evidence in the fossil record. In theory, there would have been millions of transitional forms between the major taxa in the fossil record to make evolution 'as good as cash'. But the truth is that there are massively more gaps than alleged transitions in this fossil record even up to this present time. This is despite 120 years later after Darwin and tons of fossils were unearthed. World-renowned Stephen J. Gould, paleontologist and evolutionary biologist, was candid in his assessment of the rarity of transitional critters in the fossil record. He writes:

"The extreme rarity of transitional forms in the fossil record persists as the trade secret of paleontology. The evolutionary trees that adorn our textbooks have data only at the tips and nodes of their branches; the rest is inference, however reasonable, not the evidence of fossils... We fancy ourselves as the only true students of life's history, yet to preserve our favored account of evolution by natural selection we view our data as so bad that we never see the very process we profess to study."[2]

There are two ways to understand the fossil record – one, to let it talk (which is science), and two, to impose our dogmatism on it (which is anti-science). If the fossil record can talk, it will scream of sudden appearances without ancestors, abrupt extinctions without reasons, or a continuous existence of the same critter for 'millions of years' till today in the living fossils. It is strangely silent on the gradual transition from one kind to another.

"Every paleontologist knows that most new species, genera, and families, and that nearly all categories above the level of family appear in the record suddenly and are not led up to by known, gradual, completely continuous transitional sequences."[3] (George Gaylord Simpson)

"In the fossil record, missing links are the rule: the story of life is as disjointed as a silent newsreel, in which species succeed one another as abruptly as Balkan prime ministers. The more scientists have searched for the transitional forms that lie between species, the more they have been frustrated... Evidence from fossils now points overwhelmingly away from the classical Darwinism which most Americans learned in high school..."[4] (John Adler with John Carey)

"... one of the most striking and potentially embarrassing features of the fossil record. The majority of major groups appear suddenly in the rocks, with virtually no evidence of transition from their ancestors."[5] (Douglas Futuyma)

"No wonder paleontologists shied away from evolution for so long. It never seemed to happen... When we do see the introduction of evolutionary novelty, it usually shows up with a bang, and often with no firm evidence that the fossils did not evolve elsewhere! Evolution cannot forever be going on somewhere else. Yet that's how the fossil record has struck many a forlorn paleontologist looking to learn something about evolution."[6] (Niles Eldredge)

But, evolutionists would often gag the mouth of our poor fossil record and instead, like the skillful ventriloquist, make it talk their talk – there has to be millions of transitions even though we do not see them. "There has to be but we do not see them" – it sounds familiar, we have heard that somewhere before – ah yes, another faith-based-without-evidence religion! The theory of evolution boasts of the millions of transitions for the millions of species, but the fossil record over deep time is strangely silent on their supposedly, obvious existence. Who should we listen to? Which is empirical science? The following reveals the honest evaluations of some very eminent evolutionists:

"The history of most fossil species includes two features particularly inconsistent with gradualism: 1. Stasis. Most species exhibit no directional change during their tenure on earth. They appear in the fossil record looking much the same as when they disappear; morphological change is usually limited and directionless. 2. Sudden appearance. In any local area, a species does not arise gradually by the steady transformation of its ancestors; it appears all at once and 'fully formed.'"[7] (Stephen. J. Gould)

"Paleontologists ever since Darwin have been searching (largely in vain) for the sequences of insensibly graded series of fossils that would stand as examples of the sort of wholesale transformation of species that Darwin envisioned as the natural product of the evolutionary process. Few saw any reason to demur – though it is a startling fact that... most species remain recognizably themselves, virtually unchanged throughout their occurrence in geological sediments of various ages."[8] (Niles Eldredge)

"We now come to perhaps the most serious of defects in the evolutionary theory – the complete absence of transitional forms. If life has always been in a continual stream of transmutation from one form to another, as evolutionists insist, then we should certainly expect to find as many fossils of the intermediate stages between different forms as of the distinct kinds themselves. Yet, no fossils have been found that can be considered transitional between the major groups or phyla! From the beginning, these organisms were just clearly and distinctly set apart from each other as they are today. Instead of finding a record of fine graduations preserved in the fossil record, we invariably find large gaps. This fact is absolutely FATAL to the general theory of evolution."[9] (Scott M. Huges)

How do you differentiate between a 'missing link' and a 'mistaken link'? How do you differentiate between a transition and a homologous but yet totally unrelated species by looking at the fossils? If paleontologists are honest, they will have to rely on 'it looks right to me' rather than by a foolproof, rigorous, testable, repeatable, scientific experimentation – like subjecting the law of gravity to repeatable testings in the laboratory. It will always be about a dogmatic interpretation rather than a testable evidence – "it sure looks right to me and it has to be right, end of story". The problem with fossils is that you can make the bones sing any song you like.

"A five million-year-old piece of bone that was thought to be a collarbone of a humanlike creature is actually part of a dolphin rib... The problem with a lot of anthropologists is that they want so much to find a hominid that any scrap of bone becomes a hominid bone."[10] (Dr. Tim White)

"Is Archaeopteryx the ancestor of all birds? Perhaps yes, perhaps no: there is no way of answering the question. It is easy enough to make up stories of how one form gave rise to another, and to find reasons why the stages should be favoured by natural selection. But such stories are not part of science, for there is no way to put them to the test."[11] (Dr. Colin Patterson)

Historically, many 'missing links' turn out later to be embarrassing 'mistaken links' – from the Piltdown Man to Archaeopteryx, Tiktaalik, Lucy, Ida, and scores of other mistaken links. Most of the past missing links have a certain shelf life – today, they are the 'missing links', and tomorrow, after some newer discoveries, they turn out to be another pathetic 'mistaken link' - a different or extinct species. Things have become so bad for the evolutionary camp that some would use the term 'intermediate features' instead of 'missing links', to avoid any further embarrassment. But again, how do you differentiate between intermediate features and features that belong to another unrelated or extinct species? We are back to square one.

If we were to take a step back and ask this honest question: Why is there so much controversy in the fossil record from both the creationist and the evolutionist camps? Why do the missing links turn out to be embarrassing mistaken links? Is there a place we can put our finger at and say, "Aha, this is the real culprit." Over time, I have come to the conclusion that the real problem is not about the untestable bones per se but the process or method the Darwinists use to derive at their conclusions.

There is no foolproof, surefire, scientific apparatus available to the Darwinists to test their fossilized specimens to prove they are the missing links. You can't drop this 'evolutionary ball', compute its rate of descent, and come up with a testable formula like gravity. It is a past, unobservable event. And you cannot reproduce it presently. No creature is transmutating into another kind before our eyes. And a scientific theory demands that you can observe, falsify, and reproduce it to the satisfaction of the peer review committee.

There is a wide chasm between 'it looks right to me' and 'it is right'. These missing links would be thrown out of any courtroom as evidence for evolution if, the best the Darwinists can come up with is that 'it looks right to me'. It will be laughed off and ridiculed by the legal community. But the Darwinists do not seem troubled by these fiascos. Food for thoughts – why is the Pakicetus linked to the evolution of whale and not dolphin? Both are aquatic mammals with many similar features. It is about an obvious guesswork, not science.

There is a patent disconnect between evolutionism and science – evolution speculates, science proves. And evolution is not science! Evolution is evolution, and science is science. And evolution pretends to be science but fails on an epic scale. Can't the Darwinists see that hardly anyone quarrels with the findings in physics, chemistry, or mathematics? There may be differing opinions but the observations are there unlike the unobservable evolution from the bacterium to man. And the fossilized bones will always be the untestable 'bones of contention'.

Archaeopteryx (Dinosaur-to-Bird): Archaeopteryx (ancient wing), the famous, purported intermediate between dinosaur and bird, was first discovered in the Solnhofen Limestone Formation in Bavaria, Germany, in 1861. It was supposed to be living in the late Jurassic era, between 150-148 MYA. Seven other variants were later found. It has features of both birds and supposedly dinosaurs and was, for a period of time, the icon for the evolution of dinosaur to bird.

> "Archaeopteryx: This earliest known flying bird was discovered within two years of the publication of *On the Origin of Species*, fulfilling Darwin's prediction of fossil creatures that would link major species groups – in this case, dinosaurs and birds."[12] (National Geographic)

Then, there was a tussle among the evolutionists as to whether it is more avian or dinosaurian. Archaeopteryx has claws on its wings but so has the ostrich, hoatzin, etc. Tons of papers were written on this never-ending debate. There were two intractable barriers for the theropod to evolve into bird – one, theropod dinosaurs have movable thighbones while the birds' are fixed to support their lungs; and two, theropods breathe in and out of their mouth in a tidal manner, reversing between inhalation and exhalation, while birds breathe in through the mouth and out through the body, in a circulatory fashion for efficiency of flight. However, Archaeopteryx cannot be the ancestor of modern birds as modern birds are found in the fossil record older than it. The son cannot be older than the father.

> "A prehistoric beast the size of a pheasant has become a contender for the title of oldest bird to stalk the Earth. The small, feathered "Dawn" bird lived around 160m years ago, about 10m years before Archaeopteryx, which holds the official title of the earliest bird known to science. The new species, which scientists have named Aurornis xui... pushes Archaeopteryx off its perch as the oldest member of the bird lineage."[13] (The Guardian)

> "Fossil remains claimed to be of two crow-sized birds 75 million years older than Archaeopteryx have been found... a paleontologist at Texas Tech University, who found the fossils, says they have advanced avian features... tends to confirm what many paleontologists have long suspected, that Archaeopteryx is not on the direct line to modern birds."[14] (Nature)

"For one thing, birds are found earlier in the fossil record than the dinosaurs they are supposed to have descended from," Ruben said. "That's a pretty serious problem, and there are other inconsistencies with the bird-from-dinosaur theories."[15] (Science Daily)

"But there are too many structural differences between Archaeopteryx and modern birds for the latter to be descendants of the former. In 1985, University of Kansas paleontologist Larry Martin wrote: "Archaopteryx is not ancestral of any group of modern birds." Instead it is "the earliest known member of a totally extinct group of birds." And in 1996 paleontologist Mark Norell, of the American Museum of Natural History in New York, called Archaeopteryx "a very important fossil," but added that most paleontologists now believe it is not a direct ancestor of modern birds."[16] (Jonathan Wells)

"Paleontologists have tried to turn Archaeopteryx into an earth-bound, feathered dinosaur. But it's not. It is a bird, a perching bird. And no amount of 'paleobabble' is going to change that."[17] (Alan Feduccia)

Additional Resources: *Dinosaur to Bird Evolution Creation training initiative* (YouTube) / *Formed to Fly with Dr. David Menton* (dinosaur – bird evolution refuted) – *Origins* (YouTube)

Titaalik (Fish-to-Tetrapod): Tiktaalik roseae, the 'fishapod', is a 375-million-year-old fossil fish discovered in 2004 on Ellesmere Island, Nunavut, in northern Canada. The discovery, made by Edward B. Daeschler of the Academy of Natural Sciences, Neil H. Shubin from the University of Chicago, and Harvard University Professor Farish A. Jenkins. It was touted as the 'missing link' between fish and the tetrapod.

"Tiktaalik is the perfect missing link – perfect, because it almost exactly splits the difference between fish and amphibian, and perfect because it is missing no longer. We have the fossil. You can see it, touch it..."[18] (Richard Dawkins)

But in 2009, they found footprints of tetrapods in Poland that are '18 million years' older than the Tiktaalik! Richie Dawkins' transitional Titaalik is history – it is just another passing, evolutionary bedtime story to put the uninformed public to sleep.

> "Some prints, showing individual digits, were found in limestone slabs unearthed in a quarry near Zacheɫmie, Poland, dated to about 395 million years ago — more than 18 million years before tetrapods were thought to have evolved... This would mean that large, land-roaming tetrapods would have coexisted for 10 million years with the elpistostegids — including Tiktaalik roseae, which lived 375 million years ago — a group thought to mark the transition of from fish to land-roaming animals."[19] (Rex Dalton)

> "They force a radical reassessment of the timing, ecology and environmental setting of the fish – tetrapod transition, as well as the completeness of the body fossil record."[20] (Nature)

There goes another 'perfect missing link' and the 'missing no more' illusion of the evolutionists. Dawkins' book, *The Greatest Show on Earth,* turns out to be, *The Greatest Hoax on Earth.* And real science has uncovered heaps of other 'perfect missing links' that are neither 'perfect' nor 'links' nor 'missing' at all. They were never part of the evolutionary show.

Additional Resources: *Polish footprints cause Tiktaalik Trouble* (YouTube) / *'Walking with Tetrapods: by Nature Video'* (YouTube)

Rodhocetus (Mammal-to-Whale): Dr. Philip Gingerich discovered Rodhocetus' fossils in 1992 while excavating in Pakistan. It is supposedly from the Early Eocene (47 million years ago) and apparently had primitive features seen in land mammals, but also exhibited derived characteristics found only in later ocean-dwelling species. Gingerich believes that it is an excellent candidate for a direct ancestor of modern whales.

From the drawings in the museums and textbooks, Rodhocetus has flippers and a fluke - a whale's 'tail'. In 2001, Dr. Carl Werner interviewed this leading scientist on whale evolution and discovered to his horror that Rodhocetus did not have a fluke nor flippers in the actual fossils. The following are from his DVD *Evolution: the Grand Experiment Vol. 1:*

"I went to the museum to see the actual fossils and film the interview. When I arrived, I noticed that the fossils of the most spectacular aspect of Rodhocetus were missing. There were no fossils of the arms and tail yet they had flippers and a whale's tail on the diagram. When I pointed this out to Dr. Gingerich in the interview, he retracted his claim that Rodhocetus had flippers or a fluke. His admission in this interview was simply stunning. My confidence was shaken."

In the ensuing interview, Dr. Gingerich, to his credit, frankly admitted:

"I speculated that it might have had a fluke, I now doubt that Rodhocetus would have had a fluked tail... Since then we have found the forelimbs, the hands, and the front arms of Rodhocetus, and we understand that it doesn't have the kind of arms that can spread out like flippers on a whale."[21]

This 'whale of a tale' has been featured in *National Geographic* as another 'missing link'. This is another of those just-so stories used to lend support to the elusive theory of evolution. Rodhocetus never had a fluke and flippers but is an extinct land animal! Evolutionists were suckered into using this fraud in their debates with creationists. And you can still find Rodhocetus with its imaginary fluke in museums all over the world. And you call this cutting-edge science? It is more of a cutting-edge scam! And science is supposed to be self-correcting, but the public is still conveniently kept in the dark.

Additional Resources: *Dr. Phil Gingerich Interview About Rodhocetus* (YouTube) / *Dismantling Whale Evolution* (YouTube)

Lucy (Primate-to-Man): Paleontologist Donald Johanson discovered the fossil Lucy, Australopithecus afarensis, roughly the size of a chimpanzee, in 1974, in Hadar, Ethiopia. Only 40% of the bones were found. Lucy is estimated to be about 3.2-million-year-old. She is probably the most famous 'missing link' between apelike creature and man. Lots of artistic imaginations and touch ups have been put into it to make it look 'half ape and  half human', with a fossilized thoughtful gaze in her almost human eyes.

Lucy's fossilized bones are about only 40% complete. She is basically an extinct chimp-like, knuckle-walking ape with locked wrists, and is not bipedal as is often claimed. Her inner ear is characteristic of a chimpanzee rather than that of a human. One of the spinal vertebrate was later discovered to belong to an extinct baboon (Theropithecus). Her pelvis was remodeled to make it look more humanlike. And the 400 specimens that were supposedly to have been found are 400 pieces of bones and teeth (35%) and not 400 more skeletons as they are often portrayed. They couldn't even fill a billiard table.

> "Lucy's skull is so incomplete that most of it is imagination made of plaster of paris."[22] (Richard Leakey)

> "... images of the inner ear of the specimen show it to have semicircular canals more like those of chimpanzees than of modern humans. The fluid-filled semicircular canals are crucial in maintaining balance, and so all three lines of evidence suggest that the locomotion of A. afarensis was unlikely to have been restricted to walking on two feet."[23] (Bernard Wood)

> "The fact that the anterior portion of the iliac blade faces laterally in humans but not in chimpanzees is obvious. The marked resemblance of AL 288-1 [Lucy] to the chimpanzee is equally obvious."[24] (J. T. Stern and R. L. Susman)

> "Regardless of the status of Lucy's knee joint, new evidence has come forth that Lucy has the morphology of a knuckle-walker."[25] (Richmand and Strait)

> "... the australopithecines... are now irrevocably removed from a place in the evolution of human bipedalism, possibly from a place in a group any closer to humans than to African apes and certainly from any place in the direct lineage."[26] (Dr. Charles Oxnard)

Additional Resources: *Lucy the Australopithecus Debunked in 11 Minutes* (YouTube) / *Lucy Not a Missing Link* (YouTube) / *Ape Man and the Bible: Will the Real Ape-Man Please Stand Up* (YouTube)

Let us hear what those in the know have to say about the biasness, frauds and disingenuousness in trying to prove the evolution of man:

"There is no such thing as a total lack of bias. I have it; everybody has it. The fossil hunter in the field has it... In everybody who is looking for hominids, there is a strong urge to learn more about where the human line started. If you are working back at around three million, as I was, that is very seductive, because you begin to get an idea that that is where Homo did start. You begin straining your eyes to find Homo traits in fossils of that age... Logical, maybe, but also biased. I was trying to jam evidence of dates into a pattern that would support conclusions about fossils which, on closer inspection, the fossils themselves would not sustain."[27] (Johanson, Donald C. and Maitland Edey)

"To attempt to restore the soft parts is an even more hazardous undertaking. The lips, the eyes, the ears, and the nasal tip, leave no clues on the underlying bony parts. You can with equal facility model on a Neanderthaloid skull the features of a chimpanzee or the lineaments of a philosopher. These alleged restorations of ancient types of man have very little if any scientific value and are likely only to mislead the public... So put not your trust in reconstructions."[28] (Earnst A. Hooten)

"I spoke with many Neanderthal experts in the course of making this film (for NOVA), and I found them all to be intelligent, friendly, well-educated people, dedicated to the highest principles of scientific inquiry. I also got the impression that each one thought the last one I talked to was an idiot, if not an actual Neanderthal... The more people I spoke with, the more confusing it got... Listening to the archeologists and anthropologists talk about their work (and their colleagues' work), I heard the same frustrations voiced again and again: People are driven by their preconceptions. They see what they want to see. They find what they're looking for..."[29] (Mark Davis)

The Horse Evolution: One of the iconic proofs of evolution is the evolution of the horse. The neatly drawn diagram from Eohippus to Equus has been published in biological textbooks and displayed in museums around the world. To the uninitiated, this looks convincing, but those who have studied the specifics found it incredible that it managed to sneak its way past the peer review community. The Darwinists are so eager to promote their wares and the public is so naive to buy it unquestioningly that they ended up with a blatant fraud unknowingly.

"There have been an awful lot of stories, some more imaginative than others, about what the nature of that history [of life] really is. The most famous example, still on exhibit downstairs, is the exhibit on horse evolution prepared perhaps fifty years ago. That has been presented as the literal truth in textbook after textbook. Now I think that is lamentable, particularly when the people who propose those kinds of stories may themselves be aware of the speculative nature of some of that stuff."[30] (Niles Eldredge)

"The popularly told example of horse evolution, suggesting a gradual sequence of changes from four-toed fox-sized creatures living nearly 50 million years ago to today's much larger one-toed horse, has long been known to be wrong. Instead of gradual change, fossils of each intermediate species appear fully distinct, persist unchanged, and then become extinct. Transitional forms are unknown."[31] (Boyce Rensberger)

"But perhaps the most serious weakness of Darwinism is the failure of paleontologists to find convincing phylogenies or sequences of organisms demonstrating major evolutionary change... The horse is often cited as the only fully worked-out example. But the fact is that the line from Eohippus to Equus is very erratic. It is alleged to show a continual increase in size, but the truth is that some variants were smaller than Eohippus, not larger. Specimens from different sources can be brought together in a convincing-looking sequence, but there is no evidence that they were actually ranged in this order in time."[32] (Gordon Rattray Taylor)

"Once ensconced in textbooks, misinformation becomes cocooned and effectively permanent, because, as stated above, textbooks copy from previous texts. (I have written two essays on this lamentable practice: one on the amusingly perennial description of the eohippus, or "dawn horse," as the size of a fox terrier, even though most authors, including yours truly, have no idea of the dimensions or appearance of this breed...)."[33] (Stephen J. Gould)

"The family tree of the horse is beautiful and continuous only in the textbooks."[34] (Heribert Nilsson)

Haeckel's Embryology: In 1860, Prof. Ernst Heinrich Philipp August Haeckel (1834-1919), an admirer of Charles Darwin, cooked up the 'Law of Recapitulation', also known as 'ontogeny recapitulates phylogeny', to prove different creatures will go through a similar developmental pathway in their early stages and that the human embryo repeats all the stages of its evolutionary history.

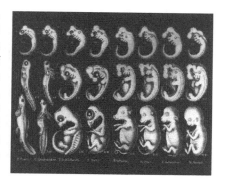

His famous but fraudulent chart has been in circulation till this day in the many evolutionary textbooks and science journals. He fudged the drawings of the different embryos in their early stages to accentuate the similarities between them and erase their differences.

> "This is one of the worst cases of scientific fraud. It's shocking to find that somebody one thought was a great scientist was deliberately misleading. It makes me angry... What he [Haeckel] did was to take a human embryo and copy it, pretending that the salamander, and the pig and all the others looked the same at the same stage of development. They don't... These are fakes."[35] (Nigel Hawkes)

> "[Haeckel] called this the biogenetic law, and the idea became popularly known as recapitulation. In fact Haeckel's strict law was soon shown to be incorrect. For instance, the early human embryo never has functioning gills like a fish, and never passes through stages that look like an adult reptile or monkey."[36] (Ken McNamara)

In 1997, embryologist Dr. Michael K. Richardson and his colleagues published the actual pictures of the embryos in question and showed the marked differences between them. This revelation blew up in the face of the evolutionary community.

> "Not only did Haeckel add or omit features, Richardson and his colleagues report, but he also fudged the scale to exaggerate similarities among species, even when there were 10-fold differences in size. Haeckel further blurred differences by neglecting to name the species in most cases, as if one representative was accurate for an entire group of animals. In reality, Richardson and his colleagues

note, even closely related embryos such as those of fish vary quite a bit in their appearance and developmental pathway. "It (Haeckel's drawings) looks like it's turning out to be one of the most famous fakes in biology."[37] (Elizabeth Pennisi)

"Surely the biogenetic law is as dead as a doornail. It was finally exorcised from biology textbooks in the fifties. As a topic of serious theoretical inquiry it was extinct in the twenties..."[38] (Keith S. Thomson)

In 1874, when exposed by his contemporary, Dr. Wilhelm His, Sr., professor of anatomy at the University of Leipzig, and a world famous comparative embryologist, Haeckel confessed to his fraud but his chart lives on – a classic example of the tenacity of manufactured data in support of an imaginary evolution. And talk about blame shifting, Haeckel had no qualms pointing out that many of his evolutionary colleagues were caught in same web of lies:

"After this compromising confession of 'forgery' I should be obliged to consider myself condemned and annihilated if I had not the consolation of seeing side by side with me in the prisoner's dock hundreds of fellow – culprits, among them many of the most trusted observers and most esteemed biologists. The great majority of all the diagrams in the best biological textbooks, treatises and journals would incur in the same degree the charge of 'forgery,' for all of them are inexact, and are more or less doctored, schematized and constructed."[39] (Elizabeth Pennisi)

But the lie lives on:

"Haeckel's confession got lost after his drawings were subsequently used in a 1901 book called *Darwin and After Darwin* and reproduced widely in English language biology texts."[40] (Elizabeth Pennisi)

Additional Resources: *Countering revisionism—part 1: Ernst Haeckel, fraud is proven, by E. van Niekerk*

It is out of the scope of this book to deal with the many other 'missing links' which, over time, were proven to be nothing more than the usual mistaken links. By and large, the fossil record reveals more about creationism than evolutionism – distinct, extinct or even living creatures are imprinted on these 'rocks of ages'. Alleged transitions are strangely more of the exceptions than the rule. If evolution were true, there would be logically millions of transitional fossilized snapshots to prove its veracity. No matter how rare fossil formations may be, there would have been heaps of obvious transitions over the 'millions of years' of deep time.

Interestingly, the search for the missing links reveals more about the Darwinists than the story of evolution. Many lookalike bones are hurriedly promoted in the science journals and museums to be the next 'missing no more' missing links. After a fifteen minutes of fame, they will inevitably be dethroned. It sounds weird but the Darwinists seem enamored in making monkeys out of themselves.

> "... perhaps generations of students of human evolution, including myself, have been flailing about in the dark; that our data base is too sparse, too slippery, for it to be able to mold our theories. Rather the theories are more statements about us and ideology than about the past. Paleoanthropology reveals more about how humans view themselves than it does about how humans came about. But that is heresy."[41] (Sean Pitman)

> "The success of Darwinism was accomplished by a decline in scientific integrity."[42] (Dr. W. R. Thompson)

In the end, the fossil record is more of a friend to the creationists than the evolutionists. Evolution predicts millions of observable transitions, but the data is sparse, questionable and mostly absent. Creationism predicts that every kind is created without ancestors and the evidence shows that it is so.

> "In most people's minds, fossils and Evolution go hand in hand. In reality, fossils are a great embarrassment to Evolutionary theory and offer strong support for the concept of Creation. If Evolution were true, we should find literally millions of fossils that show how one kind of life slowly and gradually changed to another kind of life. But missing links are the trade secret, in a sense, of paleontology. The point is, the links are still missing. What we really find are gaps that sharpen up the boundaries between kinds. It's those gaps which provide us with the evidence of Creation of separate kinds. As a matter of fact, there are gaps between each of the major kinds of plants and animals. Transition forms are missing by the millions. What we do find are separate and complex kinds, pointing to Creation."[43] (Dr. Gary Parker)

"What the "record" shows is nearly a century of fudging and finagling by scientists attempting to force various fossil morsels and fragments to conform to Darwin's notions, all to no avail. Today the millions of fossils stand as very visible, ever-present reminders of the paltriness of the arguments and the overall shabbiness of the theory that marches under the banner of evolution."[44] (Jeremy Rifkin)

"My ancestors were human. Sorry about yours."[45]

References:

1. Charles Darwin, *Origin of Species*, 1872, p. 413

2. Stephen J. Gould, *Evolution's Erratic Pace*, Natural History, vol. 86, May 1987, p. 14

3. George Gaylord Simpson, evolutionist, *The Major Features of Evolution*, New York, Columbia University Press, 1953 p. 360

4. John Adler with John Carey: *Is Man a Subtle Accident*, Newsweek, Vol. ct. 96, No. 18, November 3, 1980, p. 95

5. Futuyma, D., *Science on Trial: The Case for Evolution*, 1983, p. 82

6. Eldredge, N., *Reinventing Darwin*, Wiley, New York, p. 95, 1995

7. Stephen. J. Gould, evolutionist, Natural History, 86:14, 1977

8. Eldredge, Niles, *Progress in Evolution?* New Scientist, vol. 110, June 5, 1986, p. 55

9. Scott M. Huges. PH.D, Newsweek, November 3, 1980

10. Dr. Tim White, anthropologist, University of California, Berkeley, as quoted by Ian Anderson *'Hominoid collarbone exposed as dolphin's rib'*, in New Scientist, 28 April 1983, p. 199

11. A letter from Dr. Colin Patterson to creationist Luther D. Sunderland

12. National Geographic, 2009

13. *Early bird beat Archaeopteryx to worm by 10 m years*, The Guardian, 2013

14. Nature, vol. 322, 1986, p. 677

15. *Discovery Raises New Doubts About Dinosaur-bird Links*, Science Daily, June 9, 2009, Oregon State University

16. Jonathan Wells, *Icons of Evolution*, 2000, p. 116

17. Alan Feduccia – a world authority on birds from UNC Chapel Hill, quoted in *"Archaeopteryx: Early Bird Catches a Can of Worms,"* Science Feb. 5, 1994, p. 764-5

18. Richard Dawkins, *The Greatest Show on Earth*, p. 169

19. Rex Dalton, *Discovery pushes back date of first four-legged animal*, Nature, 6 January 2010, doi:10.1038/news.2010.1

20. *Tetrapod Trackways from the early Middle Devonian period of Poland*, Nature 463, 43-48, 7 January 2010, doi: 10.1038/ nature 08623

21. *Evolution: the Grand Experiment Vol. 1*, DVD; interview by Dr. Werner on August 28, 2001

22. The Weekend Australian, May 7-8, 1983, Magazine section, p. 3

23. Bernard Wood, *Nature* 443, 278-281, 21 Sept 2006

24. J T Stern and R. L. Susman, *American Journal of Physical Anthropology*, 80:279, 1983

25. Richmand and Strait, *Evidence that Humans Evolved from Knuckle-Walking Ancestor, Nature 2000*

26. Dr. Charles Oxnard, *The Order of Man: A Biomathematical Anatomy of the Primates*, p. 332

27. Johanson, Donald C. and Maitland Edey, *Lucy: The Beginnings of Humankind*, New York: Simon & Schusterp, 1981, p. 257, 258

28. Earnst A. Hooten, Harvard, *Up From The Ape*, p. 332

29. Mark Davis, who investigated the story on Neanderthals for NOVA

30. Niles Eldredge, Harper's, February 1984, p. 60

31. Boyce Rensberger, Houston Chronicle, November 5, 1980, p. 15

32. Gordon Rattray Taylor, *The Great Evolution Mystery*, Abacus, Sphere Books, London, 1984, p. 230

33. Stephen J. Gould, *Abscheulich! (Atrocious)*, Natural History, 2000, 109[2]: 45

34. Heribert Nilsson, *Synthetische Artbildung*, Gleerup, Sweden: Lund University, 1954

35. Nigel Hawkes, The Times (London), 11 August 1997, p. 14

36. Ken McNamara, *Embryos and Evolution*, New Scientist, vol. 12416, 16 October 1999

37. Elizabeth Pennisi, *Haeckel's Embryos: Fraud Rediscovered*, Science, 5 September 1997

38. Keith S. Thomson, *Ontogeny and Phylogeny Recapitulated*, American Scientist, vol. 76, May/June 1988, p. 273

39. Elizabeth Pennisi, *Haeckel's Embryos: Fraud Rediscovered*, Science, 5 September 1997

40. Elizabeth Pennisi, *Haeckel's Embryos: Fraud Rediscovered*, Science, 5 September 1997

41. David Pilbeam, *Review of Richard Leakey's book ORIGINS*, American Scientist, 66:379, May-June 1978

42. Dr. W. R. Thompson, world-renowned Entomologist

43. Dr Gary Parker Biologist/paleontologist and former ardent Evolutionist

44. Jeremy Rifkin, *Algeny*, New Yorker Viking Press, 1983, p. 125

45. Source Unknown

Additional Resources:

1. *Evolution Demolition* (YouTube)

2. *The Bible, Geology and Time* (YouTube)

3. *Evolution: The Grand Experiment Dr. Carl Werner* (YouTube)

4. *Dinosaur Bones Carbon-14 Less Than 40,000 Years Old* (YouTube)

5. *Real dinosaur still-soft biological tissue on ABC's 60 Minutes* (YouTube)

6. *The Kent Hovind Creation Seminar (4 of 7): Lies in the Textbooks* (YouTube)

7. *Living Fossils: Fossils that debunk evolution (Creation Magazine LIVE! 4-05)* (YouTube)

8. *Ape-Men & Human Evolution Debunked | Christian Apologetics Week 10* (YouTube)

9. *Origins - Living Fossils pt. 1 Interview with Dr. Carl Werner Program # 1206* (YouTube)

10. *Fossils and Evolution – What is the Biblical View?* (YouTube)

11. Jonathan Wells, *Icons of Evolution*

CHAPTER 3

For Nothing

The Sinking Titanic

"Darwinism is a belief in the meaninglessness of existence."[1]

The story of the 'unsinkable' Titanic is both famous and tragic. On her maiden voyage, she collided with an iceberg in the early morning of 15 April 1912 and eventually sank taking 1,517 of her passengers into the watery grave. The heroic deeds of her crew, the tragic collision with the iceberg, and the sheer terror of the sinking, have all been immortalized in books and movies.

Let us imagine in the midst of the chaos, a seaman was seen to be religiously scrubbing the deck of the Titanic. He seemed oblivious to the ongoing mayhem and went on to ensure her decks were thoroughly cleaned. "Why are you doing that?" a curious passenger inquired. "I know the Titanic is going down," said our deckhand, "but I find it meaningful and rewarding in polishing her decks." A glow of joy and a sense of satisfaction were evident on his face. However, the doomed Titanic continued her inexorable journey into the shadowy abyss below.

In due course, she sank, and over the years, her decks would eventually be encrusted with the barnacles of the deep. Our deckhand, despite all his temporal happiness and illusory meaningfulness, would soon be forgotten. And he lived his life as though he never lived. His little dash through life and his brief joy in serving on the Titanic is but a flash in the pan in the vast ocean of time. His decomposing body would soon be turned into wandering atoms, indistinguishable from the rest in the cosmos. His fleeting existence is best summed up in this science-age eulogy: from stardust to stardust – as he disappeared into the dark, eternal nothingness.

We know that such an event did not happen on the Titanic, but it happens to those whose philosophy is atheistic evolutionism. The Darwinist may find purpose and meaning in his brief existence. He can even discover fulfillment in some altruistic cause; or gain self-esteem from his work; or enjoy his wonderful family; or be in awe before a beautiful sunset. But the only problem is that it is but for the moment. The atheist can have purpose in life but not the ultimate purpose of life. When life is over, his purpose is over.

In the final analysis, whatever meaning the Darwinist may find in life has no objective meaning in the eternity to come. His life, his accomplishment, his purpose, his meaning, are but a brief moment in time. Many an atheist would happily scrub the deck of a sinking 'Titanic' and find joy in doing so, but he will usually bury his head in the sand and refuse to come to terms that the ocean of deep time will soon bury his 'Titanic' and render his earthly accomplishments a forgotten event. He is usually contented with seeking short-term meaning in life knowing there is no long-term meaning to it.

Typically, what the Darwinists will not tell you is that life, as according to Darwin, has no ultimate meaning or purpose. To get rid of God, design and life after life, they have to convince themselves and others of the meaninglessness and purposelessness of our existence. Natural selection has no reasons or goals dear to our heart. It is a wild tree of life mutating to a meaningless nowhere and destined to collapse in the Heat Death of the Universe, when the last star burns out. Evolution is about survival, not meaning or purpose. In the final analysis, it is literally a survival for nothing. Even the high priest of New Atheism Richard Dawkins recognizes that:

> "Humans have always wondered about the meaning of life... life has no higher purpose than to perpetuate the survival of DNA... Life has no design, no purpose, no evil and no good, nothing but blind pitiless indifference."[2]

> "[Genes] are in you and in me; they created us, body and mind; and their preservation is the ultimate rationale of our existence... We are their survival machines."[3]

To the Darwinist, the universe has no thoughts for man. And man, in evolutionary thinking, is just a lucky accident in a purposeless universe. Why would wondering atoms care about the meaning and purpose of life? And why would man, who is after all, nothing more than a collection of orbiting atoms, be interested in the purpose of his existence? We are but the survival machines of the unthinking genes within.

In his attempt to get rid of God, Darwin introduced evolution. And evolution turns man, who is made in the image of God, into a bucket of soulless chemicals. The gospel, as according to Darwin, is: we are chemicals from the beginning to the end, and all the illusory meaning or purpose, joy or sadness, ecstasy or pain, are nothing more than some unconscious, electrochemical reactions in the neurons of our brain. What we call reality is but a mechanistic response to an external event – of mindless molecules within reacting to mindless molecules without. In Darwinian parlance, it is:

Purpose in Life = Chemical Reaction in our Brain

Evolution has supposedly programmed into the human psyche with a creature consciousness to live and find purpose in his purposeless existence. But why? He doesn't know why but he must survive and propagate his DNA to the next generation. For what? The next generation will still be more buckets of dead molecules. Darwin seeks to liberate man from his Maker but, in so doing, he consigns man to a chemical cell. We are machines, not people; chemicals, not souls; molecules, not minds. Life has no ultimate meaning and survival has no ultimate purpose.

> "If you really think about evolution and why we human beings are here, you have to come to the conclusion that we are here for absolutely no reason at all."[4] (Dr. Susan Blackmore)

> "Although many details remain to be worked out, it's already evident that all the objective phenomenon of the history of life can be explained by purely naturalistic factors... Man is the result of a purposeless and naturalistic... process that did not have him in mind."[5] (Gaylord Simpson)

"We are as much a product of blind forces as is the falling of a stone to Earth, or the ebb and flow of the tides. We have just happened, and man was made flesh by a long series of singularly beneficial accidents."[6] (Julian Huxley)

"Darwinian evolution was not only purposeless but also heartless – a process in which... nature ruthlessly eliminates the unfit. Suddenly, humanity was reduced to just one more species in a world that cared nothing for us. The great human mind was no more than a mass of evolving neurons. Worst of all, there was no divine plan to guide us."[7] (Levine, Joseph S. and Kenneth R. Miller)

The so-called bright side of Darwinism is that we are free from God, but the dark side of Darwinism is that we are nothing more than bags of banging molecules with no real, long-term purpose, cruising along the cosmic highway from the Big Bang to the Heat Death. The complete paradigm of evolutionism, materialism, naturalism and reductionism is a meaningless existentialism coupled with a hopeless absurdism. We are nothing more than the 'story of the atoms'. This is what Darwin wants us to believe; this is what the New Atheists want us to celebrate; this is what the Evolutionists hope that we will embrace – the survival for nothing! Let us hear from William Lane Craig, the renowned Christian apologist:

"Mankind is a doomed race in a dying universe. Because the human race will eventually cease to exist, it makes no ultimate difference whether it ever did exist. Mankind is thus no more significant than a swarm of mosquitos or a barnyard of pigs, for their end is all the same. The same blind cosmic process that coughed them up in the first place will eventually swallow them all again.

And the same is true of each individual person. The contributions of the scientist to the advance of human knowledge, the researches of the doctor to alleviate pain and suffering, the efforts of the diplomat to secure peace in the world, the sacrifices of good men everywhere to better the lot of the human race – all these come to nothing. This is the horror of modern man: because he ends in nothing, he is nothing."[8]

No Maker of the Universe = No Ultimate Purpose of our Existence

And, as predictable, the New Atheists would beat the same drum and sing the same song – but this is true, but this is true – we are *From Nothing, By Nothing, and For Nothing*. But, is it scientifically true? Did something come from nothing? Is it reproducible? Is it science or a faith without evidence? Or, perhaps, more rationally, did the universe come from Someone? All physical effects have a cause, and an immaterial nothing is a most absurd candidate to be the cause of anything physical. More logically, a supernatural Someone would better qualify to be the cause of a fine-tuned 'something from nothing'.

Can dead molecules turn into a mind-boggling, highly complex, self-replicating, molecular factory we call a living cell bottom up? Has it been observed? Is it empirical science or just pure science fiction? Or, perhaps, a brilliant Designer was needed to build it top down? Which is more probable? This is a free world and the Darwinists are entitled to believe they are *From Nothing, By Nothing, and For Nothing*. And the Christians are at liberty to believe they are *From Someone, By Someone, and For Someone*. The author makes no apologies that he believes in the latter. It takes more faith to be an atheist!

Intuitively, deep in our soul, we know that we are more than bags of molecules. We have self-consciousness and self-determination; we aspire to be a somebody; find meaning to our existence; live life to the fullest; desire to survive beyond the grave; and, for many, to have a loving relationship with their Maker and heavenly Father. We are someone, not something.

But the Darwinist would seek to wrench our soul from our heart – our realities are but illusions in our brains; there is no free will but the interplays of chemicals in our head; and there is no ultimate meaning or purpose to our existence. Instead of a promised evolution, it is a guaranteed devolution – man is reduced to a meaningless monkey and a baby is no different from a purposeless piglet. This is the real heart and soul of Darwinism; this is the untold story of evolutionism; this is the final destination of atheism – we are just another piece of meat. The Darwinists are welcome to believe it, but thinking people beg to differ. Darwinism, when taken to its bitter end, is the death of all hope and the suicide of the soul.

> "When Darwin deduced the theory of natural selection to explain the adaptations in which he had previously seen the handiwork of God, he knew that he was committing cultural murder. He understood immediately that if natural selection explained adaptations, and evolution by descent were true, then the argument from design was dead and all that went with it, namely the existence of a personal god, free will, life after death, immutable moral laws, and ultimate meaning in life."[9] (William Provine)

"The real difficulty in accepting Darwin's theory has always been that it seems to diminish our significance... [Evolution] asked us to accept the proposition that, like all other organisms, we too are the products of a random process that, as far as science can show, we are not created for any special purpose or as part of any universal design."[10] (Curtis, Helena and N. Sue Barnes)

"The concept that the universe has no origin, no plan, and no norms – produces people with no purpose, no fulfillment, and no future."[11]

If Darwinism is true, it will lead to Existentialism – life has no real meaning but for us to artificially deposit meaning into it. And on its heel will be Absurdism – the search for answers in an answerless world. And that long journey will ultimately culminate in Nihilism – life has no ultimate meaning, purpose or intrinsic value in the end. In short, the world wasn't created for us and there is no reason to our existence. We are just cosmic orphans birthed through a chemical accident into an indifferent and dying universe. Dawkins is acutely aware of the whole show when he penned down his famous manifesto of a universe without God:

"In a universe of blind physical forces and genetic replication, some people are going to get hurt, and other people are going to get lucky; and you won't find any rhyme or reason to it, nor any justice. The universe we observe has precisely the properties we should expect if there is at the bottom, no design, no purpose, no evil and no good. Nothing but blind pitiless indifference. DNA neither knows nor cares. DNA just is, and we dance to its music."[12]

"Natural selection, the blind, unconscious, automatic process which Darwin discovered, and which we now know is the explanation for the existence and apparently purposeful form of all life, has no purpose in mind. It has no mind and no mind's eye. It does not plan for the future. It has no vision, no foresight, no sight at all."[13]

William Provine is an American historian of science and of evolutionary biology and population genetics, and a critic of intelligent design. In rejecting God, he is forced to conclude that there is indeed a dark side to biological evolution in classical Darwinian thinking – there is no purpose, no free will, no meaning, no objective morality, and no afterlife.

"Let me summarize my views on what modern evolutionary biology tells us loud and clear. And I must say that these are basically Darwin's views. There are no gods, no purposeful forces of any kind. No life after death. When I die, I am absolutely certain that I am going to be completely dead. That's just all. That's gonna be the end of me. There is no ultimate foundation for ethics, no ultimate meaning in life, and no free will for humans, either."[14]

The famous atheist Bertrand Russell was a British philosopher, logician, mathematician, historian, writer, social critic, political activist and Nobel laureate for Literature. He saw what many Darwinists missed out – man is going nowhere and all his accomplishments will finally be entombed in a universe in ruins.

"... man is the product of causes which had no prevision of the end they were achieving; that his origin, his growth, his hopes and fears, his loves and his beliefs, are but the outcome of accidental collocations of atoms; that no fire, no heroism, no intensity of thought and feeling, can preserve an individual life beyond the grave; that all the labours of the ages, all the devotion, all the inspiration, all the noonday brightness of human genius, are destined to extinction in the vast death of the solar system, and that the whole temple of man's achievement must inevitably be buried beneath the debris of a universe in ruins..."[15]

Michael Denton has done some deep thinking and realizes how we view the world will determine how we view ourselves. And if we are convinced we are animals, we will eventually behave like one. Potentially, many of the spiraling depression, suicides, lawlessness, immorality and killings in our society can be traced to Darwinism – a philosophy of life in which there is no God, no free will, no ultimate purpose or meaning, no good or evil, and no justice or hope beyond the grave.

"It was because Darwinian theory broke man's link with God and set him adrift in a cosmos without purpose or end that its impact was so fundamental. No other intellectual revolution in modern times... so profoundly affected the way men viewed themselves and their place in the universe."[16] (Michael Denton)

For others like Aldous Huxley, there are other hidden motivations for wanting a godless and meaningless existence – the license to indulge in unrestrained debauchery.

> "For myself, as, no doubt, for most of my contemporaries, the philosophy of meaninglessness was essentially an instrument of liberation. The liberation we desired was simultaneously liberation from a certain political and economic system and liberation from a certain system of morality. We objected to the morality because it interfered with our sexual freedom."[17]

It is said that some people think, while others think about what they think. And some people wonder superficially, while others deliberate deeply. If there is no God, no design, no purpose, then the following becomes patently obvious:

- Our makeup is but a bucket of soulless chemicals.

- All living things are mindless, molecular machines.

- We are nothing special; we are just another piece of meat.

- Our realities are but electrochemical activities in our brain.

- There is no long-term significance to our happiness or sorrow.

- We are a cosmic accident and are here for no particular reason.

- Why live on? Why suffer? Sooner or later, we will be back to stardust.

If naturalism is all there is, then we are all caged up in a cosmic cell. And all the search for the meaning of life is about which corner of the cell is best to hang around for our brief existence. King Solomon, despite his wisdom and opulence, had long concluded that if God does not exist, life has no ultimate meaning.

> "Vanity of vanities, saith the Preacher, vanity of vanities; all is vanity. What profit hath a man of all his labour which he taketh under the sun? One generation passeth away, and another generation cometh: but the earth abideth for ever."[18] (*Bible*)

"Unless you assume a God, the question of life's purpose is meaningless."[19]
(Bertrand Russell)

References:

1. Dr. R. Kirk, *The Rediscovery of Creation*, in National Review, May 27, 1983, p. 641

2. Richard Dawkins, *River out of Eden*

3. Richard Dawkins, *River out of Eden*

4. Dr. Susan Blackmore, psychologist, The Independent, 21 January 2004

5. Gaylord Simpson, noted paleontologist

6. Julian Huxley, *The Human Degree*, J.B. Lippincott Co., 1976

7. Levine, Joseph S. and Kenneth R. Miller, Biology: *Discovering Life*, Second Edition, Lexington, 1994, MA: D.C. Heath, p. 161,

8. William Lane Craig, *The Absurdity of Life without God*

9. Provine, W. B, *Dare a scientist believe in design. In Evidence of purpose: scientists discover creativity,* J. M. Templeton (ed.), New York: Continuum, 1994, p. 21–32

10. Curtis, Helena and N. Sue Barnes, *Invitation to Biology,* Third Edition, New York, NY: Worth, 1981, p. 475

11. Source Unknown

12. Richard Dawkins, *Out of Eden*, p. 133

13. Richard Dawkins, *The Blind Watchmaker*

14. Provine, W.B., Darwinism: *Science or Naturalistic Philosophy?* The Debate at Stanford University, 1994

15. Bertrand Russell, *Why I Am Not A Christian,* New York: Simon and Schuster, 1957, p. 107

16. Michael Denton, *Evolution: A Theory in Crisis,* 1985, p. 67

17. Aldous Huxley, *Ends and Means*

18. *Bible*, Ecclesiastes 1:2-4

19. Hugh S. Moorhead, *The Meaning of Life,* Chicago Review Press, December 1988

Dancing to our DNA

"The universe we observe has precisely the properties we should expect if there is at the bottom, no design, no purpose, no evil and no good. Nothing but blind pitiless indifference. DNA neither knows nor cares. DNA just is, and we dance to its music."[1]

There are only two possibilities to our reality – either there exists a Maker or we are just Molecules in Motion. In a flash of evolutionary inspiration, Dawkins saw where all this was leading to – if there were no Designer, we are just soulless DNA, and all our behaviors are nothing more than involuntary dances to its electrochemistry. The good man is good because of his 'good DNA', and the bad man is bad because of his 'bad DNA'. The rapist rapes and the killer kills because they cannot help it but to boogie to the music of their peculiar, double helix replicator. This whole Universe is turned into one big Dance Hall and every living critter is doing its soulless tango or salsa. Life is all about the unfolding DNA and its ghostly dances. It is but the physics and chemistry in our brain. And libertarian free will and human responsibility are nothing more than an illusion.

"When I think I have free will I am deluding myself."[2] (Richard Dawkins)

"Everything I know about the world tells me that there is no such thing as free will…"[3] (Lawrence Krauss)

"Free will is merely the ability to decide, and the ability to decide is nothing other than the organized interplay of shifts of atoms."[4] (Peter Atkins)

If there is no God without and no soul in us, then all that is left are materialism and molecules in motion – nothing more, nothing less, nothing else. And creature consciousness is just the interplay of the chemicals in the neurons of our brains. Our decision-making is but an illusion – we think we have the freedom to exercise our free will but it is no more than some antecedent, mechanistic response in our head to some external stimulant or demand. In a word, every thought or action is but the outcome of an involuntary, algorithmic, electrochemical reaction in our head. What begins with molecules ends with molecules. Free will is but an illusion!

Mental States = Brain States = Physical States =
Molecules in Motion = The Laws of Physics = No Free Will

We think that we deliberate and make decisions but, in truth, we did not think or decide. Instead, we did exactly according to the electrochemical configuration in our brains. This sounds really spooky – we don't really make decisions; they were already made for us by the interplays of the neurons in our head. We merely act out our electrochemical 'thoughts' gleaned from our genes and whatever input that was downloaded into our brain previously. This is exactly what Dawkins meant by the involuntary 'dancing to the music of our DNA' – you cannot help but to sway to its mesmerizing music in your behaviors. It is but the tail wagging the dog and not the dog wagging the tail.

When you follow the evolutionary trail to its logical destination, you will discover some very weird landscapes along the way – objectively, there is no free will; subsequently, there is no good or evil; and logically, there is no human responsibility or consequence. Let us humor these Calvinistic Darwinists for a moment and journey alongside with them and be entertained by their ludicrous *reductio ad absurdum*. Sam Harris, like many of his peers, advocates a hard-deterministic dogma in which the reason why the psychopaths commit their heinous acts is because they just can't help it. In his own words, Harris freely (well, not exactly freely, that is an illusion; he can't help it but have to do it; it is about the laws of physics working on the deluded neurons in his head) acknowledges:

> "In the early morning of July 23, 2007, Steven Hayes and Joshua Komisarjevsky, two career criminals, arrived at the home of Dr. William and Jennifer Petit in Cheshire, a quiet town in central Connecticut... Komisarjevsky... he bludgeoned Petit with all his strength until he fell silent... They quickly doused the house with gasoline and set it on fire... The girls died of smoke inhalation.
>
> As sickening as I find their behavior, I have to admit that if I were to trade places with one of these men, atom for atom, I would be him: There is no extra part of me that could decide to see the world differently or to resist the impulse to victimize other people. Even if you believe that every human being harbors an immortal soul, the problem of responsibility remains: I cannot take credit for the fact that I do not have the soul of a psychopath. If I had truly been in Komisarjevsky's shoes on July 23, 2007 — that is, if I had his genes and life experience and an identical brain (or soul) in an identical state — I would have acted exactly as he did. There is simply no intellectually respectable position from which to deny this. The role of luck, therefore, appears decisive."[5]

"Evil is just having the bad luck for having bad genes..."[6]

Well, there you have it, Steven Hayes and Joshua Komisarjevsky, who set fire to a home and killed three of the Petit family, are inculpable of their brutalities and murders. And so is every rape, murder and torture done to mankind – from the reign of terror by Adolf Hitler to the brutalities of Saddam Hussein. It is because of their unfortunate genes dude; just dumb luck! They cannot help it. No sense in prosecuting them. They need to be understood and pitied. Criminals are victims, not perpetuators of evil deeds. If Harris had their molecular makeup, 'atoms for atoms', he would do the same thing.

Suddenly, the whole moral terrain is transformed into some weird, out-of-this-world landscape – you should never be bitter or angry with the kid next door who rapes your daughter or the psychopath who bludgeons your son to death. You need to have compassion and understanding towards them. They can't help it! And so it is with you – if you happen to be the perpetuator of those evil deeds. According to these New Illusionists, it is liberating to be enlightened by such 'truths'. It sets us free, not only from God, but also from all human responsibilities and consequences. We can't help but do the things we do. We shouldn't feel guilty of what we can't help doing or blame others for their crimes against humanity.

Some screws definitely came loose in Harris' head! And he is not alone; scores of predestinated Darwinists are with him. Admittedly, Harris' admirers had no free will but to believe that there is no free will. They did not have a choice; it is in their genes. Or, perhaps, there was a remote possibility, on the quiet, that they did it out of their own free will? We will leave it to them to thrash it out in their revolving brains. Free will, to the Darwinist, is like a mistress – they need her but they don't want to be seen around with her. Libertarian free will point us to a living soul, and a living soul will lead us to a Creator, and that is why they seek to downplay the possibility of libertarian free will at all costs.

With that goes all the consequences of a man for all his crimes! The bottom line is that he cannot help it. To his DNA he must dutifully obey. And it is patently silly to say that he can go against his DNA to do what is right for how can unthinking DNA goes against itself? After all, DNA neither knows nor cares unless, of course, we have a mind and not just a brain – the ghost in the machine. Only a mind can deliberate and go against itself to do what is responsible; a brainless DNA is hopeless. But the Darwinists cannot admit to an independent mind because if there exists an intangible mind in us, there could be the possibility of the ultimate Mind out there.

Here is some food for thought for Sam Harris and his likes: if there is no free will, we Christians cannot help but think that we have free will. We have no choice – we are chemically predestinated – it is in our system. There is a religious 'tumor' lodged in our head that makes us believe in God and we have to boogie to the music of our DNA. So, my question is this: If you Harris acknowledge the killers kill because they cannot help it, why can't you permit Christians to believe there is God, free will, or afterlife, because they cannot help it? Why can't you let them happily dance to their religious DNA? Why must they do your meaningless, Darwinian tango?

And to extrapolate further, why not let the Islamic extremists cheerfully do their murderous jazz with their dazzling brutalities in the cosmic dance hall? They can't help it, or can they, or should they? And by the same token, they need our understanding and compassion, instead of our condemnation. For the life of me, I can never understand the backlashes of the New Atheists towards the Jihadists because both Joshua Komisarjevsky and the 9/11 Jihadists are in the same boat – they kill because they cannot help it – it is in their genes dude! It is all about 'faulty motherboards'. Why the book *God Delusion* by Richard Dawkins; or why *God is not Great* by Christopher Hitchens; or why *Letter to a Christian Nation* by Sam Harris - to discredit religions? Why not write a book – *Drown those Murderous Goons in their Disturbing Gene Pools* – to shame those predisposed to kill?

The reason why the New Atheists would write books, do debates, and attempt to right every religious wrong, is because they believe in libertarian free will and moral consciousness. Without that, it would be futile and ridiculous to reason with a religious machine that has no capacity to decide independently or to choose rightly. If they were truly convinced that there is no free will, they should not even attempt to persuade others to their cause. It is not in their genes dude! *Que Sera, Sera; Whatever will be, will be. The Killers will Kill and the Rapists will Rape, and You cannot do Anything about It.* Dawkins will be Dawkins, Harris will be Harris, and Christians will be Christians, period. It is in their immutable genes. It is hardwired into them. The laws of physics determine the orbits of the atoms in their brain. They do not have free will; they cannot reason; they can only react.

Perhaps, we should post this hilarious question to Harris: How do you feel about the fact that your wife did not freely choose you but was mechanically drawn to you? And she loved you not because she did it out of her own free will but was unthinkingly drawn to you due to her chemical makeup. And all the hugs and kisses were molecularly orchestrated by the predictable firing of the neurons in the head, possibly 5-7 milliseconds before they happened. She had no say in it and neither have you. Your love life is beginning to resemble a production line in the factory – it is all about the cogs and wheels in the machinery. It is purely mechanistic and all the romantic feelings were but an illusion. It is all about the firing or misfiring of the neurons in a deluded brain!

If our libertarian free will is just an illusion, then all our experiences is objectively nothing more than illusions relating to illusions; illusions helping illusions; illusions killing illusions; and illusions ending in illusions. From the womb to the tomb, it is but an illusory existence and experience. It is all about indeterministic molecules in motion. Why is one cluster of orbiting atoms right and another wrong, if good and evil are defined by the unguided and random firing of the neurons in our head? Or, what long-term good do the New Illusionists hope to accomplish by peddling their brand of illusion or delusion, if the world they live is nothing more than a mere illusion? Is *The God Delusion* an illusion if, by Dawkins' own admission, free will is illusory? It was, after all, written by a pack of evolving and deluded neurons in his head that thinks it is real – another obvious illusion by Dawkins' own account.

In truth, the Four Horsy Men of New Atheism lack the mental acumen to think in depth and the able foresight to see the cliff ahead. If materialism is all they got, then illusion is all that is left. What begins in illusion ends in illusion, just as what begins with molecules ends with molecules. And if illusion is all there is, their crusade to right the wrong is, at the end of the day, to manufacture more and better illusions! It is all about the laws of physics manipulating the unthinking neurons in their unthinking heads. When these New Atheists embraced materialism and evolutionism, they have inadvertently incarcerated themselves in their self-created dungeon of illusion. Truth is forever beyond their reach. Frank Turek writes:

> "But if we are all just clumps of molecules, then the laws
> of physics determine everything that we think or do. But
> if that is the case, why should we believe anything that
> anyone says – including the atheists? If we are all just the
> stuff of the laws of physics, then we don't reason, we
> merely react."[7]

When the New Illusionists talked about truth or morality from their illusory moral high ground, they were, in reality, indulging in some sort of delusional hallucination. Good isn't necessary good and evil isn't necessary evil – it is just a sachet of deluded neurons making sense of the world it is in. It is a fluid value system for the day. For the sake of argument, science may bring us to the place of morality, but science cannot tell us if it is true? At best, we think it is true. Other intellectual giants of yesteryear who have trodden down the same path of methical materialism have long concluded that truth is not only illusory but also elusive – they are beyond the chemicals of walking molecules!

"For if my mental processes are determined wholly by the motions of atoms in my brain, I have no reason to suppose that my beliefs are true. They may be sound chemically, but that does not make them sound logically."[8] (J. B. S. Haldane)

"But then with me the horrid doubt always arises whether the convictions of man's mind, which has been developed from the mind of the lower animals, are of any value or at all trustworthy. Would any one trust in the convictions of a monkey's mind, if there are any convictions in such a mind?"[9] (Charles Darwin)

"If the solar system was brought about by an accidental collision, then the appearance of organic life on this planet was also an accident, and the whole evolution of Man was an accident too. If so, then all our present thoughts are mere accidents – the accidental by-product of the movement of atoms. And this holds for the thoughts of the materialists and astronomers as well as for anyone else's. But if their thoughts – i.e. of Materialism and Astronomy - are merely accidental by-products, why should we believe them to be true? I see no reason for believing that one accident should be able to give me a correct account of all the other accidents."[10] (C. S. Lewis)

And why would an illusion want to live on in illusion; or propagate more illusions; or excel in illusions? What do they hope to accomplish in a world of passing illusions for, at the end of the day, it is but a biological sham! Why not end the painful illusion and live with the reality of meaninglessness and purposelessness? The answer is simple: somewhere deep inside us, we know we are more than molecules in motion. Even the most hardcore Darwinist would want to live his life to the fullest, find meaning in his calling, and curious about the world around him. He can experience love and hatred, joy and sadness, and a host of other human emotions. These are not the by-products of an unthinking illusion but of a real, living and conscious entity - a living soul made in the image of God, which ironically, he tries very hard to deny and obliterate. In short, you are not your brain!

On one level, Sam Harris says there is no free will but, on another level, he says you have the free will to believe there is no free will. It is tough to reason with such an incoherent and constipated brain. Let us lend him a hand - if there is no God, then there is no free will. Every decision is electrochemically predetermined, and you need not attempt to win others to your cause because those deluded religionists do not have the 'free won't' to change. Got it? Good! But if you attempt to reason with those in errors, then you do believe in libertarian free will and moral consciousness, and God pops up again. Got it? Good! And if self-consciousness, libertarian free will, and objective morality exist independently of the molecules in our brain, then you better be prepared to meet your Creator! Got it? Good! Finally, we are making some progress. Thank God!

Dawkins' dancing to the music of our DNA when taken to its logical conclusion will turn our first-person reality into a first-class illusion. Let us see how it pans out in the following fictitious conversation:

Dawkins: Hi illusion, how are you?

Darwinist: I am good, thank you.

Dawkins: Great! By the way, I forgot to tell you I am another illusion just like you.

Darwinist: Awesome! So, why are we having this illusory conversation?

Dawkins: We are here to solve some real problems with regard to the religionists.

Darwinist: If you are an illusion, and I am an illusion, and they are an illusion, and this world is an illusion, what is the problem?

Dawkins: I hate to admit it, but you are right; there is no problem. It is just another illusory happenstance by our reckoning.

Darwinist: Is this conversation real? Why am I talking to an illusion? Am I real? Or, am I just another illusion – another pack of deluded neurons that thinks it is real? It is starting to get disturbing to think that I am an illusion talking to you, another illusion. And all that I am experiencing now is not only unreal but is just another illusory encounter.

Darwinist:	And this conversation is nothing more than some mechanistic interactions between two unconscious, electrochemical systems with artificial intelligence that are defined by 'you' and 'I'. We are just two deluded 'Siri' in conversation. We are nothing more than 'Boltzmann Brains' making sense of the world we are in. And neither one of us is real! Man, this is not only disturbing but it is getting bizarre and depressive. Can someone pinch me and tell me that I am not dreaming?

Dawkins and his horsy men have nothing to offer us but a universe full of molecules, chemicals and illusions. We are nothing more than illusions living in a world of illusions, and all our experiences and accomplishments are but a delusion of illusions. This is the ultimate *reductio ad absurdum*: reality is not reality; morality is not morality; free will is not free will; truth is not truth; and we, are not really we. Everything we experience in life is but a long, unthinking, cosmic drama played out by the unthinking laws of physics acting on the unthinking molecules in our unthinking brains. We are just pieces of soulless pawns in a vast cosmic chessboard – innate, unthinking, unconscious - and being moved around by the capricious hands of purely physics and chemistry.

Francis Crick in *The Astonishing Hypothesis* sums it up aptly:

> "You're nothing but a pack of neurons... The Astonishing Hypothesis is that 'You', your joys and your sorrows, your memories and your ambitions, your sense of personal identity and free will, are in fact no more than the behavior of a vast assembly of nerve cells and their associated molecules."[11]

This is the best the New Atheists can give us after removing God out of the cosmos. They offer us fake goods for the real stuff – if there is no God, no eternal life, no reunions of foregone relationships, then all that is left is the universe of ultimate meaninglessness, purposelessness and mindless molecules in motion. And that begs the question: why bother? For, at the end of the day, everything is: "Vanity of vanities, all is vanities"[12] (*Bible*). Every Darwinist is welcome to have it, but not us as believers in the good Lord. We are more than molecules, chemicals and illusions. We have a living soul, a wonderful God, an awesome eternity to come, and above all, the unshackled freedom to cherry-pick and have it all!

If there is no God, then you are your brain.
But if there is God, then you are not your brain.

References:

1. Richard Dawkins, *Out of Eden*, p. 133

2. Richard Dawkins, *Free Will, Richard Dawkins and Lawrence Krauss*, YouTube

3. Lawrence Krauss, *Free Will, Richard Dawkins and Lawrence Krauss*, YouTube

4. Peter Atkins, *The Creation*, W.H. Freeman & Co Ltd, Oxford, 1981

5. Sam Harris' Blog, *The Illusion of Free Will*

6. Sam Harris on *Free Will, Joe Rogan Experience*, #543, YouTube

7. Frank Turek, *Stealing From God*

8. J. B. S. Haldane, *Possible Worlds*, London: Chatto & Windus, 1927, p. 209

9. Charles Darwin, *Letter to William Graham,* 3 July 1881

10. C. S. Lewis, *God In the Dock*, Grand Rapids: Eerdmans Publishing Co., 1970, p. 52–53

11. Francis Crick, *The Astonishing Hypothesis*, Charles Scribner's Sons, 1994

12. *Bible*, Ecclesiastes 1:1

The Ghost in the Machine

"You don't have a soul; you are a soul."[1]

We know intuitively that we are more than molecules in motion; we have a mind that can deliberate and make decisions freely. We can talk to ourselves, organize our thoughts, think in abstract, weigh our motives, correct our mistakes, or chart the course for our future. There is an undeniable immaterial mind in our physical brain – the ghost in the machine.

The best way to illustrate this mind and body interface is to think of the television. The volume may fail, the signals may be distorted, and some channels may be lost, but the real 'soul' of the television is not in the television itself but in the unseen broadcasting station that puts out the programs. The death of the television is not the same as the end of the station. The station lives on while the television falls apart.

Our soul is like the broadcasting station, and our body, the television. Our immaterial soul commandeers our physical body through a yet-to-be-understood interface and is independent of it. And like the many scientific challenges, we can observe them, but we don't understand how they work. And we are still figuring it out. Savvy! Our soul calls the shots and our body responds subserviently, like the intangible laws of nature governing the physical particles. And like the television, it can only respond as far as it is functionally able. We can fail in our eyesight, loose our hearing, or become bedridden, but our soul lives on.

Ah yes, the Darwinists would often point to the fact that when we have a stroke, we cannot move certain parts of our body; or when specific nerves in our brain are stimulated, some parts of our body will twitch; or that the FMRI will light up in certain parts of our brain before our decisions were made; or when we die, we die.

And so it is with the television – we can remove the volume knob and disable the sound or increase the intensity of the screen to make it brighter, but the station runs perfectly and independently of how the television is doing. Has it dawn upon the Darwinists that perhaps, it is the ghost in the machine that lights up our brain, which in turn, moves our body? Brain activity is not the same as brain causation. Perhaps, the real causal agency resides in our physical brain. Perhaps, there is an immaterial and independent 'broadcasting station' in us. The mind is not the emergent property of the brain; the mind is a separate entity from the brain.

"In the past, atheistic evolutionists suggested that the mind is nothing more than a function of the brain, which is matter; thus the mind and the brain are the same, and matter is all that exists... However, that viewpoint no longer is credible scientifically, due in large part to the experiments of Australian physiologist Sir John Eccles. Dr. Eccles, who won the Nobel Prize for his discoveries relating to the neural synapses within the brain, documented that the mind is more than merely physical. He showed that the supplementary motor area of the brain may be fired by mere intention to do something, without the motor cortex (which controls muscle movements) operating. In effect, the mind is to the brain what a librarian is to a library. The former is not reducible to the latter. Eccles explained his methodology and conclusions in *The Self and Its Brain*, co-authored with the renowned philosopher of science, Sir Karl Popper."[2]

Just because our body is physical does not mean the whole show is physical. Anyone talking to you will quickly sense there is someone intangible but very real inside your head. There is that unseen but distinctively and peculiarly 'you' housed in your molecular brain. He knows intuitively that he is not talking to a robot, or dealing with artificial intelligence, or relating to a bunch of talking neurons, but a living, independent, robust entity that can freely engage him. He knows that you will easily pass the Turing test that distinguishes between a robot and a human. This first-person consciousness is undeniably there, period.

Most of the experimentations done to prove determinism were with simple, short-term human activities like the raising of a hand or the doing of some simple calculations – the FMRI in our brain lit up before a certain hand was raised. And the results were not always 100% accurate; at times, only 60%. But there are other deeper, long-term activities in the unseen mind that point to an independent being – we can think in abstract, analyze complex problems, and make long-term decisions. It is said that it is in the long-term, complex, thinking processes like: who to marry, what job to take up, and where to go for vacation next year – things that are futuristic, years down the road, that point to something deeper than just simple, short-term, physical, brain activities like the raising of a hand. It goes beyond the immediate 'act and react' of our behaviors.

Such authorship and ownership of long-term thinking and decision-making processes reveal a robust entity with self-consciousness, self-determination and a libertarian free will. And to cap it all, it has a permanency of identity from birth to death – it is the same 'I' or 'you' or 'they' throughout all of our life.

Occasionally, it may be a frustrated 'you', or a happy 'you', or a depressed 'you', or an elated 'you', but it will always be the same 'you' throughout. It will not evolve from 'I' to 'you' or to 'someone else' despite the randomness of the firing of the neurons in our brain and the quantum indeterminacy of the orbiting atoms in our head.

And this unchanging entity comes with real, identifiable, metaphysical properties like consciousness, sensations, emotions, desires, and free will which materialism cannot account for. How do you make dead molecules have intangible feelings, desires or moral consciousness? These are non-physical phenomena which materialism rejects. If you cannot organize dead ping pong balls into a living, self-conscious being, neither can you turn inorganic, spinning atoms into a living individual with a consciousness of its own existence. The brain consists of nothing but dead molecules in motions obeying the laws of physics. Whence comes this soulish entity that knows it is alive?

In the final analysis, all our human faculties – consciousness, morality, intentionality, and individuality – all come from God. The atheists are stealing from God to lend credence to their rationality. Without God, they are back to dead molecules configured to the laws of physics. Materialism can never account for these transcendental consciousness, moral values, and free will. As C. S. Lewis observes:

> "When you are arguing against Him you are arguing against the very power that makes you able to argue at all."[3]

Science boasts of observation, falsification and reproducibility. And observational science is on the side of the reality of this intangible soul residing in the physical brain. This is how we see the world and how the world relates to us – the permanent resident in a brain with dead atoms. It is for this reason that we can reason with a child, hold an adult accountable for his crimes, and reward an individual for his altruistic deeds. No one would pause for a moment to think that he is dealing with the emergent property of a biochemical brain buzzing with predictable electrochemical activities. He knows that he is dealing with a unique, robust, permanent entity we called 'a living soul'.

On one level, the materialist says that there is nothing beyond the physical molecules but, on another level, he believes that an immaterial mind with observable self-consciousness, feelings, and desires, can emerge from the dead atoms in our brain. You can't have your cake and eat it mate – it is an evolutionary cop out and a non-explanation – a shell game to fool the simpletons. How does a collection of orbiting atoms know it is alive and has a burning desire to live for itself?

Without exception, physical things will always lead to physical things or physical phenomena, not immaterial consciousness. Water can be reduced to H^2O or transformed into a gaseous vapor or turned into solid ice. But it cannot morph into an immaterial, conscious entity with feeling, desire and intentionality. We are made of the same stuff as water – inorganic molecules of electron, proton and neutron. There is an undeniable and insurmountable firewall between physical molecules and immaterial consciousness. The Darwinist assertion that 'the mind is the emergent property of the brain' is a deliberate, misleading and desperate attempt to explain away an obvious impossibility. Molecules can be organized into a brain but not explain, nor produce, nor conjure up, a 'non-molecular' mind.

> "The problem with materialism is that it tries to construct the mind out of properties that refuse to add up to mentality."[4] (Colin McGinn)

> "How does a mental reality, a world of consciousness, intentionality, and other mental phenomena, fit into a world consisting entirely of physical particles in fields or force?"[5] (John Searle)

> "If a mental event really is a physical event in this sense, and nothing else, then the physical event by itself, once its physical properties are understood, should likewise be sufficient [*to explain*] for the taste of sugar, the feeling of pain, or whatever it is supposed to be identical with. But it doesn't seem to be.

> It seems conceivable, for any physical event, there should be a physical event without any experience at all. Experience of taste seems to be something extra, contingently related to the brain state – something produced rather that constituted by the brain state. So it cannot be identical to the brain state in the way that water is identical to H^2O."[6] (Thomas Nagel)

We can debate until the cows come home but this dualistic nature of man is just there. Rene Descartes' famous utterance: "I think, therefore I am"[7] sums up elegantly the reality of this 'ghost in the machine'. No bags of molecules can conjure up a living entity that can feel or desire. This ghost in the machine, this soul, this mind, is a taken by even the most hardcore Darwinists. They trust their minds in matters pertaining to good and evil, or truth and falsehood, but they cannot account for its causation.

And it is outside of neuroscience to find the invisible 'you'. We cannot dissect the brain to find the exact location of the neurons and synapses that defines 'you'. They are just dead molecules in its final composition. And that immaterial 'you' is just inexplicably there. You could almost touch it. And it is no illusion no matter what those no-free-will Darwinists say.

> "We'll never discover consciousness by studying how the brain works, because the brain isn't conscious. Persons are. And we aren't studying persons... I predicted that neurophysiology would continue to provide its own interesting questions, but would never give us answers concerning the nature of self-awareness."[8]

Without wading through the murky waters of determinism, compatibilism, quantum indeterminacy, causal event, altered personality due to head traumas, or REM, this Cartesian ghost in the machine quietly sits in the deep recess of our brain despite all attempts to bury it and to reduce man to purely molecules and chemicals. We know that that soul in us is not only real to us, but to all that relates to us. We have a living soul that is conscious of its existence, curious about its purpose, and wonders at its destiny. But the Darwinists belong to a different kettle of fish – they 'love the brain but hate the mind'. The existence of the mind within will lead to the Mind without to whom, someday, they must give an account of themselves.

> "And the Lord God formed man of the dust of the ground, and breathed into his nostrils the breath of life; and man became a living soul."[9] (*Bible*)

> "So God created man in his own image, in the image of God created he him; male and female created he them. And God blessed them, and God said unto them, Be fruitful and multiply, and replenish the earth... And God saw every thing that he had made, and, behold, it was very good. And the evening and the morning were the sixth day."[10] (*Bible*)

> "When we understand every single secret of the universe, there will still be left the eternal mystery of the human heart."[11]

References:

1. C. S. Lewis

2. *The Existence of God, Cause and Effect*, Apologetic Press

3. C. S. Lewis

4. Colin McGinn, *The Mysterious Flame*, p. 28

5. John Searle, *A Construct of Social Reality*, p. 9

6. Thomas Nagel, *Mind and Cosmos*, p. 41

7. Rene Descartes, *Principle of Philosophy*, 1644, part 1, article 7

8. Don Watson, *Are We Nothing but a Pack of Neurons?* Reprinted from Telicom XI, 25: 62, Feb, 1995

9. *Bible*, Genesis 2:7

10. *Bible*, Genesis 1:27-28

11. Stephen Fry quoting Ludwig Wittgenstein during a Room 101 TV program

Additional Resources:

1. *Michael Egnor: The Evidence Against Materialism* (YouTube)

Quietism of Despair

"My life came to a standstill... I could not even wish to know the truth, for I guessed of what it consisted. The truth was that life is meaningless. I had as it were lived, lived, and walked, walked, till I had come to a precipice and saw clearly that there was nothing ahead of me but destruction. It was impossible to stop, impossible to go back, and impossible to close my eyes or avoid seeing that there was nothing ahead but suffering and real death – complete annihilation...

But my family – wife and children – are also human. They are placed just as I am: they must either live in a lie or see the terrible truth. Why should they live? Why should I love them, guard them, bring them up, or watch them? That they may come to the despair that I feel, or else be stupid? Loving them, I cannot hide the truth from them: each step in knowledge leads them to the truth. And the truth is death."[1] (Leo Tolstoy)

There is a dark and depressive side to Darwinism – a truth that is seldom mentioned and is often avoided. Darwinism has a hidden doorway leading to a very different universe – a universe that transforms man into animal, his soul into machine, his mind into molecules, and his reality into electrochemical activities in his brain. While it promises liberty, it brings us into bondage; while it promises happiness, it imprisons us with despair. Darwinism, true to its intent, is a meaningless existentialism that ends with a purposeless nihilism.

Evolutionism is a race to the bottom – from the earth occupying a special place to an insignificant location parked somewhere in the backwater of the universe; from man being a precious soul made in the image of God to an accidental cosmic slime and pollution in the vast, empty space; from us having a beautiful relationship with our heavenly Father to a cold, dying universe with no One in charge; and from a life potentially full of continuing purposes to one of a meaningless end. Darwinism, when seen in its entirety, is a one-way ticket into the universe of despair.

We are just another species of animal; we are just another piece of rotting meat. And what is so great about a brain stuffed with molecules in motion blindly obeying the laws of physics? What is so noble about a gene machine propagating more unthinking DNA to the next generation? What is there to celebrate when the purpose and meaning of life are but the unconscious, electrochemical activities of a bundle of innate neurons in our head that thinks it is real? What is that to a living soul that is longing for something more lasting and meaningful than a degrading biological machine entombed in a dying universe with no future? Darwinism is heading in the wrong direction.

Life to the Darwinist is the survival for nothing and without purpose. This is the dark side of Darwinism, naturalism and reductionism. And the best part of it all is that many Darwinists seem to take pride in outdoing the last in their downhill race into the abyss of meaninglessness and nothingness. Over time, it becomes patently obvious that Darwinism is a descent into collective madness. And one wonders when the Darwinists are going to stop descending – the earth is getting less and less significant by the day and man is losing more and more of his identity as a living soul. The endgame of Darwinism is a systematic devaluation of the human self-worth and the extinguishing of his purpose of a meaningful life here and thereafter.

> "If my work helps just one person feel like a tiny insignificant speck, lost in a cold, uncaring universe, then I'm doing my job."[2]

No wonder many true-blue Darwinists are in the pit of permanent despair. The molecule-to-man evolution will inevitably end in the man-to-molecule depression. What begins with molecules ends with molecules, not the meaning or purpose of life! Only matter matters do not matter in the long run. And everything that matters is only for the present; nothing matters in the end. We are just a cosmic orphan, birthed through a cosmic accident, and destined to disappear in a cosmic blink. This is the universe of Darwin: meaningless, purposeless and patently pointless!

> "If God does not exist, then you are just a miscarriage of nature, thrust into a purposeless universe to live a purposeless life."[3] (William Lane Craig)

> "I've seen many friends, acquaintances, and colleagues fall full tilt into "Darwinian depression". It's quite a serious condition, characterized by a sinking feeling that the point of life really is to spread our genes, and that our worth as beings is completely determined by our success or failure in the Darwinian arena. The ancillary symptoms of Darwinian depression are referencing Richard Dawkins a lot, succumbing to existential despair, and drinking.

The long and short of it is that, once you start really pondering the implications of Darwinism for human life, the world – even a town as beautiful as Madison, Wisconsin – starts to look pretty dark awfully quickly."[4] (Connor Wood)

"I searched all areas of knowledge, and not only did I fail to find anything, but I was convinced that all those who had explored knowledge as I did had also come up with nothing. Not only had they found nothing, but they had clearly acknowledged the same thing that had brought me to despair: the only absolute knowledge attainable by man is that life is meaningless."[5] (Leo Tolstoy)

"If atheism is true, it is far from being good news. Learning that we're alone in the universe, that no one hears or answers our prayers, that humanity is entirely the product of random events, that we have no more intrinsic dignity than non-human and even non-animate clumps of matter, that we face certain annihilation in death, that our sufferings are ultimately pointless, that our lives and loves do not at all matter in a larger sense, that those who commit horrific evils and elude human punishment get away with their crimes scot free – all of this (and much more) is utterly tragic."[6] (Damon Linker)

"We build our life on the hope for tomorrow, yet tomorrow brings us closer to death and is the ultimate enemy; people live their lives as if they weren't aware of the certainty of death. Once stripped of its common romanticism, the world is a foreign, strange and inhuman place; true knowledge is impossible and rationality and science cannot explain the world: their stories ultimately end in meaningless abstractions, in metaphors."[7] (Albert Camus)

"For that which befalleth the sons of men befalleth beasts; even one thing befalleth them: as the one dieth, so dieth the other; yea, they have all one breath; so that a man hath no preeminence above a beast: for all is vanity."[8] (*Bible*)

Most people will usually 'auto-cruise' along the meandering highways of life doing what everyone else is doing – working hard, making money, getting married, living the good life and, towards the end of their existence, attempting to fulfill their bucket lists. Life usually revolves around a hive of endless activities of doing, getting, keeping, using, worrying, and very little about thinking on where all this will end. And before we know it, we find ourselves over the hill with death awaiting us. Life literally zips by us in quick time.

A fictitious but yet reflective story of our lives tells of a lady who once found a five-dollar note on the floor. Ever since then, she was constantly looking on the ground for more notes to collect. Over the years, she picked up various items - notes, coins, pins, et al.. And she hardly lifted up her eyes to behold a glorious sunset or enjoy the calming sounds of lapping waves.

Most of us differ very little from this lady – we found our 'five-dollar note' - there is work to be done, money to be made, and the world to enjoy. And the only time we will 'look up' is when death is at the door. It is then that we start asking these belated questions: Is this all to life? What is going to happen to me when I plunge over the cosmic cliff and free fall into eternity? Is there a God? What will happen to me, a sinner in the hands of a Holy God?

Suddenly, such questions no longer seem irrelevant; they become the only reality we have. It is said that those who are about to die know intuitively that they are standing at the edge between two worlds – this disappearing world and another – a forever, permanent existence, which they are often ill-prepared for. The cosmic lie must come to an end – life will not go on forever - we do not have a permanent address in this Darwinian world of mutation and death.

This quaint little poem sums up the brevity of life:

"When as a child I laughed and wept,
Time crept.
When as a youth I dreamed and talked,
Time walked.
When I became a full-grown man,
Time ran.
And later, as I older grew,
Time flew.
Soon I shall find while travelling on,
Time gone."[9]

Who am I? Why am I doing what I am doing? Where is all this taking me to? And what happens when life is over? All these matters of eternal values are usually swept under the carpet. And we try not to look silly by thinking about these things in private or talking about them in public. For some, they try not to get near it; for others, they pretend that it is just mere triviality. And, as the saying goes, "No one has deceived us more than ourselves."

> "Everyone knows that they're going to die,
> But nobody believes it,
> If we did, we would do things differently."[10]

The Darwinists are perfectly entitled to their hollowness in life and their hole in the ground in death. But, their story reminds me of a losing team that has a great bunch of cheerleaders but to no avail. All the cheers, chants and Rah, Rah, Rah, will come to nothing in the face of a universe that is mindless, meaningless, cold, silent and dying. Most Darwinists would echo this silly tune: we came from nothing and we are heading to nothing; life has no ultimate meaning or purpose; we are no different from an atom or an armadillo; but we should celebrate in that we are here for a brief moment of time to acquire, accomplish and enjoy - Rah, Rah, Rah!

It is akin to seeing bombs dropping on Tokyo or Berlin during World War II and the people below celebrating that they have but a few more moments before being obliterated. You got to be kidding! What is there to rejoice in a passing, purposeless and pointless world? But this is the best the Darwinists can offer us.

For others, like Lawrence Krauss, they learn to philosophize on the meaninglessness of life by postulating all kinds of fanciful but artificial construct of self-consolation. In an interview with *Vox* on his book, *The Greatest Story Ever Told - So Far – Why Are We Here*, Krauss, the loud atheist, has nothing new to offer us but the typical 'life has no ultimate meaning but we are here to assign meaning to it'. This is the best that he can offer us after removing God from the equation of life. There is nothing new under the sun - from Epictetus of old to Friedrich Nietzsche of recent years – it is the same *Amor Fati* over and over again – just learn to love your unalterable fate!

> "Of course. Nature doesn't care about our needs or demands. The earth wasn't created for us, as much as some people find that dismaying...
>
> Sure, some people find it depressing that we live in a universe that appears to have no purpose... We're here by accident, and that could be depressing for some, but I find it enlivening because we're here for a little while, we're lucky to be here, and we should enjoy our experience and make it better for our children."[11] (Lawrence Krauss)

And Krauss forgot to tell you the 'we' and 'our children' are nothing but sachets of evolving neurons governed by the laws of physics that think they are real. In short, Krauss and his children are nothing more than packets of deluded neurons!

Death will bring the Darwinist into a sharp contrast between what he believes and what will take place. In life, he claims there is no God; in death, he discovers there is no comfort. Atheism throws a twig to a drowning man in the hope that it will save him, but it can't. If there is no God, why is he afraid of death? And if he is terrified of it, where is his Comforter? Many an arrogant atheist is petrified as death approaches and his Darwinian beliefs are of no help to him.

> "Dr. Jacks tells the story of two friends who had rather blatantly proclaimed themselves to be atheists. When mortal sickness visited one of them, the other came to see him and, perhaps a little afraid lest at the last he should abandon his atheism, said to him, "Stick to it, Bill!" "But," replied the stricken man, "there is nothing to stick to!"[12]

Leo Tolstoy, the renowned giant of Russian literature, describes his depressive premonition of death in his book *A Confession*. The fear of death literally sucks the life out of him and left him with what Bertrand Russell calls 'a firm foundation of unyielding despair'.[13] In a borrowed fable, he tells of the inexorable journey into this foreboding end and the inability to enjoy the simple pleasures that life affords him. The honey will become tasteless when death becomes apparent. And the voice of death cannot be silenced but grows louder with the passage of time.

> "There is an Eastern fable, told long ago, of a traveller overtaken on a plain by an enraged beast. Escaping from the beast he gets into a dry well, but sees at the bottom of the well a dragon that has opened its jaws to swallow him. And the unfortunate man, not daring to climb out lest he should be destroyed by the enraged beast, and not daring to leap to the bottom of the well lest he should be eaten by the dragon, seizes a twig growing in a crack in the well and clings to it.
>
> His hands are growing weaker and he feels he will soon have to resign himself to the destruction that awaits him above or below, but still he clings on. Then he sees that two mice, a black one and a white one, go regularly round and round the stem of the twig to which he is clinging and gnaw at it. And soon the twig itself will snap and he will fall into the dragon's jaws.

The traveller sees this and knows that he will inevitably perish; but while still hanging he looks around, sees some drops of honey on the leaves of the twig, reaches them with his tongue and licks them. So I too clung to the twig of life, knowing that the dragon of death was inevitably awaiting me, ready to tear me to pieces; and I could not understand why I had fallen into such torment. I tried to lick the honey which formerly consoled me, but the honey no longer gave me pleasure, and the white and black mice of day and night gnawed at the branch by which I hung. I saw the dragon clearly and the honey no longer tasted sweet. I only saw the inescapable dragon and mice, and I could not tear my gaze from them, and this is not a fable but the real unanswerable truth intelligible to all.

The deception of the joys of life which formerly allayed my terror of the dragon now no longer deceived me. No matter how often I may be told, "You cannot understand the meaning of life so do not think about it, but live," I can no longer do it: I have already done it too long. I cannot now help seeing day and night going round and bringing me to death. That is all I see, for that alone is true. All else is false.

The two drops of honey which diverted my eyes from the cruel truth longer than the rest: my love of family, and of writing – art as I called it – were no longer sweet to me."[14]

Death is the one thing we fear the most and we pay the least attention. Our approach ranges from an outright denial that we will ever die to hoping against hope that when it happens we won't be there. But, in the quiet of the night, when sleep eludes us and friends leave us, and when we can be alone with our deepest thoughts, that some of these questions will return to haunt us: why am I here and what happens when life is over? And in those moments when we are free to think for ourselves and be honest with our soul, we will see that life without God is not only purposeless but also tragic.

Soon the party will be over and the music must stop. And the Darwinist, like Tolstoy, will discover there are no U-turns and no brakes to that depressive, downhill journey into Death. The arrow of time can only point forward in the direction of the grave. The mind after midnight sees a very different picture, a very gloomy landscape, in the fading twilight of Darwinism. By night, a candid atheist is tempted to abandon his faith in atheism and to half believe in God.

"My life came to a standstill... I could not even wish to know the truth, for I guessed of what it consisted. The truth was that life is meaningless. I had as it were lived, lived, and walked, walked, till I had come to a precipice and saw clearly that there was nothing ahead of me but destruction. It was impossible to stop, impossible to go back, and impossible to close my eyes or avoid seeing that there was nothing ahead but suffering and real death – complete annihilation."[15] (Leo Tolstoy)

"Pause Stranger, when you pass me by,
As you are now, so once was I.
As I am now, so you will be,
So prepare for death and follow me."
(Found on a tombstone)

And that journey into the unknown is a journey the Darwinists will have to travel alone. We live in crowds but we die one by one. We have to do our own thinking, and we have to do our own dying; nobody will do it for us. Dawkins wouldn't be there to cheer you on. Hitchens, he is already gone; he can't help himself, and he can't help you. Harris probably thinks that our fear of death is just a minor perturbation in our brain – no worries. And Dennett believes that God is just an UME (Used Mentioned Error). And yet, fear will engulf the atheist as he is hurled towards the abyss of eternity with the words of a man, a finite man, a spiritually-blinded man. The renowned British philosopher and atheist Bertrand Russell is candid about his uncertainty on his humanistic beliefs.

"I would never die for my beliefs because I may be wrong."[16]

And many atheists would pat each other on the back and reassure themselves that they are fine – there is no God, no Day of Judgment, and we are all good. But, these are just assertions, not proofs, the words of a desperate mortal, in the face of an obviously designed world and a Designer awaiting them – "The fool hath said in his heart, There is no God."[17] (*Bible*)

"A man walked into a pub and proclaimed, "There is no God". A half-inebriated man resounded, "I hope you are right; many of us here depend on you."[18]

If the Darwinist is just a collection of molecules with some electrochemical consciousness why is he terrified of death? If death is just a shutdown of his biological factory, what is he afraid of? Why should organized atoms be afraid of its rearrangements? I will tell you why: it is because the Darwinist is made in the image of God. He has a living soul, he cherishes life, he is not ready to end it all, and to meet his Maker.

Deep inside his conscience, he knows he is more than just an electrochemical machine. He has a moral consciousness that is mindful of the sins of his past; an awareness of the foreboding judgment to come; and an innate desire to have an assurance of where he is going. All the denials of God's existence, all the mocking of the believers, and all the bad-design-to-bad-God arguments, will bring the Darwinist no comfort in his dying moments. He needs real answers and assurance, but he can't find them in the meaninglessness of nothingness.

> "Whence come I and whither go I? That is the great unfathomable question, the same for every one of us. Science has no answer to it."[19] (Erwin Schrödinger)

I was once driving down a hill. An elderly lady cut across my path. And I had to brake hard to avoid hitting her. There is nothing strange about such an incident except that after seeing my car coming at her, she turned her head away from me as if she believed that if she did not look at me, I would not hit her. Perhaps, this is how some atheists relate to God – if I do not believe that God exists or think about the Day of Judgment, then nothing untoward will happen to me.

There are many things in life we do not believe will ever happen to us but they do – poverty, sicknesses, broken relationships, a sudden loss of a loved one, or being diagnosed with cancer. Our disbelief will not alter the reality of God's existence and our denial will not spare us from the coming encounter with the Creator. 'Looking away' is not the same as 'not getting hit'. Hell is a prepared place for an unprepared people.

> "And as it is appointed unto men once to die, but after this the judgment."[20] (Bible)

> "And it came to pass, that the beggar died, and was carried by the angels into Abraham's bosom: the rich man also died, and was buried; And in hell he lift up his eyes, being in torments, and seeth Abraham afar off, and Lazarus in his bosom. And he cried and said, Father Abraham, have mercy on me, and send Lazarus, that he may dip the tip of his finger in water, and cool my tongue; for I am tormented in this flame."[21] (Bible)

> "Where their worm dieth not, and the fire is not quenched."[22] (Bible)

"Remember now thy Creator in the days of thy youth, while the evil days come not, nor the years draw nigh, when thou shalt say, I have no pleasure in them."[23] (*Bible*)

"What men fear is not that death is annihilation but that it is not."[24] (Epicurus)

If God does not exist, life is meaningless and death is tragic. Every Saturday night partying will end with a Sunday morning emptiness. There will always be another empty day to reckon with – to be occupied with some activities to make it meaningful or distractions to keep us from ending our lives in despair. And we are caught in the listless current of life – there will be a job to do, a family to feed, a retirement to plan – a predictable and repetitive pattern with no escape. There is nothing new under the heavens – every generation will experience the same cycle of life – a time to be born, and a time to die.

We are like the mythical Sisyphus condemned to repeatedly roll a huge boulder up a hill only to have it roll down again. We go through nearly the same routine every day – get up tired, clean up, head off to school or work, come back tired, have our meals, go to bed, and tomorrow, we repeat the whole process with some predictable moments of happy variations and dreadful dramas.

And when we take a step back and examine the unexamined life, we discover that life not only has no objective purpose but the furthest we go is the grave. And we blindly race from one end of life to the other, seldom pausing to ask the question: for what and so what?

"If a man has no purpose, then his life is a long way to death."[25]

And when we look to Science and Evolution for answers, all we get is a blank look. Life has no real purpose darling – it is about the survival of the genes in us – feeding, fending, fleeting and fathering – just live through it and get it over with. We came from nothing, we are here by nothing, and we are heading to nothing, period. The universe is all there is, or ever was, or ever will be. Once you unravel, that is the end of your universe dude - forget about seeing your loved ones, forget about reuniting with your little baby, forget about living on forever, and forget about Paradise. Your final destination is the hole in the ground – the conclusive proof that life in the final analysis is pointless.

Epitaph on a grave: "All dressed up and no place to go."

The truly convinced Darwinist, like Leo Tolstoy, is living out the quietism of despair - very often, painful and unspoken. Life is about a long and lonely struggle with the ultimate meaninglessness of our existence and a reluctance to end it all. Purposeless, pointless, and depressive, are all parts of its furniture.

There is nothing real or lasting here or beyond the grave. The only thing that is real is a dying universe populated with dark matter, dark energy, dead molecules in motion, and a bunch of New Atheists telling us that this is an awesome discovery and a cause for our celebration! This is Darwinism in its full glory: insane, irrational and depressive. It is said that if God does not exist, everything is permitted, and the first thing permitted, is despair. In the end, we are here for nothing.

Unbeknown to many, Darwin and Darwinism have an unambiguous endgame in mind. It is encapsulated in this simple, crystal clear and inescapable conclusion: We are objectively and ultimately *From Nothing, By Nothing, and For Nothing.*

> "There is a way which seemeth right unto a man, but the end thereof are the ways of death. Even in laughter the heart is sorrowful; and the end of that mirth is heaviness."[26] (*Bible*)

> "Atheism is a long, hard, cruel business."[27]

References:

1. Leo Tolstoy, *A Confession*

2. Source Unknown

3. William Lane Craig, *The Absurdity of Life without God*

4. Connor Wood, *Darwinism: It's true. But it ain't Pretty*, March 23, 2012

5. *Confession*, tr. by David Patterson, New York: W.W. Norton, 1983, p. 33-34

6. Damon Linker, *Where are the honest atheists?* The Week, March 8 2013

7. Albert Camus, *The Myth of Sisyphus (French: Le Mythe de Sisyphe) 1942)*

8. *Bible*, Ecclesiastes 3:19

9. Henry Twells, *Hymns and Other Stray Verses*, London: Wells Gardner & Co., 1901, p. 34

10. *Tuesday with Morrie*

11. Sean Illing, Interview with Lawrence Krauss, Vox, 20 March 2017

12. J. D. Jones

13. Bertrand Russell, *"A Free Man's Worship,"* in *Why I Am Not a Christian,* ed. P. Edwards, New York: Simon & Schuster, 1957, 107

14. Leo Tolstoy, *A Confession*

15. Leo Tolstoy, *A Confession*

16. Bertrand Russell

17. *Bible*, Psalms 14:1

18. Source Unknown

19. Erwin Schrödinger

20. *Bible*, Hebrews 9:27

21. *Bible*, Luke 16:22-24

22. *Bible*, Mark 9 :44

23. *Bible*, Ecclesiastes 12:1

24. Epicurus

25. Pierre Boiste

26. *Bible*, Proverbs 14:12-13

27. Jean-Paul Sartre

Creationism to Christianity

"The heavens declare the glory of God; and the firmament sheweth his handywork. Day unto day uttereth speech, and night unto night sheweth knowledge. There is no speech nor language, where their voice is not heard. Their line is gone out through all the earth, and their words to the end of the world. In them hath he set a tabernacle for the sun."[1] (*Bible*)

The New Atheist's well-trodden argument against the God of the Bible goes something like this: first, there are so many gods and everyone claims they are right; so which one is true? And secondly, there are so many religions that are at odds with each other in their basic tenets; so no one must be true! But, on one level, the New Atheists acknowledge that there are many scientific hypotheses and they often contradict each other. In this diversity of competing hypotheses, they would celebrate. And yet, on another level, the New Atheists would accuse the theists of their inconsistency in having a variance of beliefs. They seem to be blissfully blind to this double standard in their dealings with the religionists.

We do not throw out the baby with the bathtub water just because there are differing claims to the truth – be it with the scientific or religious community. We study, debate, test and come to a conclusion with regard to the claims of each proposition. If not, there will be no conclusion of what is true or *Closer to Truth*.

And like the scientific community, we take the approach of a theory making a prediction, and then subjecting the prediction to a rigorous testing to see if the evidence tallies with the prediction. And we go through a process of elimination to arrive at a true theology. Christians are not called to believe blindly without evidence, a claim that is often parroted by these silly and naïve New Atheists. On the contrary, the Bible challenges us to study and give an answer as to why we believe in what we believe.

"But sanctify the Lord God in your hearts: and be ready always to give an answer to every man that asketh you a reason of the hope that is in you with meekness and fear."[2] (*Bible*)

"Indeed, faith is a response to evidence, not a rejoicing in the absence of evidence."[3] (John Lennox)

Let us now move on from ID to ID: 'Intelligent Design' to 'Identifying the Designer'. Part of this is already covered under the heading 'Whodunit' in the first chapter *From Nothing*. The following is an addition to the many other scientific and prophetic predictions made in the Bible:

It predicted life is in the blood:

> "For the life of the flesh is in the blood: and I have given it
> to you upon the altar to make an atonement for your
> souls: for it is the blood that maketh an atonement for the
> soul."[4] (*Bible*)

Blood is literally the life of the flesh as it provides oxygen and nutrients throughout the whole body. Without it, the creature will die. It is ironical that in 1799 President George Washington died because of a common but wrong medical practice of his day – bloodletting. It was believed then that some illnesses were caused by 'bad blood', and by cutting the veins to drain it out, the sick would be healed. If only George Washington had recognized that life is in the blood, he might have survived.

It predicted the existence of bacteria and viruses, and the practice of quarantine:

> "All the days wherein the plague shall be in him he shall
> be defiled; he is unclean: he shall dwell alone; without the
> camp shall his habitation be."[5] (*Bible*)

Between 1347 and 1352, some 25 million people, more than one-third of the population of Europe died because of the Black Plague (Bubonic Plague). Many lives could have been saved had they known of this one verse of the Bible – the practice of quarantine to combat communicable diseases.

It predicted there would be only one created couple from the beginning of time:

> "So God created man in his own image, in the image of
> God created he him; male and female created he them."[6]
> (*Bible*)

All the women today can be traced back to a single woman whom the scientists called 'Mitochondrial Eve'. And all the men alive today came from a single man: 'Y-Chromosomal Adam'. For the ladies, their lineage is traced through their mitochondrial DNA, which is passed down from mother to daughter. For the men, their connections came from their Y-chromosomes, which is inherited solely from their fathers. And the first couple lived at the same era and were much younger than the evolutionary timeline.

"The most recent common ancestors of modern-day men and women – dubbed "Adam" and "Eve" – lived during roughly the same time period, contrary to previous findings indicating that Eve was tens of thousands of years older, according to two studies published Thursday in the journal Science... But that didn't make a lot of genetic sense... How could two individuals living as much 150,000 years apart not give rise to separate species?

When they were done, they estimated that Adam had lived around 120,000 to 156,000 years ago. After repeating their analysis with the subjects' mitochondrial DNA, they concluded that Eve lived around 99,000 to 148,000 years ago - showing for the first time that both ancestors were alive around the same time period."[7]

On one level, the Bible is not a Book on science but, on another level, whenever the Bible makes a scientific prediction, it is factual. And it will be true because God made the world and He knew of its intricacies. Above all, Science and Christianity are not adversaries – they are the best of friends. God is the source of objective science and the many discoveries of science point us back to Him. Science tells us how it is done, while the Bible tells us Who did it.

The Bible is not only capable of making scientific predictions, but also prophetic predictions that are testable and falsifiable. The Bible boldly predicted the things to come before they happened. The followings are just some of the predictions of the things to come concerning the end of the world:

It predicted the State of Israel would be reborn before the world ends:

"As I live, saith the Lord God, surely with a mighty hand, and with a stretched out arm, and with fury poured out, will I rule over you: And I will bring you out from the people, and will gather you out of the countries wherein ye are scattered, with a mighty hand, and with a stretched out arm, and with fury poured out."[8] (Bible)

"After many days thou shalt be visited: in the latter years thou shalt come into the land that is brought back from the sword, and is gathered out of many people, against the mountains of Israel, which have been always waste: but it is brought forth out of the nations, and they shall dwell safely all of them."[9] (Bible)

The Roman general Titus destroyed Jerusalem in A. D. 70 and Israel ceased to be a nation thereafter. And against all odds, after the Holocaust in World War II, after six million Jews were gassed in the concentration camps by Adolf Hitler, the state of Israel was reborn on 14 May 1948. The world was cynical about this prophecy of Israel's return for almost 2,000 years, but today, no one is laughing at this uncanny prediction made in the Bible. Israel reserves the distinction as the only ethnic people in the world that returned to their homeland after almost two millenniums. All the conflicts between the Arabs and the Jews are the outcome of the fulfilment of this prophecy. The Declaration of Israel's Independence in 1948 states:

> "The Land of Israel was the birthplace of the Jewish people. Here their spiritual, religious and political identity was shaped. Here they first attained to statehood, created cultural values of national and universal significance and gave to the world the eternal Book of Books...

> After being forcibly exiled from their land, the people kept faith with it throughout their Dispersion and never ceased to pray and hope for their return to it and for the restoration in it of their political freedom...

> Placing our trust in the Almighty, we affix our signatures to this proclamation at this session of the provisional Council of State, on the soil of the Homeland, in the city of Tel-Aviv, on this Sabbath eve, the 5th day of Iyar, 5708 (14th May, 1948)."[10]

When Israel returned to their Land, God's prophetic clock started ticking, and a chain of events begins to unfold before our very eyes – the coming New World Order; the emergence of the One-World Ruler – the Anti-Christ; the Mark of the Beast – a globally controlled, cashless identification system; the explosion of knowledge and the speed of travel, etc.

It predicted the coming New World Order and Global Governance:

> "And it was given unto him to make war with the saints, and to overcome them: and power was given him over all kindreds, and tongues, and nations. And all that dwell upon the earth shall worship him, whose names are not written in the book of life of the Lamb slain from the foundation of the world. If any man have an ear, let him hear."[11] (Bible)

Towards the end of this age, countries all over the world will largely gravitate towards a One-World Government with a One-World Leader – the Anti-Christ. Presently, the political leaders of the world are awakening to the stark reality that their nations cannot survive in isolation. The onslaught of globalization, the borderless economy, the advent of the Internet, the possible environmental catastrophes facing mankind – global warming, ozone depletion, etc., and international conflicts and crises, which require multinational cooperative efforts to resolve, will inevitably force all these nations to come together in interdependence.

The latest trend in the world is towards the concept of the New World Order, globalization and global governance. The formation of international bodies like the UN (United Nations), WTO (World Trade Organization), ICJ (International Court of Justice) IMF (International Monetary Fund) and ICC (International Criminal Court) are systematically laying the groundwork for this coming New World Order. These, together with the formation of the Common Markets like NAFTA, EU and ASEAN, are drawing the nations of the world into a One-World Government.

> "Today, America would be outraged if U.N. troops entered Los Angeles to restore order. Tomorrow they will be grateful! This is especially true if they were told that there were an outside threat from beyond, whether real or promulgated, that threatened our very existence. It is then that all peoples of the world will plead to deliver them from this evil. The one thing every man fears is the unknown. When presented with this scenario, individual rights will be willingly relinquished for the guarantee of their well-being granted to them by the World Government."[12] (Dr. Henry Kissinger)

> The new EU President, Herman Van Rompuy, has proclaimed 2009 as the "first year of global governance": "We're living through exceptionally difficult times – the financial crisis and its dramatic impact on employment and budgets, the climate crisis which threatens our very survival, a period of anxiety, uncertainty and lack of confidence. Yet these problems can be overcome through a joint effort between our countries. 2009 is also the first year of global governance with the establishment of the G20 in the middle of the financial crisis. The climate conference in Copenhagen is another step toward the global management of our planet. Our mission, our Presidency is one of hope, supported by acts and by deeds."[13]

"Some even believe we are a part of a secret cabal working against the best interests of the United States, characterizing my family and me as 'internationalists' and of conspiring with others around the world to build a more integrated global political and economic structure – one world, if you will. If that's the charge, I stand guilty and I am proud of it."[14] (David Rockefeller)

"The New World Order under the UN will reduce everything to one common denominator. The system will be made up of a single currency, single centrally financed government, single tax system, single language, single political system, single world court of justice, single state religion... Each person will have a registered number, without which he will not be allowed to buy or sell; and there will be one universal world church. Anyone who refuses to take part in the universal system will have no right to exist."[15] (Dr. Kurk E. Koch)

It predicted the coming 'Mark of the Beast' – a cashless, system:

"And he causeth all, both small and great, rich and poor, free and bond, to receive a mark in their right hand, or in their foreheads: And that no man might buy or sell, save he that had the mark, or the name of the beast, or the number of his name."[16] (*Bible*)

The Anti-Christ, the coming One-World Ruler, will cause everyone to have a particular mark in his or her right hand or forehead, without which, they will not be able to buy or sell. In a word, there will be no economic transaction. Digital money will be the new, one-world currency. Cash will be history. This technology is at our doorstep – the biometric chip implants or the RFID (radio frequency identification) tags.

With this microchip implant, you can have access to your bank accounts; make cashless transactions; pay your groceries; zip pass immigrations; pull up your medical, educational or criminal records; and be in command of a host of automation in your home or office. This absolute control of personal information is the dream of every individual, government and world dictator. Although we cannot be absolutely sure about it, this biometric chip implant technology appears to be the most likely candidate for this prophecy of the coming Mark of the Beast. This seemingly innocuous and awesome technology can possibly someday in the future be 'weaponized' by the Anti-Christ to subjugate all mankind to follow and worship him. Without it, you literally cannot 'buy and sell'.

"How'd you like to avoid waiting in lines for the rest of your life? Breeze through everywhere like you owned the place. Watch lights snap on, doors open automatically, money pop out of ATMs as you approach. Never have to show an ID, buy a ticket, carry keys, or remember a password. You'd leave stores loaded with packages and waltz right past the cashiers. You wouldn't have to carry a wallet. Ever. Family and friends could find you instantly in any crowd. There's only one catch - you'd need to have a tiny little chip implanted in your body. No big deal..."[17] (Paul Somerson)

"More than 4,000 Swedes are being implanted with a microchip that contains details about their identity. The miniature technology bypasses the need for cash, tickets, access cards and even social media... The electronic tags are around the size of a grain of rice and are implanted via a syringe into the back of the hand – often above the thumb."[18] (Joe Pinkstone)

"A single electronic card may replace everything in your wallet including:

- Your cash
- Your credit cards
- Your ID cards
- Your insurance
- Your life

FUTURE: One card, or one chip, with your life on it."[19] (Time Magazine)

It is for this reason the author believes in the Jehovah God of the Bible who knows what He is talking about and not in Thor, Zeus, the Flying Spaghetti Monster, or the myriads of mythical gods. It is called the process of elimination. The Bible is uncannily accurate on matters pertaining to science and prophecy. And if it is true about these predictions, it will be true on every other revelations in the Bible.

Above all, God is not to be reduced to a science project subjected to the scrutiny and criticism of mankind. Don't you think it is really silly for a mortal man to judge the existence of the Almighty God when he should be in fear and in awe of the Creator's reality and power in plain sight? And many today that say they are looking for evidence to believe in God are usually the least concern about evidence; in reality, they are looking for loopholes to reject Him.

"Why do the heathen rage, and the people imagine a vain thing? The kings of the earth set themselves, and the rulers take counsel together, against the Lord, and against his anointed, saying, Let us break their bands asunder, and cast away their cords from us. He that sitteth in the heavens shall laugh: the Lord shall have them in derision. Then shall he speak unto them in his wrath, and vex them in his sore displeasure."[20] (*Bible*)

"The first gulp from the glass of natural sciences will turn you into an atheist, but at the bottom of the glass God is waiting for you."[21]

References:

1.   *Bible*, Psalms 19:1-4

2.   *Bible*, 1 Peter 3:15

3.   John C. Lennox, *"God's Undertaker: Has Science Buried God?"* (2011). p.15, Lion Books

4.   *Bible*, Leviticus 17:11

5.   *Bible*, Leviticus 13:46

6.   *Bible*, Genesis 1:27

7.   Melissa Pandika, *Common ancestors of modern men and women lived around the same time,* Los Angeles Times, August 02, 2013

8.   *Bible*, Ezekiel 20:33-34

9.   *Bible*, Ezekiel 38:8

10.   David Ben-Gurion, First Prime Minister of Israel, *Declaration of Israel's Independence*, 14 May 1948

11.   *Bible*, Revelation 13:7-9

12.   Dr. Henry Kissinger, Evians, France, 1991

13.   BBC News, 19-11-2009, Brussels / Available in YouTube

14.   David Rockefeller, *Memoirs*

15.   Dr. Kurk E. Koch, *Assessment of the New World*

16.   *Bible*, Revelations 13:16-17

17.   Paul Somerson, *Inside Job,* PC Computing, Oct. 1999, p. 87

18.   Joe Pinkstone, *Thousands of Swedes are getting microchip IDs inserted into their hands to swipe into homes, offices, concerts and even to access social media,* Daily Mail, 23 October 2018

19.   Time Magazine, April 27, 1998, p. 50, 51

20.   *Bible*, Psalms 2:1-5

21.   Werner Heisenberg, Nobel Laureate in Physics, 1988

Additional Resources:

1.   *Countdown to Eternity* (YouTube)

The Theory of Everything

"If everything is an accident, there's no reason to figure anything out. If everything is futile, purpose is an imaginary concept. But if everything was created, and if everything has a purpose, shouldn't it be the underlying goal of all mankind to discover that Creator and find that purpose?"[1]

The Holy Grail of science is to discover the Theory of Everything (TOE) that will harmonize all the laws of nature into a single, all-encompassing, unified theoretical framework of physics. It is speculated that that equation will probably be no longer than an inch on paper. Many great minds of science have tried and failed to find it – from Albert Einstein to Stephen Hawking, and on to a long list of theoretical physicists today. The roadblock to this discovery is mystifying. There are the laws for the big stuff – General Relativity; and there are the equations for the little things – Quantum Mechanics; and the two can't seem to reconcile. Perhaps someday, physicists will be able to harmonize them. But until then, this TOE will remain the Holy Grail of every aspiring theoretical physicist alive today.

But there is another Theory of Everything that is far more important than this physical TOE – it is the Bible's Theory of Everything – the story of mankind – where it all began, and why the world is the way it is, and how it will eventually fold up. Unlike the physical TOE, this spiritual TOE is dear to our hearts. It deals with matters that our spiritual nature craves to know – what is the ultimate purpose of my *Brief History of Time*? Is there a God who creates and owns this fine-tuned universe? How can I find Him? And what are His expectations? These are things that matter to us more than the understanding of how the cosmos works, which will inevitably lead to a pointless 'so what'.

Being made in the image of God, we long for real answers to life's burning questions that will lead us to the place of the peace that passes all understanding and the rest for our weary souls – of why we are here and where we will be going. This is sometimes known as the 'argument from desire' for the existence of God. We yearn for something that is immaterial, which we can't seem to put a finger on it – something that transcends the endless accumulation of wealth or the fifteen minutes of fame – something that will fill the God-shaped vacuum in this lonely and empty heart of ours. This inexplicable innate desire in us for the immaterial reveals both the spiritual nature of man and the existence of his Creator. Man is more than just molecules in motion; he is a living soul.

And the science of how can never satisfy the spirit of why – the curiosity of a little child and the searching of an inquisitive soul – why am I here, and is there life after life? Even the renowned atheistic philosopher Bertrand Russell was not spared from this spiritual pining for something beyond this world, something that transcends materialism. In a candid letter to Lady Constance, he revealed his eternal pains and hopeless search for that which the world could not afford him. Naturalism may satisfy him intellectually, but it starves spiritually.

> "The centre of me is always and eternally in terrible pain, a curious, wild pain, a searching for something, beyond what the world contains, something transfiguring and infinite – the beatific vision – God – I do not find it, I do not think it is to be found – but the love of it is my life – it's like a passionate love for a ghost. At times it fills me with rage, at times with wild despair, it is the source of gentleness and cruelty and work, it fills every passion that I have – it is the actual spring of life within me."[2]

It is said that God has two Books – the Book of Nature and the Book of Divine Revelation. The Book of Nature reveals the existence of the Creator behind His exquisite, fine-tuned creation in plain sight. From the wonders of creation to the complexity of living creatures, we can know the existence of the Creator, just as Paley's watch on the beach points us to the existence of the unseen watchmaker whom, despite the fact we have not seen him, we intuitively know of his existence, and that is rightly so.

We shall now close the Book of Nature and open the Book of Divine Revelation – the Bible – to take us beyond creation to explanation and expectation. And being made in the image of God, we can recognize His inescapable voice that resonates in our soul. God lives in every corner of our conscience – we can ignore, hide, or deny Him, but we cannot silence His voice within. He is there when we sin - we called it guilt. He is there when we do what is right – we called it joy. He is there in our deepest sorrows – we called it comfort. God is the *Hound of Heaven* who patiently and lovingly stalks us and longs for our return to the heavenly fold.

> "My sheep hear my voice, and I know them, and they follow me."[3] (*Bible*)

The Bible's Theory of Everything begins with the creation of the world. The first book of the Bible Genesis commences with the awesome declaration on how we get something from nothing:

"In the beginning [the beginning of time] God [the uncaused First Cause] created [something from nothing] the heaven [space] and the earth [mass-energy]"[4] (*Bible*)

After the creation of the world, God fashioned every living thing, including man, who is made in His image. And He placed Adam and Eve in the Garden of Eden, a most perfect and beautiful place, where there was no suffering nor death, but instead, an endless bliss.

All men today can be traced back to only one man through their Y-chromosome and he is widely known as the 'Y-Chromosomal Adam'. And all ladies presently will find their ancestry via their mitochondrial DNA of a single woman whom scientists call the 'Mitochondrial Eve'. Empirical science points us to the reality of the first and only couple from the dawn of civilization.

And all living creatures are reproduced through uncommon descent – every created kind reproduces their unique offspring. Smithsonian Institute reveals the Mitochondrial Eve of the sperm whale and the squid. But again, the theory must dominate the data – all Mitochondrial Eves, as according to the Darwinists, must not have been the only ancestors of their offspring. But why not? The answer is simple: the theory of evolution says it can't, period. But the data say otherwise. And all observations show that life can only come from life – biogenesis. Abiogenesis – life coming from non-life – is an article of faith.

"And God said, Let the earth bring forth the living creature after his kind, cattle, and creeping thing, and beast of the earth after his kind: and it was so. And God made the beast of the earth after his kind, and cattle after their kind, and every thing that creepeth upon the earth after his kind: and God saw that it was good.

And God said, Let us make man in our image, after our likeness: and let them have dominion over the fish of the sea, and over the fowl of the air, and over the cattle, and over all the earth, and over every creeping thing that creepeth upon the earth. So God created man in his own image, in the image of God created he him; male and female created he them."[5] (*Bible*)

This was the original plan of God for mankind – to live without sin or suffering, and to enjoy the whole of creation and a beautiful relationship with Him in a pristine environment permeated with nothing but uninterrupted love, peace and happiness. Suffering and death were foreign in the Paradise of God. But sadly, sin entered into the world and sent mankind into a tailspin.

And like all created beings – be it angels or men – there will be a probation period of testing. God placed the Tree of the knowledge of good and evil in the midst of the Garden of Eden and commanded Adam and Eve to refrain from partaking it. Will they love and obey God, or will they sin and rebel against Him? Then came Satan and successfully tempted the first couple to partake the forbidden fruit. The real problem was not the eating of a fruit but the rebellion of a heart. Man wanted to be his own god. With that, mankind lost his Paradise and had to live with the consequences of his disobedience – he was plunged into a world of sin, suffering and death – and everything miserable we now experience.

> "Now the serpent was more subtil than any beast of the field which the Lord God had made. And he said unto the woman, Yea, hath God said, Ye shall not eat of every tree of the garden? And the woman said unto the serpent, We may eat of the fruit of the trees of the garden: But of the fruit of the tree which is in the midst of the garden, God hath said, Ye shall not eat of it, neither shall ye touch it, lest ye die.
>
> And the serpent said unto the woman, Ye shall not surely die: For God doth know that in the day ye eat thereof, then your eyes shall be opened, and ye shall be as gods, knowing good and evil. And when the woman saw that the tree was good for food, and that it was pleasant to the eyes, and a tree to be desired to make one wise, she took of the fruit thereof, and did eat, and gave also unto her husband with her; and he did eat."[6] (*Bible*)

We are acquainted with the common objection: Why did God put the forbidden Tree in the Garden of Eden and allow Satan to tempt man whom He had created? Didn't He know well ahead that Adam would fall into the temptation of partaking the forbidden fruit? The real problem was not with the object of testing (Tree) or the agency of testing (Satan), but with the heart of Man. The Tree and the Tempter merely brought out what was in his heart – a willingness to contemplate the alternative to God and a brazen rebellion to disobey Him. Nobody could make the first Adam sin except he himself. It was about an inner choice and not an external tree or a talking snake. Every crook that stole from the bank cannot blame the existence of the bank but rather his freedom of choice to rob the bank. And so it is for every cheat or rape – they cannot blame the presence of easy money or pretty ladies for their crimes.

When God made man, He took a risk, and gave man the freedom to choose. He did not make a robot to obey Him at will. It is like us parents having our children – some will love us and some will reject us. In addition, God's foreknowledge is not the same as God's foreordination – God foreknew that Adam would fail, but He did not foreordain him to fall. Sadly, Adam, our Federal Head, chose otherwise and mankind lost his Paradise and instead, inherited this sin-cursed world.

> "And unto Adam he said, Because thou hast hearkened unto the voice of thy wife, and hast eaten of the tree, of which I commanded thee, saying, Thou shalt not eat of it: cursed is the ground for thy sake; in sorrow shalt thou eat of it all the days of thy life; Thorns also and thistles shall it bring forth to thee; and thou shalt eat the herb of the field; In the sweat of thy face shalt thou eat bread, till thou return unto the ground; for out of it wast thou taken: for dust thou art, and unto dust shalt thou return."[7] (*Bible*)

> "Wherefore, as by one man sin entered into the world, and death by sin; and so death passed upon all men, for that all have sinned."[8] (*Bible*)

> "We are born in sin and spend our lives coping with the consequences."[9]

With that, mankind inherited a sinful nature that is universally observed everywhere. Its reality is so encompassing that every facet of our life is affected by it. Every fabric of society is tainted with the filth of sin – some are more open and blatant, while others are more discreet and private. Lying, lusting, cheating, theft, covetousness, pride, pornography, pedophilia, adultery, fornication, rape – you name it and you will find it either in us or with the populace at large. And none is spared. All the laws of the land cannot prevent or eradicate the evils in our hearts. And every man, like the moon, has a dark side which nobody has seen and which he hopes that nobody will ever see – especially God. From the Holy Scriptures comes this:

> "For all have sinned, and come short of the glory of God."[10] (*Bible*)

> "For from within, out of the heart of men, proceed evil thoughts, adulteries, fornications, murders, Thefts, covetousness, wickedness, deceit, lasciviousness, an evil eye, blasphemy, pride, foolishness: All these evil things come from within, and defile the man."[11] (*Bible*)

> "To be alone with my conscience is hell enough."[12]

This universal sinful nature in us is encapsulated in an incident where a group of religious leaders brought a woman caught in adultery to Jesus Christ to tempt and fault Him. His answer to them was, "He that is without sin among you, let him first cast a stone at her." To the surprise of the self-righteous crowd, none could cast a stone at this adulterous woman – they were all convicted by their conscience of their sinful past.

> "And the scribes and Pharisees brought unto him a woman taken in adultery; and when they had set her in the midst, They say unto him, Master, this woman was taken in adultery, in the very act. Now Moses in the law commanded us, that such should be stoned: but what sayest thou? This they said, tempting him, that they might have to accuse him.
>
> But Jesus stooped down, and with his finger wrote on the ground, as though he heard them not. So when they continued asking him, he lifted up himself, and said unto them, He that is without sin among you, let him first cast a stone at her. And again he stooped down, and wrote on the ground.
>
> And they which heard it, being convicted by their own conscience, went out one by one, beginning at the eldest, even unto the last: and Jesus was left alone, and the woman standing in the midst.
>
> When Jesus had lifted up himself, and saw none but the woman, he said unto her, Woman, where are those thine accusers? hath no man condemned thee? She said, No man, Lord. And Jesus said unto her, Neither do I condemn thee: go, and sin no more."[13] (*Bible*)

Man's sinful nature works havoc in his life – he not only has no interest in God but seeks to run away from Him. Most of us operate on a very simple and logical premise: if God exists, we will be accountable for all our sins; but if God does not exist, we will get away scot-free. Therefore subconsciously, we will do our best to rubbish Him and disprove His existence with whatever we can get hold of – God is not good, or living critters are badly designed, or we are insignificant in the vast universe, or science has disproved God. And the avalanche of evidence for the existence of God just go past us like the water off the duck's back. Here is a candid confession from atheist professor Thomas Nagel of New York University:

"I want atheism to be true and am made uneasy by the fact that some of the most intelligent and well-informed people I know are religious believers. It isn't just that I don't believe in God and, naturally, hope that I'm right in my belief. It's that I hope there is no God! I don't want there to be a God; I don't want the universe to be like that. My guess is that this cosmic authority problem is not a rare condition and that it is responsible for much of the scientism and reductionism of our time. One of the tendencies it supports is the ludicrous overuse of evolutionary biology to explain everything about human life, including everything about the human mind... This is a somewhat ridiculous situation..."[14]

"And this is the condemnation, that light is come into the world, and men loved darkness rather than light, because their deeds were evil. For every one that doeth evil hateth the light, neither cometh to the light, lest his deeds should be reproved."[15] (*Bible*)

"Man will not go to God for the same reason a thief will not go to a policeman."[16]

With Paradise lost, man now must live his earthly life in this sin-cursed world where suffering and pain are now inevitable. Man has to elk out a living by the sweat of his brows until he returns back to dust. All these are necessary for his sake – his fallen nature needs some forms of restraint and his sinful heart needs some help to point him back to God.

"And unto Adam he said, Because thou hast hearkened unto the voice of thy wife, and hast eaten of the tree, of which I commanded thee, saying, Thou shalt not eat of it: cursed is the ground for thy sake; in sorrow shalt thou eat of it all the days of thy life; Thorns also and thistles shall it bring forth to thee; and thou shalt eat the herb of the field; In the sweat of thy face shalt thou eat bread, till thou return unto the ground; for out of it wast thou taken: for dust thou art, and unto dust shalt thou return."[17] (*Bible*)

This is the stage in which the atheists would often find fault with God – in His unwillingness or inability to prevent suffering or death in the world. He is either a bad God, or He is an impotent God, or He does not exist. Their focus is on the middle of things and they miss out the before and the after – the fall from grace and the possible redemption through the Savior Jesus Christ, the Son of God.

Most atheists' forays into theology are just overly simplistic – they focus on the suffering but conveniently ignore the sins that caused it or the benefits that brought them back to the straight path. They often neglect the righteousness and omniscience of God – He cannot sin and whatever He allows, He has a morally sufficient reason although we may not fully comprehend it presently.

Sometimes, God allows suffering to turn us from our sins:

> "Before I was afflicted I went astray: but now have I kept thy word."[18] (*Bible*)

Sometimes, God allows suffering to help man to know Him:

> "And suddenly there was a great earthquake, so that the foundations of the prison were shaken: and immediately all the doors were opened, and every one's bands were loosed. And the keeper of the prison awaking out of his sleep, and seeing the prison doors open, he drew out his sword, and would have killed himself, supposing that the prisoners had been fled. But Paul cried with a loud voice, saying, Do thyself no harm: for we are all here. Then he called for a light, and sprang in, and came trembling, and fell down before Paul and Silas, And brought them out, and said, Sirs, what must I do to be saved? And they said, Believe on the Lord Jesus Christ, and thou shalt be saved, and thy house."[19] (*Bible*)

Sometimes, God allows suffering because of our unrepentant hearts:

> "And God saw that the wickedness of man was great in the earth, and that every imagination of the thoughts of his heart was only evil continually... And the Lord said, I will destroy man whom I have created from the face of the earth."[20] (*Bible*)

Sometimes, God allows unending sufferings because of our unchanging hearts:

> "And I saw a great white throne, and him that sat on it, from whose face the earth and the heaven fled away; and there was found no place for them. And I saw the dead, small and great, stand before God; and the books were opened: and another book was opened, which is the book of life: and the dead were judged out of those things which were written in the books, according to their works.

And the sea gave up the dead which were in it; and death
and hell delivered up the dead which were in them: and
they were judged every man according to their works.
And death and hell were cast into the lake of fire. This is
the second death."[21] (*Bible*)

"He that is unjust, let him be unjust still: and he which is
filthy, let him be filthy still: and he that is righteous, let
him be righteous still: and he that is holy, let him be holy
still."[22] (*Bible*)

"Death stamps the characters and conditions of men for
eternity. As death finds them in this world, so will they be
in the next world."[23]

In attacking God for His indifference to suffering, the atheists often forget that
they are dealing with a very tiny window of time. Our time on this earth is like
a drop of water in a mighty ocean in comparison to the eternity to come. What
comparison is there with our *Brief History of Time* on earth to the eternal bliss
in heaven, or our passing sorrows here to a trouble-free world awaiting the
believers?

"For our light affliction, which is but for a moment,
worketh for us a far more exceeding and eternal weight
of glory."[24] (*Bible*)

Over the triple doorways of Milan Cathedral are three
inscriptions spanning the magnificent arches. Above one
is carved a wreath of roses, with the words, "All that
pleases is but for a moment." Over the second is a cross,
with the words, "All that troubles is but for a moment."
Underneath the great central entrance to the main aisle
is inscribed: "That only is important which is eternal."[25]

God did not intend suffering to be a permanent feature of this universe. It was
not His plan in the beginning in the Garden of Eden and it will not be His
intention for the eternity to come. We are in the middle of things now – a world
marred by sins and rebellion. When Jesus Christ, the Son of God, and God the
Son, came into this world some 2,000 years ago to taste death for mankind, it
reveals the love of God for a sinful world. God was not indifferent to man's sins
or sufferings. He came to identify with us and to die in our place. The moral of
the fictitious story here shows that God is not indifferent to our suffering.

"At the end of time, billions of people were scattered on a great plain before God's throne. Most shrank back from the brilliant light before them. But some groups near the front talked heatedly – not with cringing shame, but with belligerence.

"Can God judge us? How can he know about suffering?" snapped a young brunette. She ripped open a sleeve to reveal a tattooed number from a Nazi concentration camp. "We endured terror... shootings... torture... death." In another group a black man lowered his collar. "What about this?" he demanded, showing an ugly rope burn. "Lynched for no crime but being black!" In another crowd, a pregnant schoolgirl with sullen eyes. "Why should I suffer" she murmured, "It wasn't my fault."

Far out across the plain there were hundreds of such groups. Each had a complaint against God for the evil and suffering he permitted in this world. How lucky God was to live in heaven where all was sweetness and light, where there was no weeping or fear, no hunger or hatred. What did God know of all that people had been forced to endure in this world? For God leads a pretty sheltered life, they said.

So each of these groups sent forth their leader, chosen because he had suffered the most. A Jew, a person from Hiroshima, a horribly deformed arthritic, a thalidomide child. In the center of the plain they consulted with each other. At last they were ready to present their case. It was rather clever. Before God could be qualified to be their judge, he must endure what they had endured. Their decision was that God should be sentenced to live on earth – as a man!

"Let him be born into a hated race. Let the legitimacy of his birth be doubted. Give him a work so difficult that even his family will think him out of his mind when he tries to do it. Let him be betrayed by his closest friends. Let him face false charges, be tried by a prejudiced jury and convicted by a cowardly judge. Let him be tortured.

256

At the last, let him see what it means to be terribly alone. Then let him die. Let him die so that there can be no doubt that he died. Let there be a great host of witnesses to verify it." As each leader announced his portion of the sentence, loud murmurs of approval went up from the throng of people assembled. And when the last had finished pronouncing sentence, there was a long silence. No one uttered another word. No one moved. For suddenly all knew that God had already served his sentence."[26]

The Lord Jesus Christ, who is God in the flesh, suffered the most horrific death on the cruel cross to pay the price of our sins. The crucifixion was the worst form of torture and death the Romans could think of in punishing a man. Jesus Christ was crucified, buried and rose again on the third day. He died to bridge the gap between God's Holiness and Man's sinfulness. God's righteousness demands that sins must be punished and sinners be sent to hell forever. But, in His love, He came to taste death for us and to redeem us from the punishment of our sins. O what love is this!

"For when we were yet without strength, in due time Christ died for the ungodly... But God commendeth his love toward us, in that, while we were yet sinners, Christ died for us."[27] (Bible)

"For God so loved the world, that he gave his only begotten Son, that whosoever believeth in him should not perish, but have everlasting life. For God sent not his Son into the world to condemn the world; but that the world through him might be saved."[28] (Bible)

"An atheist once said to me, "Why doesn't your God come and physically show Himself to us?" I replied, "He did and they nailed him on the Cross."[29] (Ken Ham)

Many Darwinists would harp on the diversities of religion to rubbish them. In reality, there are only two religions – one, you must keep on keeping on in doing every possible good to save yourself, and the other, you cannot save yourself but you need Someone to save you from the coming judgment.

"While presenting the Gospel on the streets of a Californian city, we were often interrupted about as follows: "Look here, sir! There are hundreds of religions in this country, and the followers of each sect think theirs is the only right one. How can poor, plain men like us find out what really is the truth?"

We generally replied something like this: "Hundreds of religions, you say? That's strange; I've heard of only two." "Oh, but you surely know there are more than that?" "Not at all, Sir, I find, I admit, many shades of difference in the opinions of those comprising the two great schools; but after all there are but two. The one covers all who expect salvation by doing; the other, all who have been saved by something done. So you see the whole question is very simple. Can you save yourself, or must you be saved by another? If you can be your own savior, you do not need my message. If you cannot, you may well listen to it.""[30] (H. A. Ironside)

To be saved from hell by our good works won't work. The question at hand is whether we are guilty or guiltless before a righteous God and not about the degree or frequency of our sins. One sin makes us a sinner before a Holy God just as one crime makes us a criminal before society. And our good works cannot absolve us of our sins just as a criminal cannot point to his good deeds to be forgiven for his crimes. No bank robber or murderer will be pardoned because he had been a good father, or had paid his income tax, or had helped someone in need. In judicial or divine justice, it is either all or nothing.

"For as many as are of the works of the law are under the curse: for it is written, Cursed is every one that continueth not in all things which are written in the book of the law to do them. But that no man is justified by the law in the sight of God, it is evident: for, The just shall live by faith."[31] (Bible)

"For whosoever shall keep the whole law, and yet offend in one point, he is guilty of all."[32] (Bible)

How then can a sinner be justified before a Holy God? This is the eternal question. The answer lies in God coming down to save us just as a drowning man needs only a hand to lift him up to a passing boat. We cannot save ourselves and are in need of Someone to save us. We need to acknowledge our sins and to receive the Lord Jesus Christ by faith into our heart to save us. Eternal life in heaven is a free gift given to fallen man, but it is paid with the blood of the Son of God. We can do nothing to deserve it, but to humbly receive it by faith in our heart.

"Jesus saith unto him, I am the way, the truth, and the life: no man cometh unto the Father, but by me."[33] (*Bible*)

"That if thou shalt confess with thy mouth the Lord Jesus, and shalt believe in thine heart that God hath raised him from the dead, thou shalt be saved."[34] (*Bible*)

"For by grace are ye saved through faith; and that not of yourselves: it is the gift of God: Not of works, lest any man should boast."[35] (*Bible*)

Many will call this a 'cheap grace' – just believe and you will be pardoned for all your sins and be on your way to heaven. An intellectual or head belief is cheap but what differentiates a true believer from a professor of religion is a heart belief. For that, many a Christian will love God, forsake his vices, and for some, travel to the ends of the world to share his faith. Everything we do in life is the result of our inner belief or faith. We don't want to be poor because we don't believe it is good for us. We strive to be rich because we believe it serves our purpose. All our attitudes and behaviors are shaped by what we truly believe in our hearts. And that is why our eternity is conditioned on what we really believe in our heart. We will eventually do according to what we believe. Faith and work are like the heat and light of a candle; you cannot separate them.

"Sirs, what must I do to be saved? And they said, Believe on the Lord Jesus Christ, and thou shalt be saved, and thy house."[36] (*Bible*)

And so it is with the true believers in Christ – it will result in a sea change in their lives and transform them into the likeness of God. A true Christian is not a perfect person, just a pardoned person, who strives to be perfected. A professing Christian, on the other hand, is still lost in his sins, indulging in the depravities of the world. Christianity, like all other beliefs, has a fair share of hypocrites and charlatans in her bosom – the TV evangelists that prey on the simpletons; the prosperity gospel (wealth and health); the signs and wonders movement; the self-appointed messiahs; the blatant idolatries, mysticism and sins in the house of God. But the God of the conscience knows how to separate the wheat from the chaff in the Day of Judgment. There are hypocrites in the church today, but there will be no hypocrites in heaven.

"Not every one that saith unto me, Lord, Lord, shall enter into the kingdom of heaven; but he that doeth the will of my Father which is in heaven.

Many will say to me in that day, Lord, Lord, have we not prophesied in thy name? and in thy name have we cast out devils? and in thy name done many wonderful works?

And then will I profess unto them, I never knew you: depart from me, ye that work iniquity."[37] (*Bible*)

If this sin-cursed world still retains some of the original beauty of Paradise Lost, how much more glorious will it be in the coming Paradise Restored? The real world is not in this present 'Land of the Dying' but in the coming 'Land of the Living'. Our time here is but a dress rehearsal for the main event in eternity. What is life like on the other side of the great divide where fear, anxiety and death, are a thing of the past! And in its place are love, peace, joy and rest in our souls. This is what Judeo-Christianity has to offer us.

"And God shall wipe away all tears from their eyes; and there shall be no more death, neither sorrow, nor crying, neither shall there be any more pain: for the former things are passed away."[38] (*Bible*)

Darwinism boasts of unshackling us from the evils and bondages of religion. It promises us postmodern enlightenment and freedom. But when you look further down that foggy road, it reveals a universe of nothingness – you are *From Nothing, By Nothing, and For Nothing*. And the best part of it all is that you are not you but a collection of deluded neurons looking for answers in an answerless world.

Secular philosophers from Frederick Nietzsche and his obsession with Übermensch (Superman), to Bertrand Russell with his analytic philosophy, et al., are forever hopelessly lost in the unending maze of a universe that did not have them in mind. It is said that atheism, not only has lost Its way, but it has lost the address too. When we remove God from the equation of life, we will inevitably enter into the hall of mirrors with no exit!

"Human philosophy is the art of knowing more and more about less and less until we know everything about nothing."[39]

"Ever learning, and never able to come to the knowledge of the truth."[40] (*Bible*)

In Christianity, an awesome and unrealized universe opens up to us – a world where there is Someone who made us, loved us, and longed to give us the true desires of our hearts. Biblical Christianity leads us to the place of a beautiful relationship with the Designer of this amazing Universe. It defines our reality, articulates our real reason for living, and gives the deeper meaning to our existence. God is our Abba or 'Daddy'. He is there in our sorrow; He is there in our joy. He corrects us when we go astray, but He never forsakes us. And He is there even when the world leaves us. We are amazingly *From Someone, By Someone, and For Someone*!

> "The Lord is my shepherd; I shall not want (lack). He maketh me to lie down in green pastures: he leadeth me beside the still waters. He restoreth my soul: he leadeth me in the paths of righteousness for his name's sake. Yea, though I walk through the valley of the shadow of death, I will fear no evil: for thou art with me; thy rod and thy staff they comfort me."[41]

"I am come that they might have life, and that they might have it more abundantly."[42] (*Bible*)

References:

1. *Origin of the Universe*

2. Bertrand Russell, *Letter to Lady Constance*

3. *Bible*, John 10:27

4. *Bible*, Genesis 1:1

5. *Bible*, Genesis 1:24-27

6. *Bible*, Genesis 3:1-6

7. *Bible*, Genesis 3:17-19

8. *Bible*, Romans 5:12

9. Source Unknown

10. *Bible*, Romans 3:23

11. *Bible*, Mark 7:21-23

12. Source Unknown

13. *Bible*, John 8:3-11

14. Nagel, Thomas, Professor of Philosophy and Law, New York University, *The Last Word*, p. 130–131, Oxford University Press, 1997

15. *Bible*, John 3:19-20

16. Source Unknown

17. *Bible*, Genesis 3:17-19

18. *Bible*, Psalms 119:67

19. *Bible*, Acts 16:26-31

20. *Bible*, Genesis 6:5-7

21. *Bible*, Revelation 20:11-14

22. *Bible*, Revelation 22:11

23. Nathaniel Emmons

24. *Bible*, 2 Corinthians 4:17

25. Source Unknown

26. Source Unknown

27. *Bible*, Romans 5:6-8

28. *Bible*, John 3:16-17

29. Ken Ham, *Answers in Genesis*

30. H. A. Ironside

31. *Bible*, Galatians 3:10-11

32. *Bible*, James 2:10

33. *Bible*, John 14:6

34. *Bible*, Romans 10:9

35. *Bible*, Ephesians 2:8-9

36. *Bible*, Acts 16:30-31

37. *Bible*, Matthew 7:21-23

38. *Bible*, Revelation 21:4

39. Source Unknown

40. *Bible*, 2 Timothy 3:7

41. *Bible*, Psalms 23:1-4

42. *Bible*, John 10:10

The New Neanderthals

> The New Atheist's utterances sound like deep wisdom
> because we do not think deep enough. If we do, they
> sound really stupid.

The Neanderthal is supposedly a subspecies of the human race according to the Darwinist. In some way, the New Atheist resembles the Neanderthal – both are ugly and dumb. When we sift through their loud and irrational ranting, we will discover there is very little grey substance beneath their skull. Behind the mask of an assumed intellectual, they are, in reality, very muddled up and terribly ignorant of how silly they come across to thinking people. Richard Dawkins encourages us to think critically, let us take heed to his advice. Let us turn his gun on his species, the New Atheists, and see how patently primitive they are.

> "Skeptical rational inquiry is always the best approach...
> we can think independently, be truly open-minded. That
> means asking questions, being open to real corroborated
> evidence. Reason has liberated us from superstition and
> given us centuries of progress. We abandon it at our
> peril."[1]

Richard Dawkins: "Faith is one of the world's great evils, comparable to the smallpox virus but harder to eradicate."[2]

> "I am not attacking any particular version of God or gods.
> I am attacking God, all gods, anything and everything
> supernatural, wherever and whenever they have been or
> will be invented."[3]

The New Atheist would pick up a couple of religions that behave badly, then lump all the religions of the world together and rubbish them. If the Islamic Jihadists are evil, so are all the other religionists. Therefore, all religions are evil. Let us see how patently silly such an argument is. Theo Hobson puts it aptly in *Richard Dawkins has lost: meet the New New Atheists*:

> "The events of 9/11 were the main trigger for the
> explosion of this latent irritation. There was a desire to
> see Islamic terrorism as the symbolic synecdoche of all of
> religion. On one level this makes some sense: does not all
> religion place faith above reason? Isn't this intrinsically
> dangerous? Don't all religions jeopardies secular freedom,
> whether through holy wars or faith schools? On another

level it is absurd: is the local vicar, struggling to build community and help smelly drunks stay alive, really a force for evil – even if she has some illiberal opinions?

When such questions arise, a big bright 'Complicated' sign ought to flash in one's brain. Instead, in the wake of 9/11, many otherwise thoughtful people opted for simplicity over complexity. They managed to convince themselves that religion is basically bad, and that the brave intellectual should talk against it."[4]

Let us take a couple of atheists like Joseph Stalin and Mao Zedong, and parade their brutalities. Between them, they killed tens of millions of their people. After which, let us link them with atheism. There you have it – all atheists are potentially evil people and there is no fear of God to restrain them. Are these Neanderthals silly enough not to know that there are good religionists and bad religionists, good atheists and bad atheists, and good scientists and bad scientists? As it is wont to say, "One swallow does not a summer make." The difference does make a difference. Let us borrow a page from Oxford professor John Lennox:

"I've learned to distinguish between the greatness of God and the inexcusable evil that has been done by those professing his name. And so I do not deduce [as Christopher Hitchens does] that God is not great, and that religion poisons everything. After all, if I failed to distinguish between the genius of Einstein and the abuse of his science to create weapons of mass destruction, I might be tempted to say science is not great, and technology poisons everything."[5]

The author, like almost all religionists, is on the same page as Richard Dawkins on 9/11. There are religions and religionists who abused their faiths to perpetuate violence, but the vast majority of religions do not advocate such atrocities but rather condemn them. Instead, they advocate love, kindness and altruism. If so, why does Dawkins condemn the religionists that condemn 9/11? Wisdom would demand that we do not lump all religions into one basket and label them as 'evil'. Such reasoning reveals the infantile nature of these Neanderthals. The thinking populace does not subscribe to the ludicrous and simplistic conclusions of these Primitive Atheists.

Steven Weinberg: "I don't need to argue here that the evil in the world proves that the universe is not designed, but only that there are no signs of benevolence that might have shown the hand of a designer."[6]

The common objection is: if God is good, there will not be any evil and suffering in the world. And since there are, God is not good and He does not exist, period. They travel the same path as Epicurus of old:

> "Is God willing to prevent evil,
> but not able?
> Then he is not omnipotent.
> Is he able, but not willing?
> Then he is malevolent.
> Is he both able and willing?
> Then whence cometh evil?
> Is he neither able nor willing?
> Then why call him God?"

In the first place, does it dawn on these New Atheists that they have, at best, proven there is a 'bad God' and not that there is 'no God'. Many in Germany thought Adolf Hitler was a benevolent ruler but later found out that he was, in essence, a cruel despot. Does that prove Hitler never existed? A bad Hitler is not the same as no Hitler!

Secondly, they are dealing with a God who knows the end from the beginning. And He has the best of reasons for allowing what He allows in a world that has turned its back on Him from the dawn of civilization. The world would not shed a tear for a baby Hitler, Stalin, Mao or Pol Pot, had they died a horrible death at birth. These have been the cause of unimaginable tortures and deaths. Conversely, not all sufferings are due to potential evils, some are for the best of reasons – like the drawing of indifferent people to know God or the turning away of sinners from their foolish ways. Many atheists are taking potshots at God and Theodicy at which they are terribly unschooled.

> "Imagine someone holding forth on biology whose only knowledge of the subject is the *Book of British Birds*, and you have a rough idea of what it feels like to read Richard Dawkins on theology."[7] (Eagleton, T.)

> "But I think first that these people do a disservice to scholarship. Their treatment of the religious viewpoint is pathetic to the point of non-being. Richard Dawkins in *The God Delusion* would fail any introductory philosophy or religion course. Proudly he criticizes that whereof he

knows nothing… Conversely, I am indignant at the poor quality of the argumentation in Dawkins, Dennett, Hitchens, and all of the others in that group… I have written elsewhere that *The God Delusion* makes me ashamed to be an atheist. Let me say that again. Let me say also that I am proud to be the focus of the invective of the new atheists. They are a bloody disaster and I want to be on the front line of those who say so."[8] (Michael Ruse)

Thirdly, the 'bad God' argument does not do away with the existence of God just as the 'good God' argument does not prove there has to be a God. If this world were a Shangri-La or an Utopia, does that prove that God exists? I doubt any atheist will buy that argument. The 'bad God' argument is a philosophical and not a scientific argument against the existence of God. It is not experimental science and does not do away with God, just as the existence of some unethical scientists does not do away with the reality of good science. Science deals with demonstrable mechanism and phenomena, not character. A house points to a builder regardless of whether he is good or evil. And creation points to a Creator regardless of our interpretation of His character or dealings with us.

"Science is about facts, not norms; it might tell us how we are, but it couldn't tell us what is wrong with how we are. There couldn't be a science of the human condition."[9] (Jerry Foder)

Dawkins' book *The God Delusion* is barking up the wrong tree. His famous accident with a truckload of evolutionary Thesaurus is a total waste of breath against the existence of God. It is, at best, a personal vendetta against God and, at worst, a sophomore attempt at interpreting Theodicy.

"The God of the Old Testament is arguably the most unpleasant character in all fiction: jealous and proud of it; a petty, unjust, unforgiving control-freak; a vindictive, bloodthirsty ethnic cleanser; a misogynistic, homophobic, racist, infanticidal, genocidal, filicidal, pestilential, megalomaniacal, sadomasochistic, capriciously malevolent bully."[10]

I am pretty sure that Dawkins' children would adopt some of these invectives to describe him when Dawkins deals harshly with their attitude problems. And so will many other kids resort to such language against their parents' misunderstood love and necessary discipline. God punishes because of man's sins, and Dawkins would focus on man's punishment at the exclusion of his sins and, with a twisted logic, transform a loving and just God into an 'unforgiving control freak'. Would Dawkins be a vindictive person if he administers due justice to an assailant who attempts to hurt his children or be jealous if some man tries to seduce his wife? Would he sit by passively and watch them carry out their evil acts on his family so that he would not come across as a control freak or a jealous husband?

Fourthly, the doing away of God does not remove the suffering of this world – it merely eliminates all hope of divine help and comfort, as well as eternal justice and rewards. And the only answers to their atheistic cries are the silence of the universe and the reverberating echoes of their deluded persuasions: THERE IS NO GOD, NO PURPOSE, NO REASON, NO JUSTICE, DUDE; JUST GRIT YOUR TEETH AND SUFFER! THIS IS WHAT WE HAVE BEEN TOLD AND THIS IS WHAT WE ARE TO EXPECT! IT IS ALL ABOUT DARWINIAN EVOLUTION DUDE! This is the best you will ever get from the devolving minds of these primitive Neanderthals.

Lastly, the Darwinist will presume to judge God as evil but borrow his moral judgment from the moral laws of God written in his conscience. The whole evolutionary shebang cannot account for objective good or evil. A lion killing a lamb is all about the survival of the fittest and has nothing to do with matters pertaining to right or wrong. And so is one man taking the life of another in strict evolutionary thinking. At which point in time does one ape killing another become evil? We are, after all, supposedly evolved from some apelike creature – we are but a more refined ape!

Many philosophers and honest Darwinists have attempted to get from 'is' to 'ought' (what is to what ought) through the mechanism of materialism and reductionism, and have failed utterly. Where did molecules get their moral values from? What is the physics of right or the chemistry of wrong? What is the formula for 'good', or where to hang 'evil' on the periodic table of elements? And evolution deals only with behavior (survival of the fittest), not belief (survival of the righteous). Morality is none of its concern. Its primarily focus is about survival, not morality. At best, it can only speak of herd's preferences. But such democratized morality can be utterly wrong.

> "Perhaps the unbeliever takes "good" to be whatever evokes public approval. However, on that basis the statement, "The vast majority of the community heartily approved of and willingly joined in the evil deed," could never make sense. The fact that a large number of people feel a certain way does not (or should not rationally) convince anybody that this feeling (about the goodness or evil of something) is correct."[11] (Bahnsen)

267

To judge God as evil is to assume that there is an objective good. And to assume there is objective good is to believe that there exists a transcendental moral law. And that points to the ultimate Lawgiver. Evolutionism has no workable apparatus to provide for objective morality – you cannot get from molecules to morals – not even via Sam Harris' *Moral Landscape* constructed from the amoral desires for human flourishing and the escape from human miseries. And the moral laws within point to a moral Lawgiver without. So, by calling God evil, the Darwinists have unintentionally proven He exists!

> "Why do intellectually honest atheists admit that, without God, objective moral values cannot exist? Because it is the logical result of taking atheistic philosophy to its natural conclusion. If there's such a thing as evil, you must assume there's such a thing as good. If you assume there's such a thing as good, you assume there's such a thing as an absolute and unchanging moral law on the basis of which to differentiate between good and evil. If you assume there's such a thing as an absolute moral law, you must posit an absolute moral lawgiver, but that would be God – the one whom the atheist is trying to disprove. So now rewind: if there's not a moral lawgiver, there's no moral law. If there's no moral law, there's no good. If there's no good, there's no evil. Which is just what Richard Dawkins admits to...
>
> This fact produces what is called the moral argument for the existence of God, which can be stated in the following way:
>
> Laws imply a Law Giver There is an objective Moral Law Therefore, there is a Moral Law Giver
>
> True objective moral good cannot be defined without purpose, and purpose cannot be defined without a cause. Without God – the cause of everything – all that is left is time + matter + chance. And such a combination only produces chaos; not an absolute moral framework."[12]

And to top it all, Darwinists like Dawkins, believe that there is no God, no good and no evil. And then they turn around to accuse God of being 'evil'. These Neanderthals can't even think straight! Does it dawn on the Darwinists that all perceived evils may not be 'evil', but are just the amoral, naturalistic, predicted, Darwinian 'dancing to the music of our DNA'? The lion's DNA is designed to kill and live – it is no fault of the lion. There is no such thing as an evil lion. And so it is with us; we are just 'tangoing to our DNA' in objective Darwinian thinking – there is no good or evil – just natural selection, random mutation, and the evolving of the fittest.

"The universe we observe has precisely the properties we should expect if there is at the bottom, no design, no purpose, *no evil and no good*. Nothing but blind pitiless indifference. DNA neither knows nor cares. DNA just is, and we dance to its music."[13]

Good and evil are not part of the materialist's worldview – they are immaterial, intangible and invisible – like a transcendental God or dancing angels. Molecule is physical while morality is non-physical. Molecules cannot produce morality, and morality is beyond molecules! And our brain is just a collection of molecules; whence comes this immaterial moral framework? Can the molecules in Dawkins' brain help us understand how he gets his moral values from an undesigned, purposeless universe consisting of nothing but molecules in motion obeying the laws of physics? Or, how did the dancing to the music of our unconscious and unthinking DNA waltz its way up to a moral high ground?

Evolution Is as Real as Gravity:

"Evolution by natural selection is much more than just a hypothesis, and is as much a valid and well-accepted scientific theory as the theory of gravitation. What Darwin did for biology is on par with what Newton did for physics — and mathematics plays an important role in both theories."[14] (Wim Hordijk)

"Some claim that evolution is just a theory, as if it were merely an opinion. The theory of evolution – like the theory of gravity – is a scientific fact. Evolution really happened. Accepting our kinship with all life on Earth is not only solid science. In my view, it's also a soaring spiritual experience."[15] (Neil deGrasse Tyson)

The Darwinists generally parrot the same garbage that biological evolution is as real as gravity or as good as cash. You got to be kidding! The law of gravity is observable and testable while the evolution of the bacterium to man is speculative and unobservable. Physicists are generally too smart to fall prey to equating gravity with evolution. Let us hear from David Klinghoffer:

"What's wrong with this? Thoughtful reader Jonathan nails it: "I'll be interested when a physicist proclaims 'gravity is as real as evolution.'" Yes, evolution needs to associate itself with something factual, whereas gravity has no such need. That is kind of telling...

Whether the comparison is to gravity, or to cancer, or to any empirical observation, we consider it to be a fact because we can observe it. Whether or not we can explain it, and to what degree we can explain it, has no bearing on the observation itself. So Gould is correct that gravity does not go away when scientists debate rival theories to explain it.

But we do not observe humans evolving from apelike ancestors. That is the claim of evolution, and it is a claim that suffers from substantial scientific problems. That is not a comment on evolution; it is a scientific fact.

Yes evolutionists do debate rival explanations for how the species originated, but there is no observation of evolution that "doesn't go away" during the debate. There is no fact of evolution to fall back on while evolutionary explanations encounter scientific problems."[16]

Have the evolutionists ever wondered why hardly anybody quarrels with the veracity of gravity while there are endless controversies with the hypothesis of evolution? It is because the evolution of molecule to man is religiously assumed but has never been observed while the law of gravity can be rigorously tested and consistently repeated before our very eyes! Gravity can stand on its own two feet while evolution needs a crutch.

Christopher Hitchens: "I challenge you to find one good or noble thing which cannot be accomplished without religion."[17]

Simply put, what good things a religionist can do, the atheist can do too. A man does not need religion to be good. He can be altruistic without a religious belief. So, what does that prove? Nothing! In the first place, hardly any religionist lays claims to the proposition that you need religion to do a good or noble thing. It is a straw man argument: Hitchens puts up a straw man and then viciously attacks it and walks away seemingly triumphant with a supposedly knockout argument against the religionists. Most thinking people see through his ruse.

The central question is about the existence of God and not about the good that an atheist or a theist can do. The atheists can be good because they are made in the image of God and His moral laws are written in their hearts. Ask Hitchens how he gets his moral values from the spinning molecules in his brain! That would be an interesting discussion and you will see his bridge to nowhere.

"For when the Gentiles, which have not the law, do by nature the things contained in the law, these, having not the law, are a law unto themselves: Which shew (show) the work of the law written in their hearts, their conscience also bearing witness, and their thoughts the mean while accusing or else excusing one another."[18] (*Bible*)

"But if this is the case, what explains the existence within us of this inner moral code or compass? According to atheism, human beings and all their thinking processes are simply the accidental by-products of the mindless movement of atoms within an undesigned, random, and purposeless universe. How then can we attach any ultimate meaning or truth to our thoughts and feelings, including our sense of justice? They have, on this view, no more validity or significance than the sound of the wind in the trees."[19] (James Bishop)

By the way, Hitchens conveniently forgets to tell you that atheists can be just as immoral as the sinning religionists. Theo Hobson writes:

"In previous generations, the atheist was keen to insist that non-believers can be just as moral as believers. These days, this is more or less taken for granted. What distinguishes the newer atheist is his admission that non-believers can be just as immoral as believers. Rejecting religion is no sure path to virtue; it is more likely to lead to complacent self-regard, or ideological arrogance."[20]

Hitchens, like most Neanderthals, is vacuous in his thinking by not differentiating between epistemology and ontology – atheists can know what is good and evil because God's moral laws are written in their hearts (epistemology), but they cannot get their moral values from molecules but from the God of the molecules (ontology). Morality can only come from a moral Being, not molecules! Even Hitchens will tell you that, when it comes to moral perfection, the whole of mankind, whether believers or non-believers, fails miserably. It is for this reason that we need a Savior to save us from our sins.

"For there is not a just man upon earth, that doeth good, and sinneth not."[21] (*Bible*)

"We all come from the same mold – and some of us are moldier than others!"[22]

Steven Weinberg: "Religion is an insult to human dignity. With or without it, you'd have good people doing good things and evil people doing bad things, but for good people to do bad things, it takes religion."[23]

This may be true for a handful of religionists like the Islamic extremists but not for the majority of other believers. The contrary is also true – for some bad people to be good, it takes religion. Religion has transformed many a drunkard and druggie into a responsible citizen. This proves nothing! The truth is, for most good people to do bad things, it takes ideology, not necessary religion – what one chooses to believe or interpret rather than what one is exposed to. The same people in the same religion with the same book can do things very differently – some will build a mosque while others will blow it up.

> "Atheism deserves better than the new atheists whose methodology consists of criticizing religion without understanding it, quoting texts without contexts, taking exceptions as the rule, confusing folk belief with reflective theology, abusing, mocking, ridiculing, caricaturing, and demonizing religious faith and holding it responsible for the great crimes against humanity. Religion has done harm; I acknowledge that. But the cure for bad religion is good religion, not no religion, just as the cure for bad science is good science, not the abandonment of science."[24] (Sacks, Jonathan)

Good theists and atheists can commit some of the most heinous crimes due to their ideology or indiscretion, and not necessarily because of religion or the lack of it. Many good people became irreligious Marxists, Communists or Fascists, and brutalized millions. You don't need a religion to be evil; you need a wrong belief – an ideology. Weinberg would have failed miserably in a philosophy course by not distinguishing the difference. Well, what do you expect from a devolving Neanderthal? No wonder they are no longer in the gene pool.

"We are all born ignorant, but one must work hard to remain stupid."[25]

References:

1.   Richard Dawkins, *The Enemy of Reasons*

2.   *"Is Science a Religion?"* The Humanist, January 1997

3.   Richard Dawkins, *The God Delusion*, p. 57

4. Theo Hobson, *Richard Dawkins has lost: Meet the New New Atheists*, The Spectator, 13 April 2013

5. John Lennox

6. Steven Weinberg, Professor of Physics, University of Texas at Austin, Winner of the 1979 Nobel Prize in Physics, *A Designer Universe?* April 1999

7. Eagleton,T., *Lunging, Flailing, Mispunching*, London Review of Books 28(20), 19 October, 2006

8. Michael Ruse, *Why I Think the New Atheists are a Bloody Disaster*, From the blog Science and the Sacred (retrieved: 30/10/10)

9. Jerry Foder, *Why Pigs Don't Have Wings*

10. Richard Dawkins, *The God Delusion*

11. Bahnsen, *Always Ready*, p. 168

12. *Compelling Truth*

13. Richard Dawkins, *Out of Eden*, p. 133

14. Wim Hordijk, *Evolution: It's as real as gravity!* Plus Magazine, July 13, 2016

15. Neil deGrasse Tyson

16. David Klinghoffer, *The "Evolution Is as Real as Gravity"* Talking Point, Evolution News and Talking Point, June 29, 2017

17. Attributed to Christopher Hitchens, Source Unknown

18. *Bible*, Romans 2:14-15

19. James Bishop, *Evidence leads atheist writer & lecturer*, Philip Vander Elst, to Christianity, August 28, 2017

20. Theo Hobson, *Richard Dawkins has lost: meet the new new Atheists*, The Spectator, 13 April 2013

21. *Bible*, Ecclesiastes 7:20

22. Source Unknown

23. Attributed to Steven Weinberg, Source Unknown

24. Sacks, Jonathan, *The Great Partnership: Science, Religion, and the Search for Meaning,* New York: Schocken, 2011, p. 11

25. Often attributed to Benjamin Franklin, Source Unknown